KAFKA

THE
TERROR
OF
ART

D0809699

KAFKA

THE
TERROR
OF
ART

by
MARTIN GREENBERG

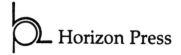 Horizon Press   New York

For Paula

PREFACE

Every Poet his own Aristotle.
—BYRON

This is a book about Kafka's art. More specifically, it endeavors
to describe and define his main narrative form—what I call the
"dream narrative"—and trace its evolution from its beginnings
to its culmination in *The Castle*. Kafka is an easy writer to appreciate, a hard one to understand; his antithetical art combines
very great simplicity with tortuous complexity, starkness with
obscurity. It is able to do so without falling into artificiality
thanks to its natural truth of form, thanks to a form which is
true to nature. And the nature to which it is true—the natural
phenomenon whose truth Kafka makes his own—is the dream.

In his early years, during his twenties, Kafka did not quite
know what to do with himself as a writer. He was conscious of

possessing literary gifts, even great literary gifts, but how should he employ them? What should he write? Most of what he wrote he burned. In 1910, at Max Brod's suggestion, he began to keep a diary, at first simply in order to exercise his pen. The minor successes this great storyteller achieved in this period were not even stories but short compositions in a meditative vein. And then his imagination found in its own characteristic way of working the form it needed to unfold itself—proving once again that in the modern age every genuine poet has to be his own Aristotle and himself lay down the laws his art is subject to. Or in the words of Coleridge (of which the epigraph from Byron is a succinct résumé): "No work of true genius dare want its appropriate form; neither indeed is there any danger of this. As it must not, so neither can it be, lawless! For it is even this that constitutes its genius—the power of acting creatively under laws of its own origination." This book is about Kafka's appropriate form—about the dream-narrative form and the modern substance it is an appropriate form for.

My hope is that as well as throwing light on Kafka this study will also throw some light on modern literature in general, though now it is completed I am more conscious of my debt to other writers on modernism than of any new perceptions of my own. I have been struck like other critics by the way in which the modern movement continued the Romantic one, and continued its internationality. Hence the epigraphs from the English Romantic poets in a book about a modern writer of German.

The quotations from Kafka's works which appear in the text are taken from the published translations. I have often revised them, however, sometimes drastically, to bring out an omitted or slurred meaning; such omissions and slurrings are inevitable in all translation. Sometimes I have changed them to correct an outright error or simply to improve them—though the lovely English of the Muirs' translations, so modest and so fluent, touched with the genius of someone who was himself a great poet, leaves little room for the latter.

The Muirs translated *Gemeindevorsteher* (in *The Castle*) as "Superintendent." In a subsequent edition this was changed by other hands to "Mayor," also unsatisfactory. I have taken another stab at it and used the term "Village Head."

All emphases in quotations from Kafka are my own. Kafka himself, with his characteristically even tone, almost never indicated emphases.

I should like to thank the John Simon Guggenheim Memorial Foundation for its generosity in awarding me a fellowship that made possible, for a time, the complete immersion in Kafka into which he draws one and which he seems to require.

MARTIN GREENBERG

CONTENTS

KAFKA

THE
TERROR
OF
ART

1 ART AND DREAMS

There is a surprising entry in Kafka's diary which he made on February 19, 1911, when he was twenty-seven years old:

> The special nature of my inspiration . . . lies in this, that I am capable of everything and not just of what goes into a particular piece of work. If I write down the first sentence that comes into my head, for instance, "He looked out of the window," it already has perfection.[1]

One does not expect from Kafka such confidence in his literary powers. Yet the truth is that he never doubted his abilities as a

3

writer; what he doubted was his ability to realize his abilities, his power to fulfill what elsewhere in the diary he calls his "literary destiny." [2] Even so, however, his saying that his every sentence possessed perfection seems an extraordinary assertion. What he meant by this, I believe, was that his prose had *style*. Other writers of German were capable of this and that particular piece of work, but they did not possess a general literary capability. Kafka is here declaring his general literary capability, his style, which he had been developing with laborious care ever since he was a schoolboy going to the German Gymnasium in Prague.

Great style is an uncommon thing in any language, but it is more uncommon in German than it is in English (and more uncommon in English than in French). Prose is truest to its own nature when it is rational and clear, persuasive rather than overpowering, sober rather than striking. The very best style, what we call classical style, is ruled by intelligence and a scrupulous sense of truth, which give it a certain modesty. Such is Kafka's style. His prose strives toward the classical in its effort to "express new and profound ideas in a perfectly sound . . . style," [3] in its effort to "raise the world into the pure, the true, the unchangeable." Only if he could do that, he said, would his work give him "happiness" rather than just the "momentary satisfaction" he got from the glittering effects of a story like "A Country Doctor." [4]

As a Prague-born speaker of German, Kafka had an unsure instinct for the tongue and worried about the niceties of grammar and idiom.[5] But his concern for purity of style, which goes far beyond correct usage, had nothing to do with the requirements of the German language, only with his own requirements. English prose insists on style, French prose insists even harder, but German prose does not. German offers itself, so to speak, as naked syntax. Most writers of German, since the language makes no authoritative demand on them, get along more or less without a style, merely elaborating the special language needed for particular kinds of work. Those German writers who have fashioned literary styles for themselves have had to build them from the ground up.

But if Kafka possessed a style that was "capable of everything," it was still impossible for him in 1911, when he was already twenty-seven, to point to a particular piece of work that he had been able to achieve satisfactorily in his pure, clear, truthful prose. Another year and a half went by, bringing his twenty-eighth and twenty-ninth birthdays, and then on the night of September 22–23, 1912, he wrote *The Judgment*, the first of his great stories, in a sudden triumphant release of his imaginative powers. A few weeks later this was followed by *The Metamorphosis*. And in this same productive period of 1912, which he always looked back on as a unique time in which he had enjoyed the "full possession of all my powers" and "a clear head," [6] he wrote a good part of the novel *Amerika*, started some time before he wrote *The Judgment*.

The Judgment marks a decisive turning point in Kafka's work and he immediately recognized it as such. The same day that he finished the story, he described its composition in a diary entry which exults at having discovered, in the nighttime hours, the way to write "with such coherence, with such a complete opening out of the body and the soul":

This story, *The Judgment*, I wrote at one stretch on the night of the 22nd–23rd from ten o'clock in the evening to six o'clock in the morning. I could hardly draw my legs from under the desk, they had got so stiff from sitting. The terrible strain and joy, how the story unfolded before me as if I were advancing over water. At times during this night I was carrying my own weight on my back. How everything can be said, how for everything, for the strangest ideas, a great fire is prepared in which they perish and rise up again. How it turned blue outside the window. A wagon went by. Two men walked across the bridge. At two I looked at the clock for the last time. As the maid walked through the anteroom for the first time, I wrote the last sentence. Putting out the lamp and the light of day. The faint heart pains. The tiredness that disappeared in the middle of the night. Going in trembling to my sisters' room. Reading aloud. Before that, stretching in front of the maid and saying: "I've been writing till now." The way the undisturbed bed looked, as though it had just been brought in. The conviction confirmed that with my novel writing I am in the shameful lowlands of writing. This way is the *only* way to write, only with such coherence, with such a complete opening out of the body and the soul. Morning in bed. Eyes clear still. All sorts of feelings during the writing, for example delight at having something fine for Max's *Arkadia,* thoughts about Freud, of course . . . of course too about my "Urban World." [7]

The entry shows that Kafka wrote *The Judgment* in a kind of seizure in which his ordinary constraints and inhibitions fell away so that the story seemed to write itself. Some months later, when he was correcting the proof sheets of the story, he said that it had come out of him "like an actual birth." [8] Although Kafka cultivated his style with painstaking effort, most of his manuscripts show very few corrections—his hand moved as if possessed across the page, the sentences flowing with uncanny smoothness. (Characteristically, he tended to delete whole sentences, paragraphs and pages and to substitute new writing for them; he wrote anew, rather than correcting.) His mode of creativity was inspiration rather than making. He was the inspired poet rather than the poet as maker. He did not make or construct so much as he transmitted, even though what he transmitted was shaped at every point by the pressure of his conscious art. Through him "another" voice makes itself heard.

Only so could Kafka write. What he abominated was "constructions," the deliberate contrivances of the calculating consciousness. When his confidence deserts him, then he cries out that *Alles erscheint mir als Konstruktion*—that everything looks like an artificial construction to him, false and dead, as opposed to the "power of life" that he feels.[9] Inspiration meant the spontaneous expression of his more intuitive, more unconscious side, with its truer grasp of reality, with its grasp of the hidden living rather than the mentally constructed reality:

> For us there are two kinds of truth, as they are represented by the Tree of Knowledge and the Tree of Life. The truth of [purposeful] striving and the truth of [purposeless] being at rest [*Die Wahrheit des Tätigen und die Wahrheit des Ruhenden*]. In the first, good separates itself from evil, the second is nothing but

good itself, knowing neither of good nor of evil. The first truth is given to us actually, the second only intuitively. That is the sad side of it. The happy side is that the first truth is of the moment, the second of eternity, which is also why the first truth fades away in the light of the second.[10]

The soul is sick because it is divided against itself, knowledge against life. Our ignorance is wiser than our knowledge because our knowledge has become separated from our life. Like Kleist, who influenced him so strongly, he believed that "every first inclination, whatever is involuntary, is beautiful; but everything is distorted and displaced as soon as it understands itself." Thought, the deliberating consciousness of man, has lost its creative power, civilization its creative life. Kafka has the head of the castle village say to K. about the oppressive castle bureaucracy, that tremendous representation of the rationalizing consciousness: "Nothing here is done without taking thought." * [11] Reason, consciousness, conscience no longer serve the self to find its true way, but are the means by which an oppressive world rules it for ends not its own.

Yet Kafka is the opposite of an irrationalist or an antinomian who preaches liberation from law and reason in a post-ethical paradise of pure instinctual truth, even though he sometimes seems to talk that way in his aphorisms. His aphorisms are often rhetorically one-sided, whereas his stories are always imaginatively complex. And the note in his stories is not only one of protest against the unjust law, but of striving for the true law that is absent from the world. "Where was the Judge whom he had never seen?" Joseph K. asks as he is being executed. "Where was the High Court, to which he had never penetrated?" [13] Although our thinking has become the enemy of our life, only through our thinking can we recover our life. Only when life and reason, life and conscience, life and law are reunited, shall we be reborn. As Kleist puts it in his essay "On the Puppet Theater,"

* Cf. D. H. Lawrence to Bertrand Russell: "Nothing is born by taking thought. That which is born comes of itself." [12]

7

we must "eat of the Tree of Knowledge a second time in order to fall back into a state of innocence"—we must rediscover our innocence through *increased* consciousness. (But that is "the last chapter of the history of the world.") Kafka said to Gustav Janouch, the very young friend with whom he used to walk and talk in the early 1920's: "The poet has the task of leading the isolated and mortal into eternal life, the accidental into conformity to law." [14]

But if Kafka is an inspired poet rather than a maker-poet, why did he have to wait until the writing of *The Judgment* for the channels of his inspiration to become unstopped? We have works of his that go back to 1904 and we know that his pen was busy even earlier than that—why should he have had to wait till 1912, till he was twenty-nine, to produce a story of some fifteen pages which, suddenly bursting out with powerful effect, starts him on his course as a major writer? Because in writing that story he discovered the narrative form which made it possible for him to "free" the "gigantic world" that he had "in his head," [15] because with *The Judgment* he discovered "the only way to write." He had been shaping a style that was capable of everything and had been making tentative, laborious efforts (one judges by the very few writings of his early period which escaped destruction at his own hands) in the direction of a composition which leaned now toward poetic fantasticality and now toward prosaic realism, when the discordant elements of composition, poetic and prosaic, sprang together in *The Judgment* into a narrative form modeled on the dream. Kafka became a major writer when he discovered his dream narrative. *The Judgment* was the beginning of a development that advanced through *The Metamorphosis*, fell back in *Amerika,* still faltered in *In the Penal Colony,* and then succeeded on a large scale in *The Trial* and *The Castle.*

The dream-narrative form made it possible for his imagination to plumb depths of the self which were otherwise out of reach. The inward, introspective, visionary character of a main tendency of modern literature is carried by Kafka to a very far point indeed. With him, literature gropes its way to the very bottom of the mind, seeking the unconscious self in its very condition of hiddenness, in all its turbidity and strickenness.

His writing was a struggle with himself. He speaks in his diary of his "hatred" of introspection,[16] but it is an "inescapable duty" which he must carry out even though it "tears him apart" and threatens him with "madness." [17] Kafka's writing is a brave effort to penetrate the depths of his life-fear and his life-failure. Though there is a morbid admixture of self-abasement and self-abnegation in it, his dominant effort is to affirm himself in spite of fear and failure, *through* his fear and failure. Georg Bendemann in *The Judgment* executes his father's verdict on himself and drops into the river, but the story is as much an outcry as a surrender, and ultimately K. sets out to conquer the castle of fear of the world-as-given by taking its measure with his exact surveyor's instruments.

The theme of Kafka's work is the theme of his life: the struggle of the self with itself to be itself. The struggle starts out as a psychological one (although ontological overtones are never absent), but then becomes more and more ultimate. One of the reflections that he jotted down in the years 1917–1918 is almost a curse: *Zum letztenmal Psychologie!*—which may be freely translated as, "From now on, to hell with psychology!" [18] Kafka's struggle with himself to be himself in spite of the adverse influences of father, family, education, and milieu became more and more the universal struggle of the self to be in spite of all the forces of nonbeing. It took courage to stare into the Gorgon's face of universal senselessness and despair without flinching away cynically or idealistically or religiously or in any of the innumerable ways there are of flinching; and in fact he was always on the point of turning to stone.* Milena Jesenská, the courageous, vivid-spirited Czech woman who burst into his dead

* "I'm less and less able to think, observe, make things out, remember, talk, share anything, I'm turning to stone, that much I can make out." [19]

9

man's life (as he called it) in 1920, says about him in one of her vehement letters to Max Brod:

> . . . [H]e . . . never escaped to any such sheltering refuge. . . . He is absolutely incapable of lying, just as he is incapable of getting drunk. He possesses not the slightest refuge. For that reason he is exposed to all those things against which we are protected. He is like a naked man among the clothed.[20]

Kafka represents the struggle of the self with itself to be, in the form of a dream. The truth revealed in the dream is the real truth and asserts itself against the official truth of the waking self which is an official lie. The dream is an intuitive avenue to the truth; it is a part of what in one of his notebooks he terms "man's intuitive capacity," which, "though it often misleads, does lead, does not ever abandon one."[21] His stories exercise a magical effect, but his magic is not the magic of illusion but of revelation. His gift is only superficially a gift for the fantastic and unreal. In fact his art is devoted to reality. We see this in his style, which is sober to the point of plainness, and in his humble realistic detail. Yet at the same time it is modern in its profound feeling for the mystery of reality, which is felt as a mystery of hidden depths.* "*The Metamorphosis* is a terrible dream, a terrible conception," young Janouch said to him. "Kafka stood still. 'The dream reveals the reality, which conception lags behind. That is the horror of life—the terror of art.'"[22] The conceiving consciousness lags behind—fails to grasp, indeed seeks to stifle knowledge of—the reality that is known unconsciously and re-

---

* The more the modern movement recedes into the past the clearer it becomes that it was a continuation of what Alfred North Whitehead in *Science and the Modern World* called the Romantic "protest on behalf of value" and "against the exclusion of value from the essence of matter of fact." In Kafka's life and work this protest took the form of an intense need and longing for a permanent center and source of value which would redeem the world from emptiness. The quest for this ultimate led him, by introspection, out of the world of modern matter of fact, whose reality excluded from its essence the "indestructible something" Kafka sought, deep within the solitude and silence of his inner self.

vealed in dreams. The horror of life lies in the fact that the self is split in this way rather than being whole, so that we do not know who we are or what we do. The terror of art lies in the representation of the hidden reality, with its shattering effect.

One reason for the starkness of Kafka's style is his renunciation of metaphors. For Kafka, metaphors were embellishments that obscured rather than revealed the clear lines of things; they were not "true." In rigorously excluding figures of speech from his prose, he was reacting against the turgid, rhetorical style cultivated by his Prague contemporaries, among whom were Franz Werfel and even Rainer Maria Rilke. The German dialect spoken in Prague by a narrow official and bourgeois class at the beginning of the twentieth century, when Bohemia made part of the Austro-Hungarian Empire, formed a little island in the Slavonic sea and was not a truly living language; the Prague writers, in straining to surmount its linguistic poverty, jumped over into extravagance and artificiality.[23] Kafka went the other way, *with* rather than against the limitedness of Prague German. By building on the very poverty of the language, which he purified and strengthened, Kafka was able to arrive at his classically plain style. Of course, his "classicism" has a more than local explanation. He was not only reacting against the Prague *littérateurs*, he was reacting against "literature" in general. Everywhere in Europe (and America) around the end of the nineteenth century, literature had become literary—affected and unreal, conventional and false, working a worn-out machinery of words and ever more words. It was not the first time European literature had been overtaken by debility. But now the revitalization that followed this decline was to an unusual extent the work of provincials and outsiders: the Irishmen Joyce and Yeats, the American Eliot, the French half-Jew Proust, the coalminer's son Lawrence, and Kafka, both a provincial and an outsider. All these men were able to see from their vantage point on the periphery how literature was caught in the lying surface of things and tried in their different ways to strike through to the truth.

Kafka's way was antiliterary—through the renunciation of literary effects.

And yet at the same time that Kafka turned away from metaphor as a stylistic element because it derogated from the strict truthfulness he aimed at in his prose, metaphor became the very basis of his narrative art. Most of his stories are founded squarely on a single metaphor; they are the literal enactment of an abstraction, the embodiment in a concrete image of an idea. The death sentence literally passed on Georg Bendemann in *The Judgment* is a metaphor for the father's condemnatory opinion of his son. Gregor Samsa's metamorphosis into vermin is a metaphor for his banishment from "the human circle." [24] Joseph K.'s literal trial metaphorically expresses his spiritual trial. The wound the country doctor is helpless to heal is the spiritual sickness of "this most unhappy of ages" [25]—the whole story rests on the medical image. In German the word for castle (*Schloss*) also means lock—the castle of the novel is locked against all K.'s efforts to fight his way into it, a fortress of impersonal mediate authority which expresses the tyranny of automatic social, biological, and psychological processes, barring the way to the ultimate self-authority of the individual person freely choosing himself and choosing to be free.[26]

Kafka's stories are essentially metaphors, images. He said to Janouch (about Karl Rossmann and the stoker in *Amerika*): "I was not describing [actual] people. I was telling a story. They are images, only images." [27] His narrative art lies in the elaboration, the unfolding of a basic image, rather than in the traditional representation of an action. The Kafka story is not dramatic but visionary; it does not move from the beginning through the middle to the end of an action, it progresses through intensities of seeing toward an ever deeper vision. Nothing really happens in the typical Kafka story, not even death. Death is already there, implicit in the situation of the story. The protagonist sees more and more clearly till he sees his own death. K. says to Olga in *The Castle:* "If a man has his eyes bound, you can encourage him as much as you like to stare through the blindfold, but he'll never see anything. He'll be able to see only when the blindfold is removed." [28] The Kafka story is a removing of blindfolds.

Kafka's kind of metaphor—the literal expression in a concrete image of an abstraction—works essentially like dream metaphors. Embarrassment, in a dream, is not a long word with two *r*'s and two *s*'s; it is being naked in public. In a dream about someone who "makes you sick" you literally throw up. The literal dream image supplies the basic structure of Kafka's dream narrative. The breakthrough that he made in writing *The Judgment* was a breakthrough to a narrative form based on dream literalism.

Literalism is at the heart of his art. It is responsible for the elemental quality of his stories, which in *The Castle* reaches an epical level. That novel is a great conception of the imagination because of its elemental simplicity: there are K., the village, and the castle, and over everything the snow, nothing more. And yet the simple, concrete image of the castle world is able to embrace the entire modern world, expressed as an unfree bureaucratic automatism—Kafka is able to imagine the modern world in its entirety through the literal image of his novel.[29] Only the literal expresses the truth; the abstract weaves a web of mortal confusion. Kafka's classicism of style and modernism of feeling are one in his literalism; the prosaic literalness of his style and the poetic literalness of his narrative are one.

Kafka's work of course consists of more than dream narratives, but they represent the major part. Stories like *The Great Wall of China*, "The Hunter Gracchus," *Investigations of a Dog* are not dream narratives; they have virtually ceased to be narratives at all and have become a kind of thinking in images, imaginative reasonings in which an image is not represented or delineated in the usual way, or unfolded through a process of enactment as in his own dream stories, but, as it were, excogitated—a good name for these peculiar compositions is "thought-stories." When the thought-story becomes highly condensed and succinct —as for instance in "An Imperial Message" and "Before the

Law," both of which are excerpts from larger works which they sum up—it resembles the traditional parable. But the old parable illustrated a meaning already established in some other realm of discourse, whereas the thought-story elaborates a meaning which exists only through the image it excogitates.[30]

A number of Kafka's works fall somewhere in between the dream narrative and the thought-story, straddling the two forms. "A Country Doctor," for example, shares characteristics of both forms. But in spite of the brilliance of its writing there is something unsatisfactory about it; it challenges one to read it as a narrative and yet it is most successful as a thought-story. At the end of his life, in his last novel, Kafka was able to unite his two story forms: *The Castle* is a dream narrative in that the castle image is unfolded by a process of enactment, yet at the same time it is a thought-story in that the process of enactment is an excogitation of the castle image by K. and his interlocutors in the lengthy colloquies which make up most of the novel.

Kafka found his way to the dream narrative through his own experience. He was acquainted with Freud's work,* but he did not acquire his knowledge of dreams and depths of the mind by getting up the psychoanalytic literature. He "was not an academic student of the mind. He was however a meticulous observer of his own mental activity" [32]—his notebooks and diary, with their intensely introspective contents and wealth of recorded dreams, make that very plain. His conception of the dream indeed is in a narrow sense opposed to Freud's. Freud stressed the hallucinatory nature of dreams, the illusory fulfillment they give to wishes. Like art, Freud thought, they deal in illusion. With characteristic moral rigor he saw dream distortion as a "dishonest" attempt to conceal the very wish the dream is trying to satisfy. Dreaming is an underhanded enterprise, a sort of truancy which the schoolboy unconscious tries to hide from the

* The biographer of his early years writes: "Kafka became acquainted with psychoanalysis relatively early, at the very latest through a series of lectures given at the Fanta house [in Prague] around 1912." [31]

schoolmaster consciousness. With equally characteristic moral rigor Kafka saw in the fantastic incoherence of dreams the stammering efforts of the humble client unconscious to make its true petition heard against the angry shouts and denunciations of the bureaucrat consciousness. For him, as we have seen, the dream is the opposite of hallucinatory, it is truth-telling and creative—"the dream reveals the reality."

Kafka inherits directly from the same tendency of European thought and feeling that Freud inherited from: the tendency that sees man at odds with himself and his own works; the tendency that, with Rousseau, sees civilization as a question to be weighed rather than as given, that weighs the cost exacted by "the progress of the sciences and the arts." In the background of the influences that shaped Kafka's thought looms the figure of Goethe, dim but grand, as it looms behind Freud; that he was an adherent of Nietzsche in his youth we know[33]; and in the foreground of the influences is the well-loved Kleist (and also Flaubert)—all representatives of the tendency to question the traditional consciousness and conscience of European civilization.

But Kafka also inherits from Freud. Freudian ideas undoubtedly influenced Kafka and may indeed have helped him to find himself as a writer in 1912. Kafka's subjective world of apparent irrationality hiding a heart of meaning is Freudian through and through. His literal and mythopoeic quality is Freudian. His conception of the dream is in the larger sense the same as Freud's; both understood it as an expression of unconscious experience. Kafka was preternaturally self-absorbed and, Freud or no Freud, would have lived in his own subjectivity and dreams. But one may suppose that Freud's ideas encouraged him to take his dreams more seriously than he might otherwise have done. And Freud's impress, one guesses, rests on Kafka's concern with "the opposition between fathers and sons," as he puts it in his diary in 1911.[34] In his diary entry (really an essay on the character of the literature of small nations—he has in mind Czech and Yiddish literature) he lists the "dignifying of the opposition between fathers and sons, with the possibility of discussing it," as one of the benefits of literary activity. Perhaps Freud's influence, direct or indirect, helped to give him the courage to understand his quarrel with his father as a worthy contest rather than a puerile one, which he could "discuss" in his stories rather than turn away from ashamed. The three works that he achieved in such a sudden outburst in the fall of 1912, *The Judgment, The Metamorphosis,* and a substantial part of *Amerika,* are all concerned with the opposition between fathers and sons.* Later Kafka expands and deepens that opposition beyond the psychological sphere into an antithesis established in the very ground of modern existence, which he expresses in the opposition between the individual and the huge bureaucracies of *The Trial* and *The Castle.* But at first he remains within a sphere that one may broadly term Freudian. The fathers whom he portrays in his early stories, and notably in *The Judgment,* are Freudian cartoons. Bendemann Sr. in the latter story thunders like a little Jehovah, but the effect of the story is to expose his pretensions to almightiness. The story does more than that; but it is thoroughly "Freudian" in its exposure of the arbitrary, purely personal nature of the father's authority over the son. It reduces the father to a human "comedian" (as his son calls him) rather than elevating him into a god, just by letting his poor flesh exercise the powers of a god.

Kafka defends the human by exposing the all-too-human basis of inhuman authority; he "reduces" the bigger than human to the human in characteristic psychoanalytical fashion. But he is also concerned, as he moves from his early to his middle and last years, with defending the human against being itself reduced psychoanalytically to "nothing but" this or that illness or "neuro-

* " 'The Stoker' [Chapter One of *Amerika*], *The Metamorphosis* . . . and *The Judgment* belong together outwardly and inwardly, there is an obvious and still more a hidden connection between them whose demonstration, by bringing them together in a book with some such title as 'The Sons,' I should hate to forego. . . . I am no less concerned about the unity of the three stories [as a group] than I am about the unity of each one of them." Letter to his publisher, Kurt Wolff, April 11, 1913.[35]

sis," and here he becomes positively anti-Freudian—"From now on, to hell with psychology!" If in his first important works he wishes (among other things) to show that the all-too-human father possesses godlike power over the son only because of the latter's spiritual captivity ("neurosis"); and if later in *The Trial* Joseph K. submits to the arbitrary godlike authority of the world-as-given because of his spiritual impotence, and if in *The Castle* the land-surveyor K. tries to bring the power of critical intelligence to bear on the arbitrary godlike authority of the world-as-given in his struggle for spiritual freedom—if in all this Kafka struggles to "reduce" the bigger-than-human to the human according to the finest ethos of psychoanalysis, he is always steadfast on the other hand in his search for a faith in "something indestructible," [36] something eternal which does not lie beyond man but within him. He hates the presumption that would reduce all hunger for belief in something permanent, all "matters of faith," [37] to "nothing but" psychological matters. Insofar as religious faith is such a hunger, Kafka respects it. But Kafka does not affirm God, however negatively or paradoxically, in his work. He does not care about God, he does not care about theism or atheism, he leaves all that behind; his world is entirely the human world. But he does care about the "indestructible" in the human world. "Man cannot live without a permanent trust in something indestructible in himself," he says in one of his "Reflections on Sin, Pain, Hope and the True Way,"*

and at the same time that indestructible something as well as his trust in it may remain permanently concealed from him. One of the ways in which this concealment can express itself is as faith in a personal God.[38]

One of the ways in which the indestructibly human is concealed from us is through faith in a personal God. But another, opposite way of concealing it is to call the longing for such trust in something indestructible a neurotic illness. A letter that he wrote to Milena Jesenská in 1921 or 1922 runs as follows:

* The title is the editor's (Brod's), not Kafka's.

You say, Milena, you don't understand it. Try to understand it by calling it illness. It's one of the many manifestations of illness that psychoanalysis believes it has uncovered. I don't call it illness and I consider the therapeutic part of psychoanalysis a hopeless error. All these so-called illnesses, sad as they may appear, are matters of faith [Glaubenstatsachen], efforts of human beings in distress to find an anchorage in some maternal ground or other. . . . Such anchorages, which have a hold in real ground, are not a private possession of individuals which they can surrender, but are established from before in man's nature and go on forming his nature (as well as his body) in the direction already laid down. And they think they are going to cure that? [39]

Religious faith—which, as we have seen, Kafka distinguishes from belief in God—the hunger for a lasting meaning, is not an illusion of mankind but a true spiritual striving implanted in man's nature from before, an anchorage in real ground; trust in something indestructible is man's hope, not man's illness. When Joseph K. dies seeking the judge whom he has never seen, the High Court to which he has never penetrated—seeking the indestructible something in himself in which he may trust—he dies in true spiritual anguish and not in neurotic illusion. When K. crosses the wooden bridge into the castle village he stands "gazing into the apparent emptiness above him" [40]—the emptiness is only apparent, the castle is really there, his goal is a real goal and not a neurotic obsession. Kafka called his "fear," which is the subject of the following letter, "perhaps the best part" of him:

The most beautiful of your letters (and that means a lot, for as a whole they are, almost in every line, the most beautiful thing that ever happened to me in my life) are those in which you agree with my "fear" and at the same time try to explain that I don't need to have it. For I too, even though I may sometimes look like the bribed defender of my "fear," probably agree with it deep down in myself, indeed it is part of me and perhaps the best part. And as it is my best, it is also perhaps this alone that you love. For what else worthy of love could be found in me? But this is worthy of love. [41]

In an earlier letter he had written that "this fear is after all not my private fear—it is simply that, too, and terribly so—but it is as much the fear of all faith since the beginning of time." [42]

And yet there is a deep defensiveness in his calling the whole "therapeutic part" of psychoanalysis a hopeless error. He himself is guilty of a reckless "nothing but" when he writes, in a letter to Brod, that "there is only one sickness, no more, and this one sickness medicine hunts blindly like an animal through endless forests." [43] By tracing every illness, mental and bodily, to a universal spiritual one, to a question of faith, he justified his doing nothing about himself here and now.* In the end he chose to stay the way he was. Which is only to say that he chose to be the writer he was. To accomplish his literary destiny he needed to fail in his life. Or in the words of Sartre: "The genuine poet chooses to lose, even if he has to go so far as to die, in order to win. I repeat that I am talking of contemporary poetry. . . . This is the deeper meaning of that tough luck, of that malediction with which he always claims kinship and which he always attributes to an intervention from without; whereas it is his deepest choice, the source and not the consequence of his poetry. He is certain of the total defeat of the human enterprise and arranges to fail in his own life in order to bear witness, by his individual defeat, to human defeat in general." [45]

Kafka called medicine blind and psychoanalytic medicine hopeless, but he took a lively interest in every kind of half-

* In talking to Janouch about his insomnia, he made a rather different general pronouncement on illness:

"Perhaps my insomnia only conceals a great fear of death. Perhaps I am afraid that the soul—which leaves me in sleep—will never return. Perhaps insomnia is only an all-too-vivid sense of sin, which is afraid of the possibility of sudden judgments. Perhaps insomnia is itself a sin. Perhaps it is the rejection of the natural."
I remarked that insomnia is an illness.
Kafka replied, "Sin is the root of all illness. That is the reason for mortality." [44]

To call sin the root of all illness is no longer to reduce illness to nothing but something else, it is to grant it its complexity. In seeing illness and death as sin, which is to say as an aberrancy in, a "fall" from human nature, Kafka is at one with the great tradition of human redemption of which psychoanalysis is also a part.

cracked nature cure. He was looking for salvation, though only half seriously, not for anything as mediate as "medical assistance." Max Brod writes:

> Franz's attitude to nature cure methods and similar reform movements was one of very intense interest, tempered by the good-natured irony he felt toward the follies and eccentricities which accompany these movements. Fundamentally he saw in efforts to create a new, healthy man by utilizing the mysterious curative powers freely offered us by nature, something extremely positive which agreed with many of his own instincts and convictions.[46]

Vegetarianism, fruit-and-nut diets, fresh air regimens, anthroposophy, sun-bathing, nudism—Kafka dabbled in them all, always to be sure with a certain irony. When Rudolf Steiner lectured at the Fanta house in 1911,[47] he was an attentive listener to the theosophist's mystagogic utterances ("Downfall of the Atlantic world, the Lemurian downfall," "Ahrimanian powers") and recipes ("two liters of emulsion of almonds and fruits that grow above ground level"), which he duly noted in his diary.[48] He describes his visit to Dr. Steiner irreverently, and yet he visited him; the account he gives the doctor of the "confusion" of his life—because of the irreconcilability of his two professions of insurance company official and writer—is in dead earnest. He does not ask Steiner seriously how to clear up the confusion, he only asks him, half-seriously, if his taking up theosophy would not constitute a third endeavor which would only add to the confusion. Kafka does not record what Steiner said to him. He does record what Steiner said to Frau Fanta when she complained to him about her bad memory: "Don't eat eggs." Thus he consulted a doctor to whom he was able to give a serious account of a fundamental impasse in his life, but whose own words he did not have to take seriously. He was ready to talk seriously about himself to somebody to whom he did not have to listen seriously.

Anything that promised a salvation which he could regard half-jokingly drew him like a magnet. But he did not believe in the possibility of real salvation. Or rather he believed in it as a possibility, but *only* as a possibility. "The Messiah will come," he said, "only when there is no longer any need for him, he will come only the day after he comes, he won't come on the last day, but on the last day of all." [49]

That is, the Messiah will come only when it is too late, when everything is over and done with; that is, the Messiah will never come; that is, there is no Messiah. Salvation is an illusion.

But at the same time he is saying that the Messiah will come only when it is too late because the world will already have been saved; and so the Messiah will never come, and there is no Messiah, but for the very opposite reason—because salvation is already present in human existence. (The Messiah will not come because there is no miraculous agency but only human life; the Messiah will have come already because human life is the miracle.)

In this glittering paradox, in which the apes of feeling mimic the rationality of discourse in order to mock it, all Kafka's hopelessness as well as all his hope is expressed. The Messiah will not come in any case—without hesitation Kafka brushes aside all supernaturalism and religious irrationality. But his not coming is the source of hope as well as despair. It is not that hopelessness was strong in him and hope weak even if never quite dead. Hope, too, was strong in him. The given world, his own given self were so hopeless, so immovable, but the world as it might be within itself, himself as he might be within himself, promised paradise. Another of his aphorisms runs:

> The expulsion from Paradise is in the main eternal: So it is indeed true that the expulsion from Paradise is final and life in the world unavoidable, yet the eternalness of the event (or, expressed in temporal terms, the eternal repetition of the event) makes it possible nevertheless that not only might we live in Paradise permanently, but that we are actually permanently there, no matter whether we know it here or not.[50]

If the expulsion from paradise is eternal, then we dwell eternally in it: for we have to keep on being in it in order to keep on being driven out of it.

Kafka, with his sense of unlimited human possibility, is in the line of Rousseau. He goes back still further to the Jewish messianic tradition. But he also goes back, at the very same time, to a Jewish rationalist tradition which sardonically postpones the coming of the Messiah to "the day after he comes." He reflects the essential hopelessness of his own father, and so many of the fathers of Jewry, on whose sense of the possibilities of life the gates of the ghetto still remained shut. "In us," Kafka said to Janouch, the ghetto "still lives—the dark corners, the secret alleys, shuttered windows, squalid courtyards. . . ." [51] But he also reflects the essential strength of his own father and so many of the fathers of Jewry: the strength to endure, to endure in spite of everything, feeling despair but not yielding to it finally, defeated but not ever giving in. In him one feels a hope of life that somehow outlasts life itself, a hope after all hope is gone, the Messiah who will come the day after he comes.

On one side stood the possibility of marriage, of children, of human connection and contentment—everything he understood by life in the world (what he called Canaan)—but also defection from his own spirituality; writing and the freezing solitude of his own subjectivity and spirituality stood on the other (what he called the wilderness).[52] He had to die as a human being to live as a writer, to lose in order to win. It was an old (by now it is a conventional) attitude of the modern age,* but with him it was not an attitude, it was his life, the antithesis that he lived and died from.

The breath of life-in-the-world that his love affair with Milena Jesenská brought him, the joy and sanity of human relationship

---

* Mann's *Tonio Kröger* is a *locus classicus* for its expression. Flaubert, whose moral resignation was so different from Kafka's own rigor, based his existence on a split between literature and life. "A love that was normal, regular, permanent and solid would take me out of myself too much, would worry me. I should return to active life, physical truth and, finally, to the common path. And it's precisely that which has proved harmful every time I've tried it," Flaubert wrote to Alfred Le Poittevin. To Louise Colet he wrote words which Kafka echoes almost exactly: "Perhaps it's my heart which is impotent. I'm exhausted by the deplorable mania for analysis." [53]

that it brought to the stony solitude, the snowy waste he inhabited, was for him a storm that he hoped would "fly out of the window . . . I cannot after all keep a storm in my room."* [54] Another letter to her remembers as

> perhaps the best time of your life [he is addressing himself at this point] those eight months in a village about two years ago where you thought you'd finished with everything, where you were free . . . in the shelter of your illness [his tuberculosis], and when at the same time you didn't have to change much of yourself, but had only to retrace more firmly the old narrow outlines of your nature (after all, your face under the gray hair has hardly changed since your sixth year).[55]

The best time of his life was when he thought he was finished with the world once and for all and did not need to make the effort to change himself. In a letter written to Max Brod after his affair with Milena had ended, he said, touchingly but obstinately:

> You'll be talking to M., I'll never have that happiness again. When you do, talk about me as if about a dead man, I mean as far as concerns my "outside," my "extraterritoriality." When Ehrenstein paid me a visit the other day, he said something to the effect that in M. life put out its hand to me and I had the choice of life or death; that was rather too grandly said (not about M. but about me), but essentially it was true, the foolish thing about it was, he seemed to think I had a choice. If there were still a Delphic oracle and I had questioned it, it would have answered: "The choice of life or death? How can you hesitate?" [56]

He would not change himself, he would not change his life direction, and yet he would not stop condemning himself for not changing himself. He wandered stubbornly (but also helplessly) in the wilderness, yet he was convinced that Canaan was the only proper place for a human being. He quoted the Talmud which says that a man who has no wife is not a proper human

---

* But later on in the affair Kafka was ready to join with Milena, provided she would break finally from the husband to whom she was unhappily married. She wasn't able to.

being.[57] He is the mouse in his "Little Fable" whom the cat eats up because it is unable to change its direction:

> "Alas," said the mouse, "the world is growing smaller every day. At the beginning it was so big that I was afraid, I kept running and running, and I was glad when at last I saw walls far away to the right and left, but these long walls have narrowed so quickly that I am in the last chamber already, and there in the corner stands the trap that I must run into." "You only need to change your direction," said the cat, and ate it up.[58]

He is the mouse who cannot change his direction, but he is also Franz Kafka, the writer, who has arranged it all: the mouse, the trap, the cat, the fable.

If Kafka found himself as a writer when he found his dream narrative, this discovery did not originate entirely within himself; he did not fetch it up entirely from the depths of his own subjectivity and dreams, with more or less assistance from Freudian ideas. Although his preoccupation with his own dreams was extreme (in 1911 Max Brod noted in his diary that "nothing but Kafka's own dreams seem to interest him any more" [59]), all of literary Prague at the turn of the century seemed preoccupied with dreams and nightmares. Klaus Wagenbach speaks of the "hothouse atmosphere" of the Bohemian capital in those years and describes its literary productions as a "gruesome waxworks of the most fantastic figures. . . . A good deal of that airless, oppressive dream world entered into Kafka's work. . . ." [60] His writing not only came out of his own private head, it also came out of historical and sociological circumstances which he shared with others. Kafka was a German-speaking Jew of the old (Imperial) Prague in the years immediately preceding the First World War and the collapse of the Austro-Hungarian Empire. It has often been remarked that as a German speaker he was cut off from the Czechs,* and as a Jew

---

* Kafka's father had migrated as a young man from the Bohemian countryside to Prague, where he gave up his native Czech for German. Kafka was distinguished from most of his Prague contempora-

from the Germans. But as a Western Jew—as, in his own words, "the most typical Western Jew": so he describes himself to Milena[61]—he was not only cut off from traditional Judaism and the bits and pieces of it that survived in the Prague community, he was also cut off from his fellow Western Jews. ("What do I have in common with Jews, I have hardly anything in common with myself. . . ." [62]) For to be "the most typical Western Jew" was to be naked and alone even in the midst of the naked and alone, even in the middle of what had been the old Prague ghetto; it was to be somebody, he writes in the same letter to Milena, to whom "nothing is granted," "not one calm second," somebody for whom it was the case that "everything had to be earned, not only the present and the future, but the past too. . . ." As the most typical Western Jew, Kafka lived that "nothingness" to the limit. The others scattered on the run in every direction, seeking a positive association—a past, present, and future—in Zionism, or Marxism, or Orthodox Judaism, or socialism, or German nationalism, or conversion, or bohemianism, or literature, or what have you. Kafka too tried some of these but he could never carry any of them through and remained in Prague with his "nothingness." On May 3, 1915, he writes in his diary:

> What is there of a past or a future to support me? The present is a phantom state, I don't sit at the table but hover around it. Nothing, nothing. Emptiness, boredom, no, not boredom, only emptiness, meaninglessness, weakness.[63]

His estrangement from the world and from himself of course had sociological as well as personal reasons. In its sociological aspect it showed itself in a sense of unreality which he shared with his contemporaries in Prague (most of whom were Jews) and which found expression in a literary genre of nightmares peculiar to the Bohemian capital at the turn of the century. The sense of unreality reflected the situation of Austria-Hungary, an ancient empire whose outward panoply concealed an advanced

ries by knowing Czech; he strongly sympathized with Czech nationalism.

stage of inner decay. The traditional external forms, political, social and moral, hid the truth within; under the placid surface of things breakdown threatened. Something of this situation went into the making of a Freud, who saw with the clear judgment of a physician and an outsider the toll in illness and debility that the split took and extended his observations of the symptoms he noted in Vienna into a universal diagnosis. But most of Kafka's contemporaries exploited the sense of unreality and alienation for its sensational interest, producing second-rate works that specialized in the extravagant and outré. They exploited the dream for its bizarre effects. He used it for its truth.

Kafka also used the Prague German dialect for its truth. In Prague, Wagenbach writes, German was, actually, a foreign tongue, "a kind of officially subsidized language employed on holiday occasions . . . dry and artificial, a foreign element." [64] Kafka's contemporaries tried to deny the lifelessness and alien character of *Prager Deutsch* by a forced vivacity and colorfulness of style. But Kafka accepted its essential foreignness, as he accepted his own foreignness in all things, building his style on the actual character of Prague German (as mentioned earlier) rather than trying to invent another character for it—building his style, that is, on the truth of Prague German.

The foreignness of the German language in Prague made it possible for him to take "a detached view of individual words which did not occur either in daily use or in the [*Prager Deutsch*] dialect. Individual words, especially out-of-the-way ones, were taken literally, revealing their original meaning. This way of taking language literally is quite pronounced in Kafka's work. . . ." [65] Here we have the linguistic basis of Kafka's psychoanalytic imagination. Kafka's tendency in his first works is to penetrate the abstract covering of custom and convention and reveal the original, concrete significance of language. He analyzes German words into their original elements. His imagination, working in the same way that the mind works in dreams, seeks its truth in the primitive concrete hidden within the abstract conventional.[66] Thanks to his distance as a Prague Jew from the German language, he is able to see it in an "analytic" way.

In his early works, however, this literalist tendency is limited to individual words and phrases and does not reach as far as fundamental narrative conception. In his early works he has not yet discovered his highly poetic form of the dream narrative based on a single literal image whose unfolding is the Kafka story. Without much interest of their own (except for the short pieces collected in *Betrachtung* [*Meditation*],[67] the works he wrote before *The Judgment* are interesting for the light they shed on Kafka's development as a writer.

2   *JUSTIFICATIONS*

OF NONBEING

Although Kafka's pen was busy from his adolescence on, little of his early work has survived. Undoubtedly he destroyed a great many of his manuscripts: "Burned a lot of awful old papers today," he notes in his diary on March 11, 1912.[1] He was as severe a judge of his work as he was of himself. But if he judged his own work harshly one may hope that he also judged it well and never burned anything of real literary value. True, he threatened to burn some of his best work too, especially the never-completed manuscripts of his novels, yet he never did; although his testamentary notes to Max Brod say that he would really like every page of his destroyed, that was impossible in the case of his published stories and most unlikely in the case of his unpublished writings which, as he well knew, his friend was not about to put a match to. There was a certain consistency in his wishing to make a bonfire of everything he had written, but there was an equal consistency in his asking it of a friend who had always struggled to elicit Kafka's work from him and make it known.

The two chief early works, the novella *Description of a Struggle,* and the novel fragment "Wedding Preparations in the Country," would seem to confirm such a view of Kafka's judgment of his own work. For these two compositions, which he really meant to destroy—they escaped burning only by the accident of getting lost among Brod's papers—have little intrinsic value. The earliest one, *Description of a Struggle,* written in 1904–1905[2] when Kafka was twenty-one, is a series of loosely connected descriptions and conversations that hardly make a story. The novella begins prosaically enough: it is midnight at a party and a few people get up to leave. The narrator is sitting alone at a table and is annoyed to see a new acquaintance, who is flushed from kissing his girl in the next room, coming to join him. Thus, at the very start of Kafka's work the theme is one of a stubborn-helpless solitariness in the midst of the feast of life, estrangement from the wedding of the world (the erotic component of the theme is strong and immediate). The narrator is not only estranged from the world, he is also estranged from himself: "Hardly were we outside when I evidently began to feel very gay"—separated from himself, he must say that he "evidently" began to feel gay. A few lines later, after slapping his acquaintance on the back, "I suddenly no longer understood his mood, and withdrew my hand. Since I had no use for it, I stuck it in the pocket of my coat." [3]—his contact with another human being dies as soon as it is born and he withdraws his hand ("Whew, what a cold hand!" the acquaintance says about it later), which is an object of embarrassment to him now that it has committed the indiscretion of touching somebody, and puts it in his pocket as if it were something separate from himself.

It is only with Part II, when the narrator suddenly jumps onto the shoulders of the acquaintance, that the story veers off into a phantasmagoria of dissolving and re-forming landscapes dotted with extraordinary figures that carry on declamatory conversations within conversations. There is nothing dreamlike about this, or it is dreamlike only in a loose and inaccurate sense of the word. The work is a phantasmagoria rather than a dream, shifting images of the intellect deliberately cast by a magic lantern rather than a theater of subjective reality. *Description of a Struggle,* for all its pictorial quality, is a series of reflections, thoughts expressed in a vocabulary of bizarre pictures, a kind of graphic *pensées,* rather than anything like a real novella. Kafka declared as much himself when he rejected the work as a whole but quarried it for individual sketches and short pieces which he published separately, along with other short pieces, under the title of *Meditation.*

The novella as a whole, with its Zarathustrian invocations, apocalyptic conversations, and a yellow fat man borne on a litter through an Oriental landscape (inspired by an old Japanese woodcut, Brod reports, that Kafka was very fond of [4]) has an artificial, even precious quality reminiscent of its time, which was the Orientalizing *fin de siècle.*[5] It belongs to that highly contrived, intellectualized literature which Austria especially has produced and which is so thin-blooded and local underneath its cosmopolitan sophistication. This literature, whose stamp is on such eminent writers as Robert Musil and Hermann Broch, cannot really survive outside the milieu that gave it birth. Kafka owed much to his time and place, but it was precisely this aesthetic preciousness and parochialism which he had to transcend to become more than just another Prague *littérateur.*

Yet if *Description of a Struggle* is artificial in its form, the style is already moving toward that classical spareness which is fully achieved for the first time in *The Judgment.* And on the level of reflection, the story announces themes that will occupy Kafka the rest of his life. It is very much a young man's work on the aesthetic side, derivative, uncertain, and unsuited to what is struggling inside him to come out; but on the side of thinking, as thoughts, it has his ageless and eternal quality, which is simply the effect of his eternal struggle with nonbeing, a struggle that has neither youth nor age. It is the same struggle waged by Georg Bendemann in *The Judgment*, Gregor Samsa in *The Metamorphosis*, Joseph K. in *The Trial*, and K. in *The Castle*—except that in those works the struggle is actualized rather than just being thought about. The struggle that his first work describes is a failing one against the impossibility of living—Part II is entitled "Proof That It's Impossible to Live." Thus the supplicant says to his interlocutor that he hopes "to learn from you how things really are, why it is that around me things melt away [*versinken*] like fallen snow, whereas for other people even a little liqueur glass stands on the table as steady as a statue." [6] In the midst of the completely artificial genre of narrative that Kafka is employing here, he expresses with unaffected directness his sense of overwhelming dissolution, of everything melting into nothing, which others do not seem to feel. The supplicant wants to learn "how things really are"—to find out how things really are will be the aim of everything that Kafka writes. In the "Conversation with the Supplicant" that Kafka published separately in a magazine in 1909, he revised the above passage to make the point explicit and carry it further:

> There has never been a time in which I have been convinced from within myself that I am alive. You see, I comprehend the things around me only through such collapsing conceptions [*hinfälligen Vorstellungen*] that I always feel things once were real but now are dwindling away [*versinkend*]. I have a constant longing, my dear sir, to catch a glimpse of things as they may be before they show themselves to me. I feel that then they are calm and beautiful. It must be so, for I often hear people talking about them as though they were.[7]

The world simply will not stand up straight and solid for him but dwindles and founders because the "conceptions" that once sustained it and kept it from dissolving in an anarchic flood are now "collapsing." This is the same thing (though only at the level of ideas) as Yeats's "Things fall apart; the centre cannot hold."

31

Only where Yeats sees this historically, Kafka feels it on his own body, as it were; he feels in his own brain the failing hold of the center, it not only fails historically, it fails in him. For Yeats it is the failure of the traditional order. For Kafka it is the failure of the indispensable primary order of existence itself. In *Description of a Struggle*, however, he can only think about this; later he is able to realize it concretely in a narrative.

The germ of the novella is contained in a passage in a letter that Kafka wrote to Brod on August 28, 1904,[8] and which he incorporated practically unchanged into the work. In it he expresses astonishment at the confidence with which people can ask a question and expect an answer, at the assurance with which they live in a world that he experiences as being, in Kleist's phrase, so infirm (*gebrechlich*):

> When as a little child I opened my eyes after a brief afternoon nap, still not quite sure I was alive, I heard my mother up on the balcony asking in a natural tone of voice: "What are you doing, my dear? Goodness, isn't it hot?" From the garden a woman answered: "Why, I'm having my tea on the lawn." They spoke casually and not very distinctly, as though the woman had expected the question, my mother the answer.[9]

In the letter, in place of the last line quoted above, he made a more explicit comment: "Then I marvelled at the assurance with which people are able to go on living." The most banal incident of this kind for Kafka is a "marvel." In the letter the scene is said to have taken place "the other day"; in the novella the supplicant says it happened when he was a "little child." Kafka's wonder and astonishment at the world, that it stands up straight and strong for others and for himself is always collapsing, he makes into a child's astonishment—the astonishment of a child awakening from sleep. A child's astonishment runs right through his work. He marvels at the ordinary because for him there is nothing ordinary, nothing assured. Subsequently in the later works childish wonder becomes a radical criticism of the modern reality.

And even at the beginning the wonder is critical, although in the rather snobbish way of the young Prague *littérateurs* who turned their noses up at their parents' bourgeois world; it expresses itself in a defiant challenge to conventional reality and in a modish "justification of [his own] non-being." [10] When the supplicant leaves a party and passes out into the Prague night, he feels himself called into question by the world's otherness and retorts:

"What is it that makes you all behave as though you were real? Are you trying to make me believe I'm unreal, standing here absurdly on the green pavement? You, sky, surely it's a long time since you've been real, and as for you, Ringplatz, you never have been real." [11]

The second piece of writing from the early years is a fragment of a novel, "Wedding Preparations in the Country." Written a year or so after the *Description,* it marks a definite development in narrative style, if not an improvement in literary interest. Nothing remains of the artificial phantasmagoricalness of the earlier work; the oddly detached realism of the first part of the *Description* now prevails throughout, a kind of spookiness which expresses the menace of nonexistence. And it is the plainest kind of realism, based on the minute description of things; plain indeed to the point of being gray. But something of that prosaicness so intense that it turns into a kind of magic, which is the quality of Kafka's mature style, is just beginning to be present. The story begins:

When Eduard Raban walked through the entrance hall into the open doorway, he saw that it was raining. It was raining just a little.

On the sidewalk directly in front of him many people were walking by at different speeds. Every so often one of them would step out and cross the road. A little girl was holding a tired puppy in her outstretched hands. Two gentlemen were exchanging information. One moved his hands, which he held palm-upward, up and down in a regular motion, as though he were balancing a load. Then one caught sight of a lady whose hat was covered with ribbons, buckles and flowers. And hurrying past came a young man with a thin walking stick, holding his left hand, as though paralyzed, flat against his chest. Now and then men who were smoking came by, bearing small upright elongated clouds along in front of them. Three gentlemen—two holding top coats over their crooked forearms—several times walked forward from the front of the buildings to the edge of the sidewalk, observed what was going on there and then went back again without interrupting their conversation.[12]

Raban (the first of several parallel names for Kafka that occur in his stories), who is unhappily on his way to join his fiancée for a short holiday in the country, observes the world in almost hallucinatory detail across the same gulf of separation which one noticed in the *Description*. The novel fragment is a register of what he sees on the street, in the railroad car and in the station omnibus—all passing in anxious review before his stranger's eyes—accompanied by his musings and reveries. What is described is Raban's consciousness but not his "stream of consciousness"; Kafka does not try to represent the flux of Raban's mental life as it is actually experienced, but stands back of it as it were (but still inside Raban's head—which is his own head) and notes its contents with a kind of scientific detachment. His way of writing here is analytic and, as in *Description of a Struggle*, produces thoughts and observations, but not a living story. Only when he hits on the literal image in which the unconscious reality is enfolded, is he able to penetrate the depths of consciousness by unfolding the image in a narrative; then his way of writing, which was analytic and unawakened, becomes "psychoanalytic" and alive.

Evidently the novel was meant to describe a man who found it "impossible to live" in the world, and specifically to marry—a note of Brod's in 1924 describes its subject matter as being the "anxieties of somebody who wishes to marry." [13] For Raban, work is impossible, love is impossible, life is impossible:

". . . One works so excessively at the office that afterwards one is too tired even to enjoy one's holidays properly. But even all that work doesn't give one a claim to be treated lovingly by everyone, on the contrary one is alone, a total stranger, and only an object of curiosity. And as long as you say 'one' instead of 'I' it's nothing at all and one can tell this story, but as soon as you admit to yourself that it is you yourself, you feel as though transfixed and start with terror." [14]

The last sentence of the quotation points directly ahead to Kafka's greatest works, to their pure subjectivity which expresses the terror of saying "I" to yourself instead of "one." But at this point he is still unable to really "tell this story"; he is only able to think about it. In *The Metamorphosis* he says "I" and Gregor Samsa wakes up to find himself changed into a gigantic bug. In "Wedding Preparations" Eduard Raban can only imagine himself, in a reverie, being changed into a bug. Dreading going out into the world to visit his fiancée, he thinks of taking refuge in a daydream as he used to do as a child:

"I don't even need to go to the country myself, it isn't necessary. I'll send my dressed up body. If it stumbles out of the door of my room, the stumbling will indicate not fear but its nothingness. . . . I myself am meanwhile lying in my bed, the yellow-brown blanket drawn smoothly over me, exposed to the breeze that blows through the seldom aired room. The carriages and the people in the street drive and walk hesitantly on polished ground, for I am still dreaming. Coachmen and pedestrians are shy and every step they take forward they ask as a favor from me, by looking at me. I encourage them, they meet no obstacles . . . I have, as I lie in bed, the shape of a big beetle, a stag beetle or a cockchafer, I think. . . .

"The shape of a big beetle, yes. Then I would pretend that I was hibernating and squeeze my little legs against my bulging belly. And I would whisper a few words of instruction to my unhappy body, which stands stooping close beside me. Soon I am done—it bows, it goes off swiftly and it will take care of everything in the best way possible, while I rest." [15]

Bedroom, bed, blankets—the furnishings of the Kafka dream narrative are all here, but unable to come to life, thoughts in Raban's head rather than living images.

The strong, even obsessive descriptive emphasis of "Wedding

Preparations," which was already present in *Description of a Struggle,* will remain a permanent feature of his writing, able in the future to make his dream of the world real where now it fails to show, as Kafka wished to in his early writing, the real world as a dream—as "a nothing, a dream, a dim hovering." [16] Wagenbach in his biography connects the descriptive emphasis with the prominent place given to description in the instruction Kafka received at the German Gymnasium. He also sees the influence of natural science in Kafka's exact, exhaustive notation of detail —thanks to an admired teacher of natural history who was a convinced Darwinist, the sixteen-year-old, otherwise without scientific inclination, read Darwin and Haeckel and came under the influence of scientific naturalism.[17] (This is not to gainsay the other influences that encouraged Kafka's descriptive tendency, among which are Kleist's novelle with their extreme circumstantiality of style.) The young Kafka also was a socialist and an atheist and belonged to a student organization whose purpose was to combat clerical influence. Hardly any account has been taken of this "naturalistic" side of Kafka's; there is little trace of it in Brod's biography and criticism until recently has overlooked it. But it was very prominent in his formative years and remained a part of him in some sort to the very end. The matter has importance because it indicates Kafka's literary as well as intellectual provenance. His literary origins lie in realism-naturalism, in much the same way that Joyce's and Mann's do. "Kafka's work has its starting point in naturalism rather than expressionism, improbable as that may sound. . . . The early Franz Kafka is concerned above all with the detailed 'description' and exact representation of everything that exists, just like the 'thorough-going naturalist' Arno Holz, Emile Zola and others," writes Wilhelm Emrich.* [18]

This shift in the same writer, from realism to something whose

* Professor Emrich's exhaustive study, which interprets Kafka's images and ideas solely within the framework of his own writings, helps to pull the writer out from under many of the alien notions heaped on him.

varied forms and expressions are lumped together under the name of symbolism, happened often enough at the turn of the century. The novelist starts out in the old realistic mode and then, dissatisfied, turns back for help to that very "poetry" which the realistic novel had had to get rid of so as to find its truth. The transition is as clearly marked as one could wish in Joyce. It also occurs in Lawrence and Mann; and before them, in an anticipatory way, in James and Conrad. And before all these its course is laid down in Flaubert. "Anything is interesting if you only look at it long enough," Flaubert said.[19] Eduard Raban registers the contents of the world in something like the spirit of this remark, except that the confusion and dismay which underlie such a saying have not yet reached awareness in Flaubert, whereas they menace Kafka with the impossibility of living. If everything is equally interesting, then everything is equally uninteresting— underneath Flaubert's remark yawns the void of nothingness, which he was still able to feel only as a mood of ennui and disgust, but which Kafka experienced to the full. Flaubert's observation seems to express the confidence of a scientific attitude which, faced by the crumbling of the old European spiritual order, is ready to study everything and make its own sense of it, putting things together into a new order. In fact, however, he is without that confidence. He has no confidence in the world, only in literature. Flaubert invents symbols (for the traditional symbols have lost their power) so as to make a literary world of his own even as the world itself is falling apart for him—"each of his books is a 'forest of symbols,'" to quote Martin Turnell.[20] Literature replaces life.

Kafka doesn't share the modern writer's inordinate confidence in literature, in the power of words to make things real; or he shares it only wryly, recognizing it as hubris, as a claim to create like God.* Although Kafka keeps out of his "creation" as scrupu-

---

* Stephen Spender praises this ambition: "The imagination has been restored in modern literature to its position of Verb. The reinstating of imagination as primary, central, the verb, was perhaps the attitude responsible for the greatest modern achievements: works like

lously as Stephen Dedalus' artist-God, utterly rejecting the role of an author who mixes in everywhere and arranges things to suit his own conceptions, he does not stand off at a distance contemplating his handiwork with detached, nail-paring satisfaction—he keeps out of his story as a stage-managing author just precisely by flinging himself right into the middle of it as K., without retaining a shred of advantage for himself as the author. Kafka reinvents the world too, but in despair, for his world has a negative basis. Kafka does not write stories that triumph over life through his art; his art is based just precisely on the defeat which follows from the fact that the "indestructible something," without which it is impossible to live, remains concealed from him.[22]

A last fragment from the early years, the seven pages of a story called "The Urban World" which Kafka wrote into his diary in 1911, carries the development of his narrative right to the brink of *The Judgment*. The subject of the story is the "opposition between fathers and sons"—between "Oscar M., an oldish student," and his angry father.

> Oscar M., an oldish student—if you looked at him close up his eyes were frightening—stopped short one winter's afternoon in the middle of a snowstorm on an empty square, in his winter clothes and overcoat, wearing a shawl around his neck and a fur cap on his head. His eyes blinked in thought. He was so lost in thought that once he took his cap off and rubbed its kinky fur against his face. Finally he seemed to have made up his mind and turned homewards with a dancing movement.
>
> When he opened the door to his parents' sitting room he saw his father, a smooth-shaven man with a heavy, fleshy face, seated at an empty table, facing the door.
>
> "At last," the latter said, when Oscar had barely set foot inside

the last novels of Henry James (particularly *The Golden Bowl*), *Finnegans Wake*, Yeats's Byzantium poems, the *Duineser Elegien*, put these writers in the Godlike position of being isolated within their own creations, of having to reinvent the world and all its values within their art." [21]

the room, "stay by the door, please, I'm so furious with you I don't know what I might do."

"But Father," Oscar said, and noticed only when he spoke how he had been running.

"Silence," his father shouted and stood up, blocking a window. "Silence, I say. And keep your 'buts' to yourself, do you understand?" At the same time he gripped the table with both hands and carried it a step nearer to Oscar. "I simply won't put up with your good-for-nothing existence any longer. I'm an old man, I hoped you would be the comfort of my old age, instead you are worse than all my ailments. Shame on such a son whose laziness, extravagance, wickedness and (why shouldn't I say so to your face) stupidity are driving his old father to the grave!" Here his father stopped, but his face worked as if he were still speaking.

The style is purely realistic. The meditative, thinking character of all that Kafka has written hitherto has at last disappeared. Now he is no longer "thinking about" something, he is telling a story. He has learned to say "I" instead of "one." The utter objectivity of language is the stylistic aspect of his courage to be directly subjective and confront himself.

But the story trails off disappointingly in the conversation with the friend Franz. Beginning with abrupt effect with the father's attack on the son (the fact that it is a death struggle is slyly hinted at in the elder M.'s conventional phrase about his being driven to the grave), it fails to break through the surface reality in a metaphorical extension and consummation of its meaning. Instead, a tendency to silly word play in the exchange between father and son, which signals the collapse of inspiration, becomes an outright embarrassment in Oscar's conversation with Franz.

What remains, then, from the early years in the way of accomplished literary work are the short pieces that Kafka assembled from *Description of a Struggle* and from his diary and published under the title of *Meditation*—a handful of pages. I think the critic must approve Kafka's literary self-judgment. His longer works had failed and he abandoned them; but some of the reflections scattered through his writings shone with authentic value and these he brought together to make up that curious little work. Or at least to the English reader the work seems curious. For the kind of ideas that Kafka expresses in these pieces, in English literature would go into poems or in some cases even essays. German literature is not so severe about forms; but if this imposes less of a check on mere effusiveness, it also affords more opportunity for direct expression. The engaging trait of these meditations is the way in which they give trusting, unaffected utterance to intimate feelings which are at the same time general ideas. The work has a unity which is not at first apparent, based on its meditative, melancholy tone and its theme and perspective of estrangement. One needs to read the pieces over and over; gradually they acquire a surprising force:

THE TREES
For we are like tree trunks in the snow. Apparently they lie lightly poised and with a little push one could dislodge them. No, one can't, for they are stuck fast to the ground. But see, even that is only apparent.

Four short simple sentences evoke the receding vistas of appearance of *The Trial* and *The Castle,* Kafka's dialectic of hope and despair. It needs only a little push to move us; but only apparently so because we are stuck fast; but that too is only apparent —it needs more than a little push to move us, and yet we are not stuck fast.

"The Sudden Walk" consists of two sentences: a marvelously flexible one, a page long, in which the repeated "when" clauses are so many wing beats fighting to lift "you" clear of the trammels of the family:

When it looks as if you had made up your mind finally to stay at home for the evening, when you have put on your house jacket and sat down after supper with a light on the table to the piece of work or the game that usually precedes your going to bed, when the weather outside is unpleasant so that staying indoors seems natural, and when you have already been sitting quietly at the table for so long that your departure must occasion surprise to everyone, when, besides, the stairs are in darkness and the front door locked . . .

and which culminates in the climactic "then" clause in which "you" finally soar away into the upper air of freedom; and a short staccato sentence of peroration that wraps the victory up. The elation of "The Sudden Walk" is followed (and refuted) by the graveyard depression of "Resolutions." "Outing in the Mountains" takes nothingness seriously (i.e., treats it as indeed something, by playing on the word "nobody") and so makes a bitter witticism about lack of human relation:

> "I don't know," I cried soundlessly, "I just don't know. If nobody comes, then nobody comes. I've done nobody any harm, nobody's done me any harm, but nobody will help me. A lot of nobodies! Yet that isn't really so. It's just that nobody helps me—otherwise a lot of nobodies would be rather nice. I'd love to go on an outing —why not?—in the mountains with a lot of nobodies. Of course in the mountains, where else? How these nobodies crowd against each other, all these outstretched arms linked together, all these feet treading on each other's heels! . . . Our throats are free in the mountains! It's a wonder that we don't start singing."

Standing "on the tram," in the sketch of that name, Kafka feels "completely unsure of my footing in this world, in this town, in my family." He notices, across the void of separation in which he moves, a girl standing ready to get off at the next stop; the piece describes her minutely:

> She is as distinct to me as if I had run my hands over her. She is dressed in black, the pleats of her skirt hang almost still, her blouse is tight and has a collar of white fine-meshed lace, her left hand is braced flat against the side of the tram, the umbrella in her right hand rests on the second top step . . .

and on and on. His naïve astonishment at her mere being-ness casts doubt on her reality—is she really there or is she an apparition? It is the same question he asks about himself. But to treat her being as a question rather than as given, is at the same time to translate it out of the sphere of the ordinary into that of the miraculous. Where all existence is in doubt, life itself, the most banal kind of life, becomes an object of amazement, a miracle. And so he wonders, "How is it that she is not amazed at herself, that she keeps her lips closed and makes no such remark?"

Meditation opens, with evident intention, with a piece about the unthinking happiness of childhood, "Children on a Country Road"—one of Kafka's finest short sketches; it closes with "Unhappiness" (a less satisfactory one), in which he is visited by a child ghost (that is, the ghost of childhood). "Children on a Country Road" evokes the separateness and secrecy, inside the adult world, of the child's world. Adults exist at some far remove: "I was given my supper by candle light. Often both my arms were on the wooden board and I was already tired as I bit into my bread and butter." (It is like the food that lowers itself into the canine world from on high in *Investigations of a Dog.*) The "tired," melancholy boy gets up "with a sigh" when he is called out into the evening by his friends for a breathless run. "What are you sighing for? What's wrong? Has something dreadful happened that can never be made good? Shan't we ever recover from it? Is everything lost?" But "nothing was lost":

> We ran our heads full tilt into the evening. There was no daytime and no nighttime. . . . Like cuirassiers in old wars, stamping and springing high, we drove each other down the short alley and with this impetus in our legs a farther stretch along the main road. Stray figures went into the ditch, hardly had they vanished down the dusky escarpment when they were standing like newcomers on the field path above and looking down.
>
> "Come on down!"—"Come on up first!"—"So's you can push us down, no thanks, we're not such fools."—"You're afraid, you mean. Come on up, you cowards!"—"Afraid? Of the likes of you? You're going to push us down, are you? That's a good one."
>
> We made the attempt and were pushed head over heels into the grass of the roadside ditch, tumbling of our own free will. Everything was equally warm to us, we felt neither warmth nor chill in the grass, only one got tired.

It is Eden, except that one gets tired. So that when the boy's time is up and he says goodbye, he doesn't head for home but

> for that city in the south of which it was said in our village:
> "There you'll find queer folk! Just think, they never sleep!"
> "And why not?"
> "Because they're fools."
> "Don't fools get tired?"
> "How could fools get tired!"

The tiredness that the "fools" don't feel in the city in the south, the tiredness that the boy would like to escape, is the same tiredness that the bureaucrat Poseidon feels from the "endless work of administering all the waters." [23]

> Poseidon got tired of his ocean. The trident fell from him. Unmoving he sat on a rocky coast and a gull, dazed by his presence, described wavering circles around his head.[24]

It is the same tiredness that causes the castle officials to perpetually nod. It is the tiredness of rationalized existence, of an existence whose conscious purposes and processes are an exhausting "operation," divorced from unpurposed true existence.[25] The unpremeditated, ceaselessly flowing vitality of true existence, which Kafka suggests in the impetuous sentences describing the boys' run, belongs to children and fools, to the childish, foolish true self buried deep inside one, out of reach.

Against the happiness of childhood is the "Bachelor's Ill Luck":

> It seems so dreadful to stay a bachelor, to become an old man struggling to keep one's dignity while begging for an invitation whenever one wants to spend an evening in company, to lie ill gazing for weeks into an empty room from the corner where one's bed is, always having to say good night at the front door, never to run up a stairway beside one's wife, to have only side doors in one's room leading into other people's living rooms, having to carry one's supper home in one's hand, having to admire other people's children and not even being allowed to go on saying: "I

have none myself," modeling oneself in appearance and behavior on one or two bachelors remembered from one's youth.

That's how it will be, except that in reality as well, both today and later, one will stand there with a palpable body and a real head, and therefore, too, a real forehead, for smiting on with one's hand.

Once again there is the very long sentence, managed with virtuoso skill, that one saw in "A Sudden Walk," only now it has a dirgelike rise and fall that dies away defeated in the last clause. The naked expression of feeling in this piece, which came straight out of Kafka's diary with only a few changes, is breathtaking; it mediates life as directly as possible and abhors "literature." He sets his feeling down, which has nothing interestingly sad about it—it is the humblest possible feeling—like a dog lays its head in one's lap. But having set it down, he sees that it is inescapably words on a page—literature after all. And so he says in the final sentence, with resigned brevity: "That's how it will be, *except that in reality as well,*" and not only in diary entries and published books, his bachelor's fate is dreadful—always he struggles to break down the wall of words that separates literature from life, but knows that that consummation must await the coming of the Messiah on the day after he comes.

Looking back on his earliest work in 1920, Kafka summed it up as follows in one of the autobiographical jottings grouped under the rubric "He":

Many years ago I sat one day, in a sad enough mood, on the slopes of the Laurenziberg. I went over the wishes that I wanted to realize in life. I found that the most important or the most delightful was the wish to obtain a view of life (and—this was necessarily bound up with it—to convince others of it in writing) in which life, while still retaining its natural fullbodied rise and fall, would simultaneously be recognized no less clearly as a nothing, a dream, a dim hovering. A beautiful wish, perhaps, if I had wished it rightly. . . .

But he* could not wish in this fashion, for his wish was not a

* The passage switches from the first to the third person.

wish, but only a vindication of nothingness, a justification of non-being, a touch of animation which he wanted to lend to non-being, in which at that time he had scarcely taken his first few conscious steps, but which he already felt as his element. It was a sort of farewell that he took from the illusive world of youth; although youth had never directly deceived him, but only caused him to be deceived by the utterances of all the authorities he had around him. . . .[26]

This appraisal of his early writings, if we may judge them by *Description of a Struggle* and "Wedding Preparations in the Country," is harsh but accurate. He had wished to show the life around him as real and solid and at the same time as "a nothing, a dream, a dim hovering." But it wasn't a true wish because what he really had in mind was to show *up* the world around him, to thumb his nose at the "authorities" who had deceived him in his youth, by a snobbish justification of what was just his deepest anguish, his nothingness, the nonbeing "which he already felt as his element." Kafka is condemning himself for having yielded to something in the Prague environment that came to gross expression in "those snobs who run around as mystics and orthodox believers only because every tailor, schoolteacher and journalist is a believing atheist"—to quote Franz Werfel.[27]

From trying to show up reality as a dream, he turns in *The Judgment* to the dream as a way of revealing reality, passing out of the parochial literary milieu of Prague into a frontier region of world literature. He characterized his later writings as follows in another of these autobiographical notes:

Everything he does seems to him extraordinarily new, it is true, but also, consistent with the incredible outpouring of new things there is, extraordinarily amateurish, indeed scarcely tolerable, incapable of becoming history, breaking the chain of the generations, cutting off for the first time at its most profound source the music of the world, which before him could at least be divined. Sometimes in his arrogance he is more afraid for the world than for himself.[28]

Kafka recognizes the radical character of his stories, which he seems to class with the avant-garde art that was being produced

in such profusion at the time, but with his habitual self-depreca-
tion he wishes to dismiss them as being as amateurish as they
are novel. Gliding, however, along the rails of his self-condemnation he passes half-involuntarily into an almost extravagant
description of the revolutionary break they represent with traditional literature. And he concludes with a sentence that expresses his feeling (which he calls arrogant) of possessing literary powers great enough to unsettle the world's foundations:
"Sometimes in his arrogance he is more afraid for the world than
for himself." Kafka knew that his work was an attack on the
modern world—a work of criticism. *He* doesn't after all cut off
the music of the world at its source, all he does is describe a
world in which that reality is reflected. Wagenbach says truly
that Kafka's writing continues a Jewish tradition which at first
sight would seem to be completely closed to fiction: the modern
Jewish tradition of criticism, which makes such an important
part of the general critical tradition of modern times, represented by Heine, Marx, Freud, and Einstein.[29] Because he is
aware of this, Kafka says he sometimes feels more afraid for the
world than for himself.*

* This "arrogant" fear for the world rather than for himself plays
its part in *The Castle*, where K. is the attacker and at the beginning
prone to "fits of easy confidence." [30] When the Bridge Inn landlady
pleads with K. to give up his crazy plan of seeking an interview with
the official Klamm, he asks her if she is not "afraid for Klamm." [31]

3 THE LITERATURE
OF TRUTH

"Reality's dark dream!"
—COLERIDGE

I said earlier that Kafka's imagination is a "psychoanalytic" one. Not because he studied Freud but because he grasped intuitively the split in the self and the struggle of the unacknowledged part against the public part. The single images unfolded in his dream narratives reveal the primitively literal at the heart of the abstract. Of all his stories, *The Judgment* furnishes perhaps the clearest demonstration of his psychoanalytic vision—clearest because least complicated by other considerations. The true starting point of his work, it is primarily a psychological story; although even here, at the start, his utterly simple images suggest an unlimited depth of significance and not only psychological depth.

47

The image that *The Judgment* unfolds is one of paternal condemnation and execution; it is the story of a father's sentencing his son to death. The essential metaphor of the story is contained in the title, *Das Urteil*. *Urteil* (like the English "judgment") has both the literal ("primitive") legal-judicial meaning of "sentence" or "verdict," and the abstract meaning of "critical estimate," "opinion." The literal death *sentence* reveals the murderous truth buried underneath the abstract surface of the father's *opinion* of the son. The destructive paternal judgment is laid bare symbolically in an actual condemnation to death.

This, however, is only to give the formula of the symbolism of the story. It misses the unusual dynamic character of the symbolism. For the relation of the literal to the abstract, of the image to the idea, in this story (as in *The Trial* and *The Castle*) is not the usual symbolical one. The usual symbolical relation is given rather than being at issue in a work, fixed rather than in question, even when the symbolism is not traditionally established but is purely personal and arbitrary as in the case of modern symbolical literature. Bloom wanders through the confusion and uncertainty of the modern city, but amid all the uncertainty one thing is certain and that is his symbolical status as Ulysses. Bloom is Ulysses—on the rock of that metaphor the novel is built. Though everything may be uncertain in the world, *Ulysses* by James Joyce is certain. The modern world may totter over an abyss, but not the imaginative symbolical world created by the writer's art. Literature remains, if nothing else. In *Death in Venice* the whole order of civilization is symbolically shaken by the upheaval, inside Aschenbach, of demonic forces from the "abyss." But art remains unshaken. Art indeed is one of the forces of the abyss undermining civilization, rather than being undermined with it—it is a disease and disorder of life along with cholera, Italian duplicity, and illicit love. It is true that Mann thus calls art into question. What he questions, however, is its *moral justification* and therefore its "legality," not its existence. What the dazzling art of *Death in Venice* affirms is just its own triumphant existence, through an ironically classical style and symbolism which mock the morality of civilization and glorify the amoral power of art.[1]

But in *The Judgment* it is just its own symbolism, and therefore its existence, which is at issue. What the story is about is just the question of whether it shall have a symbolical meaning, or whether its symbolical meaning shall be overthrown by the action of the story. Shall the father be a figure of Godlike authority to his son, with the power to give life and take it away? Or shall he simply be a man like other men, and a doddering old man at that? ("We are all simply men here, one as much as the other," K. says to the priest in *The Trial*.[2]) Shall his father's judgment of Georg be a "sentence" of death on him, or one man's "opinion" of another? Is his father God, or a "comedian"[3] playing God? The struggle in the story, which takes place entirely inside Georg's subjectivity, is between his "primitive," "childish," irrational conception of his father, the existence of which his confident behavior at the beginning of the story would deny, and the appreciation of his father as being just a man. What the story is about is Georg's struggle against his "neurotic" submission to his father's "comic" pretensions to absolute authority; it is a "psychoanalytic" story through and through.

Georg's life hangs on the question of whether or not his father shall prevail over him in his own soul as a symbol. In the upshot the symbolical (which is to say the "neurotic") triumphs within Georg and he executes himself at his father's command. But suppose Georg had triumphed over his "neurosis," that is, had been able to reduce his father from a symbolically inflated figure to one that he is able to perceive in its literal dimensions? In that case the symbolical would have been overthrown by the—truth. The truth threatens to "expose" the lying symbolical and cancel the story. In Kafka's work, where everything tends toward the ultimate, there is an ultimate antagonism between literature and truth; by implication *The Judgment* raises the possibility of the "overcoming" of literature by truth.

Language tries symbolically to bridge the split between consciousness and existence, between our thinking and what is. In

Joyce and Mann the symbolical relation is static, expressing the split as an unchanging condition. In *The Judgment* the symbolical relation is dynamic, expressing the split as an active contention within the soul, which thus has the possibility of being resolved. Heal the rupture between consciousness and existence and the need for symbols—and so for literature in general—apparently vanishes. That is one of the meanings of paradise for Kafka: the place where no books are.

Joyce and Mann, as different as they are, are literary men, "wordmen," poet-makers of a supreme art-reality. For them words and symbols do finally express and uphold existence. Joyce writes about Stephen Dedalus: "Words which he did not understand he said over and over to himself till he had learnt them by heart: and through them he had glimpses of the real world about him." [4] Literature does finally reach reality. For Kafka literature and life are ultimately divided. Words are abstractions which miss the concrete truth of life; they are ultimately a veil hiding existence, although he tries to refine them to the highest degree of transparency. Like one of his bureaucracies, like the doorkeeper before the law in the parable the priest tells Joseph K. in *The Trial*, language stands between the individual and truth, blocking the way with its abstract imperviousness. Kafka is not a poet-maker but a poet-seer. Everywhere in him there is the anti- (or super-) literary effort to transcend literature and reach existence. The effort smacks a little of the early and the ancient (the classical) because words and existence were much more closely united for the ancient writers than they are for us. For them, however, such a union was not the result of transcendent vision but was given in the simplicity of early culture. In our own time the reunion of literature and existence must be the goal of a sheerly "Romantic" effort at transcendence. A transcendental longing lives at the heart of the classical pellucidity of Kafka's prose.

But such considerations outrun *The Judgment*, which is after all only a beginning in these directions.

For all its brevity *The Judgment* is a novella rather than a short story. The short story, being literary and prizing art, deals with what it can deal with and does not try to cram the whole story in. The novella on the other hand—the old Italian novella of the kind that Kleist and Stendhal wrote—is, literally, "news" and tries to tell the whole extraordinary story of some unheard of happening.* For the old novella it is not art that is extraordinary but what happens in life. The roughly carpentered, impatient old novella form has been refined by Kafka's hand into the simple-subtle form of his dream narrative, but its aim remains life-truth rather than literary art. Here, on the ground of a literature of truth rather than of art, Kleist, Stendhal, and Kafka are united.

The Judgment describes an "unheard of occurrence," in Goethe's words, but one so unheard of that it has passed beyond the limits of empirical reality into a dream world of poetic (metaphorical) reality. You can only call the reality of *The Judgment* metaphorical, however, by standing outside the story; it is an analytical statement. To experience the story you have to read it from inside, standing in Georg's shoes. Read from inside, the metaphor is felt as literally true. You have to stand inside the story and outside the story. This of course is what happens with dreams. Dreaming, one feels the dream as literally true; awake, one analyzes it as a metaphor. Kafka's art unites feeling and analysis; it asks that you should respond to its reality directly and wholeheartedly without standing off at a distance, and also that you should interpret it by analysis. It is an art that unites poetic vividness with intellectual subtlety.

The dream suggested to Kafka a narrative mode for expressing the absence that he felt of any ground but his own self to stand on. In his stories the narrator, like the dreamer, sees and hears only what is inside his own head. He knows the world only

* Goethe defined the old novella as follows: "Was ist eine Novelle anders als eine sich ereignete, unerhörte Begebenheit?" (What else is the novella but an unheard of occurrence that has taken place?)—Goethe to Eckermann, January 29, 1827.

as it is reflected inside himself. The evolution of modern narrative shows a more or less steady surrender of the traditional Godlike claim of the storyteller to omniscience. In *The Judgment* the distance between the narrator and his narration has dwindled to the vanishing point. As Friedrich Beissner writes, the Kafka narrator does not "manipulate his characters like a puppeteer or . . . explain the external facts and the external course of events to the reader through some knowledge he possesses by virtue of his detachment—rather he has completely transformed himself into the lonely Georg. . . ." [5] Georg is Kafka the narrator.* Why then does Kafka not write "I" instead of "Georg"? Why doesn't he use first person narrative rather than third person narrative? Because in the dream "I" appears to the dreamer as "him"—the self looks at the self and judges itself.†

Kafka's narrative mode eliminates every trace of the traditional hauteur of detachment of the narrator from his narration, and yet in the very unity of the narrator with his narration there is the detachment of the self standing off from itself and judging itself. The dream did not provide Kafka with a model for expressing mere senselessness or nihilistic phantasmagoria. Although he was driven back on his own self, that self was not simply helpless vis-à-vis the world but owned resources, and notably the power of judgment.‡ Judgment is as strong a quality in

* Not Kafka, but "Kafka the narrator."

† Kafka began *The Castle* as a first person narrative but then changed it back to the third person narrative he used in his earlier work. His narrative method was not a self-consciously worked out system which he knew how to use unerringly—he errs in *Amerika* and *In the Penal Colony*—but was more or less intuitively apprehended.

‡ The Romantic conviction that the self, through the power of imagination, creates the human reality, is still strong in Kafka, only it has lost its joyful confidence. With Coleridge he might have said that "we receive but what we give/And in ourselves alone does Nature live"—except that for lack of the knowledge of "something indestructible" the shaping spirit of Imagination hideously misshapes the world into what the ode on *Dejection* calls "Reality's dark dream!" But Kafka never stops believing that man has the power to dream the reality of paradise.

Kafka as the eeriness with which his name is associated; indeed the never defeated effort to judge and reason correctly in the midst of nightmarishness is an essential element of the Kafka eeriness. His dream stories are not helpless outcries or mere delusions, but like the creative dream itself they unite poetry and judgment in the dream image which is a criticism of the self and through the self a criticism of the world.

The Judgment turns upon the conflict between Georg's self as he thinks he is, would like to be and in part is, and his self as it really is, sleeping outside of his awareness but starting awake in the dream—between the apparently successful young business-man whose reverie opens the story and the helpless Georg for whom his father's word makes all things be or not be, the Georg who dies saying, "Dear parents, I have always loved you, all the same." There is the mystery of the friend in Russia, who is doubtless another side of the narrator's self—but more about him later.

The story opens on Georg looking out of the window of his room on a Sunday morning in spring, immersed in his own thoughts.* A successful young merchant, he has just finished a letter to an old friend now settled in Russia belatedly announc-

* Georg is a Kafkan window-gazer, a looker-out on the world like the "meditator" of *Meditation,* two of the pieces of which are called "Absent-minded Window-gazing" and "The Street Window." The latter piece states the meaning of window-gazing:

> Whoever leads a solitary life and yet now and then wants to attach himself somewhere, whoever, according to changes in the time of day, the weather, the state of his business and the like, suddenly wishes to see any arm at all to which he might cling—he will not be able to manage for long without a window looking on to the street. And if he is in the mood of not desiring anything and only goes to his window sill a tired man, with eyes turning from the public to heaven and back again, not wanting to look out and having thrown his head up a little, even then the horses below will draw him down into their train of wagons and tumult, and so at last into the human harmony.[6]

One must understand Georg as somebody who is striving to make himself part of "the human harmony."

ing his engagement to a well-off girl. His lengthy reverie turns around his unsuccessful misanthropic friend whom he has hesitated to tell about his business successes and most recently about his personal success in becoming engaged. There is a touch of condescension in his thoughts and more than a touch of impatience; he would like to advise his difficult, lonely friend to give up his unsuccessful Russian venture but cannot be sure that he would not be worse off at home. In the course of Georg's reverie we learn the main facts about his life: that he shares the household with his father, that his mother died two years before, and that since then he has taken an active part in the family business, which his father used to run dictatorially, so that it has bloomed surprisingly.

When Georg crosses from his own room to his father's, which he hasn't visited for months, he is surprised how dark it is. The darkness is the interior darkness of his own self. As his father rises to meet him, his heavy dressing gown swinging open and the skirts fluttering, Georg thinks, with a touch of surprise: "My father is still a giant of a man." His surprise at his father's strength increases as they talk: "In business hours he's quite different, he was thinking, how solidly he sits here with his arms crossed." In the light of day, his father appeared elderly and enfeebled; at the level of dreams—at the symbolical level—he sits with solid strength.

Georg has come to tell his father that he has written the news of his engagement to his friend in St. Petersburg.

> "To St. Petersburg?" asked his father.
> "To my friend there," said Georg, trying to meet his father's eye. . . .
> "Oh yes. To your friend," said his father, with emphasis.

His father's interrogative echoes and emphases undermine Georg's words so that they begin to ring hollowly. Then finally his father speaks, "lengthening his toothless mouth"—there is a constant shuttling back and forth in Georg between seeing his father as a dodderer and seeing him as a giant. The latter's speech is a querulous complaint about things being done since the mother died "that aren't right," his not being "equal to things any longer," his failing memory, how "our dear mother's death" affected him more than it did Georg—ending in a sudden thrust at his son:

> "But since we're talking about it, about this letter, I beg you, Georg, don't deceive me. It's a trivial affair, it's hardly worth mentioning, so don't deceive me. Do you really have this friend in St. Petersburg?"

Georg's response to the elder Bendemann's questioning the existence of his friend in Russia is one of "embarrassment," in which fear of his father (who can simply wipe a friend out of existence with a question) and fear that his father has become senile— fear of the giant, fear for the dodderer—are mingled. Georg resolves to take better care of his father in the future, to see to it that he eats properly, to call in a doctor, to exchange rooms with him—he resolves to treat him as ailing and incapable and to put him to bed at once. He is concerned for his father, but his concern is also a mask that hides his fear for himself—his fear that the old man may overthrow the successful, independent Georg who is about to cap his triumphs with marriage. His putting his father to bed is both an act of solicitude and a counterattack.

When Georg undresses the old man and notices remorsefully (and critically!) his "not particularly clean" underwear, he decides to take him into his own future household. "It almost looked, on closer inspection, as if the care he meant to lavish there on his father might come too late." This is the high point of Georg's perception of his father's weakness (for the latter is indeed dangerously weak), but also the high point of his conceit about his own strength vis-à-vis the elder Bendemann's.

The father submits to being put to bed; the senile way he plays with his son's watch chain while being carried there and hangs onto it when he attempts to lay him down, gives Georg a "dreadful feeling." Bendemann Sr. draws the covers up and looks at Georg "with a not unfriendly eye." The comedy the father and son are acting reaches its climax in the father's repeated question about whether he is "well covered up now." "Don't worry, you're well covered up," Georg replies soothingly.

At this point the novella explodes into a nightmare in whose lurid light the "primitive" truth about Georg Bendemann and his father is revealed.

> "No!" cried his father, cutting short the answer, threw the covers off with a strength that sent them all flying in a moment and sprang erect in bed. Only one hand lightly touched the ceiling.
>
> "You wanted to cover me up, I know, my young sprig, but I'm far from being covered up yet. And even if this is the last strength I have, it's enough for you, too much for you. Of course I know your friend. He would have been a son after my own heart. That's why you have been playing him false all these years. Why else? Do you think I haven't cried for him? And that's why you had to lock yourself up in your office—the Chief is busy, mustn't be disturbed—just so that you could write your lying letters to Russia. But thank goodness a father doesn't need to be taught how to see through his son. And now that you thought you'd got him down, so far down that you could set your bottom on him and he wouldn't move, then my lordly son makes up his mind to get married!"

The father understands "covered up" as meaning "buried," the bed Georg wishes to confine him to as a grave, their relations as a death struggle. The covers that he flings off are all those trappings of civilization which conceal the primitive battle to the death between fathers and sons. Suddenly we are pitched out of history back into natural history, into a world a good deal like that of Freud's *Totem and Taboo*.* In the eyes of the father the son's succession as head of the family business is a usurpation, never mind his own failing strength. For the father, the son's life as a man is his own death; his life needs his son's defeat. Therefore he hits out cruelly (and comically—he is indeed a comedian, as Georg calls him) at Georg's engagement:

> "Because she lifted up her skirts," his father began to flute, "because she lifted her skirts like this, the nasty creature," and mim-

* Freud was writing his book in the same year of 1912 that Kafka wrote *The Judgment*.

56

icking her he lifted his shirt so high that one could see the scar on his thigh from his war wounds, "because she lifted her skirts like this and this you made up to her, and in order to make free with her undisturbed you have disgraced your mother's memory, betrayed your friend and stuck your father into bed so that he can't move. But he can move, or can't he?"

And he stood up quite unsupported and kicked his legs out. His insight made him radiant.

The bellowing old man, cavorting in his bed, is transfigured by his insight into the truth of what is going on between him and his son; he hisses with self-gratulation over his own shrewdness. Bendemann Sr. takes Georg's engagement as a blow at himself, just as if he were the leader of a horde and it was one of his own mates Georg was coveting. That is why he calls Georg a child and a devil in the same breath, just before he pronounces the death sentence:

"An innocent child, yes, that you were, truly, but still more truly have you been a devilish human being!"

It is out of natural innocence, in the fulfillment of his most natural instincts, that Georg reaches for a wife; but in reaching for a wife he oversteps the "law" which gives all wives to the father and becomes a "devil." Child or devil is the alternative his father confronts him with—"childish" submission to sheerly arbitrary authority or "devilish" defiance of it. We are down to a level of the soul which reflects the earliest times, before there ever was a written law.[7]

And how wrong is the old man about his relations with his son? Georg recoils from his father, thinking how

a long time ago he had firmly made up his mind to watch closely every least movement so that he should not be surprised by any indirect attack, a pounce from behind or above. At this moment he recalled this long-forgotten resolve and forgot it again, like a man drawing a short thread through the eye of a needle.

So Georg knew all along that a battle was going on between himself and his father! But he "forgot" it, and even as he recollects it now he forgets it again.

But the Georg who is wrestling for possession of his own soul and who tries to see his father as a man like any other struggles desperately against the other Georg who bends hypnotically to the father's command. He calls his father a comedian (and bites his tongue the very next instant). Of course he has been playacting, the father replies; what else but guile was left to him in his "back room, plagued by a disloyal staff, old to the marrow of my bones"? When this tribal *Urvater*, this hunting forefather, boasts to Georg that he is still the stronger one and that "I have your customers here in my pocket!" the son seizes on the insignificant phrase and takes it literally so as to persuade the world (and through the world himself) that his father is an "impossible figure," in a passage of penetrating shrewdness:

> "He has pockets even in his nightshirt!" said Georg to himself, and believed that with this remark he could make him an impossible figure for all the world. Only for a moment did he think so, since he kept on forgetting everything.

He can't stop forgetting!

The elder Bendemann tells the "stupid boy" that he has been secretly communicating with his friend in Russia all along.

> ". . . [H]e knows everything a hundred times better than you do yourself. . . ."
>
> In his enthusiasm he waved his arm over his head. "He knows everything a thousand times better!" he cried.
>
> "Ten thousand times!" said Georg, to make fun of his father, but in his very mouth the words turned into deadly earnest.

His own words turn against him (for the father and the friend have indeed been in cahoots with one another), his attempt to reduce his father from a symbol to a human being is defeated; the time for his sentencing "to death by drowning" is at hand. As he rushes—or rather "feels himself driven"—from the room, down the stairs and to the riverside, "the crash with which his father fell on the bed behind him was still in his ears"—the condemnation uses up the father's last-remaining strength. "Dear parents, I have always loved you, all the same," Georg whispers abjectly just before he drops into the river.

58

At this moment an unending stream of traffic was just going over the bridge.

The powerful pulse of the life of the world that the son was unable to reach and make part of, the "human harmony" that he wished to join, beats in the story's last words. (Kafka likened the last sentence to an orgasm.[8]) He dies pathetically, a tiny falling figure against the indifferent ceaseless streaming of human life.

The puzzle of the story is the friend in Russia. Is it possible to account for him in a way that is convincing rather than just ingenious? I think he can be accounted for, I do not think he can be justified; he is the one failure in a story of vivid, succinct art.

Kate Flores' suggestion that Georg's expatriated friend is a side of Kafka himself, the Kafka who was a writer and a bachelor, just as Georg is another side of Kafka, is surely right.* [9] Throughout Kafka's work Russia figures as an image of the most extreme solitude, which stands for his own solitude as a writer. In the original draft of "The Sudden Walk," which he wrote into his diary some nine months before *The Judgment,* he concludes his description of his sudden bolting from the bosom of the family one evening as follows:

> . . . then for that evening you have so completely got away from your family that the most distant journey couldn't take you farther and you've lived through what is for Europe so extreme an experience of solitude that one can only call it Russian.[11]

In the second volume of the *Diaries* there is the fine unfinished story, "Memoirs of the Kalda Railroad," which begins:

> At one time in my life—it is many years ago now—I had a post with a small railroad in the interior of Russia. I have never been so forsaken as I was there. For various reasons that do not matter

---

* Freud remarks, in "The Relation of the Poet to Day-dreaming," that "the psychological novel in general probably owes its peculiarities to the tendency of modern writers to split up their egos by self-observation into many component-egos, and in this way to personify the conflicting trends in their own mental life in many heroes." [10]

now, I had been looking for just such a place at the time, the more
solitude ringing in my ears the better I liked it. . . .[12]

In still another place in his diary he notes: "The infinite attraction of Russia." [13]

In *The Judgment* the friend in Russia is described as a man
who "was resigning himself to becoming a permanent bachelor"
—Kafka had just met the woman to whom he later became engaged (twice over) but never married, and was carrying on a
tortured debate with himself that lasted his entire life over the
question of marriage, which he was painfully convinced was irreconcilable with his writing. The friend's unspecified business,
which is doing so poorly, is (as Mrs. Flores points out) Kafka's
own business of writing, in the doldrums too until he wrote this
story. The necessity for such biographical references indicates
Kafka's failure to realize *in the story* the meaning he intended
the friend to have.

Georg's friendship with the man in Russia (i.e. Kafka's bent
toward "Russian solitude" and literature) imperils his marriage;
that is explicitly stated when his fiancée, "Fräulein Frieda Brandenfeld," * says: "Since your friends are like that, Georg, you
shouldn't ever have got engaged at all." The two friends are in
an uneasy relationship in which each refuses to accept the other
as he is. Georg would like to persuade his friend, "who had obviously run off the rails," to give up and come home; the friend on
his side has tried to persuade Georg to emigrate to Russia.
Georg's writing the news of his engagement to St. Petersburg is a
first step toward a rupture with his friend; his marriage would
have completed the rupture (i.e. been the end of Kafka as a
writer). But the father intervenes at this point and saves the
friend (Kafka the writer-bachelor) from being "betrayed" by
Georg:

* "Frieda has as many letters as F[elice] and the same initial,
Brandenfeld has the same initial as B[auer], and in the word 'Feld'
a certain connection in meaning as well." [14] (Felice Bauer was the
name of Kafka's first fiancée.)

"But your friend hasn't been betrayed after all!" cried his father, emphasizing the point with stabs of his forefinger. "I've been representing him here on the spot."

The father, "representing" the interests of the friend, stops the marriage and condemns Georg (Kafka the man) to death.

The theme of *The Judgment* is "the opposition between fathers and sons." But Kafka intended to represent the conflict between marriage and writing as an integral part of the father-son opposition (as I will try to show more clearly in a moment). Here he failed. The friend in Russia is unable to come alive in the story with the meaning that Kafka wished him to have. He remains a ghostly ineffectual presence, a mystery whose explanation must be sought in Kafka's life.

Kafka's failure, I think, can be traced to his inability, in these years of trying to marry, to see beyond the injuries his father had done him, recognize his bachelorhood as his own choice and embrace his fate as a writer—to a confusion in his understanding of his own responsibility for his life. This confusion shows up in the story in the puzzling, contradictory representation of the relations between the father and the friend in Russia. The father's attitude to the friend, we learn from Georg's words, was hostile at first: he "used not to like him very much. At least twice I [Georg] denied him before you [*vor dir verleugnet*], although he was actually sitting with me in my room. I could quite understand your dislike of him, my friend has his peculiarities." To placate his father, Georg has twice denied his peculiar friend before him (i.e. repudiated his connection with Kafka the writer). But when the father flings the covers off and denounces Georg, he claims the friend as his own: "Of course I know your friend. He would have been a son after my own heart." He has been writing to him all along, he roars at his son some pages later; "in his left hand he crumples your letters unopened while in his right hand he holds up my letters to read through!" (That is, Kafka the writer-bachelor heeds only his father's "messages" and ignores all communications from Kafka the man.)

Yet the father's sudden embrace of the friend menaces the latter's life. No sooner does the elder Bendemann trumpet his proprietorship in the friend than Georg sees him "lost in the vastness of Russia."

> His friend in St. Petersburg, whom his father suddenly knew too well, touched his imagination as never before. Lost in the vastness of Russia he saw him. At the door of an empty, plundered warehouse he saw him. Even now he stood among the wreckage of his showcases, the slashed remnants of his wares, the falling gas brackets. Why did he have to go so far away!

The better the father knows the friend the more the latter is "lost in Russia"—indeed he knows him "too well." And the contempt the father feels for the friend, in spite of his saying he would have been a son after his own heart, is unmistakable in his last words about him; he is only using him against the Georg who is fighting his father for his life:

> "How long a time you've taken to grow up! Your mother had to die, she couldn't see the happy day, your friend is going to pieces in that Russia of his [*in seinem Russland*], even three years ago he was yellow enough to throw away. . . ."

Bendemann Sr. is no friend of writing!

The contradictions in the father-friend relation can be explained only out of the biographical sources. In the "Letter to His Father" Kafka says that his father was the never-ending theme of his writing:

> My writing was all about you, all I did there, after all, was to complain about the things I couldn't complain about on your breast.[15]

The friend is joined to the father in the story as Kafka the writer was joined to the obsessive theme of his father; the friend is in "league" with the father against Georg, as Kafka the writer-bachelor was "leagued" with his father against Kafka the man who had recently met Felice Bauer and was thinking hard about marriage. In the sentence immediately following the one quoted above, Kafka betrays the perplexity in his own understanding of himself as a writer which is responsible for the failure in the story:

> It [his writing] was an intentionally long-drawn-out leave-taking from you, something, to be sure, which you were the cause of, but which took its course in a direction determined by me.[16]

Kafka is saying that his father was the reason why he was a writer (although the kind of writer he became was his own doing), by having banished him from the world to the freezing inhuman solitude ("Russia") in which only writing was possible. (In the diary entry of January 28, 1922, two and a half years before he died, he wrote: " . . . [W]hy did I want to quit the world? Because 'he' [his father] would not let me live in it, in his world." *) In making the father the ally and support of the friend in Russia, Kafka is trying to give objective narrative expression to his sense of his father's responsibility for his being a writer. But this is to try to express a negative responsibility in positive terms and produces the absurdity that the closer father and friend in the story are allied, the nearer to perishing in Russia the latter is. The contempt the elder Bendemann shows for Georg's friend, who "is going to pieces in that Russia of his, even three years ago he was yellow enough to throw away," flagrantly contradicts his saying that the exile would have been a son after his own heart. It betrays the contempt Herrmann Kafka felt for his son's life of devotion to writing. Kafka's father's contempt for him is a negative fact that cannot be accommodated within the positive metaphor of the alliance of Bendemann Sr. and the friend in Russia—just as Kafka's own writing is a positive thing

---

* Above all for Kafka "living in the world" meant being married, and marriage was a sphere preempted by his father:

> . . . [M]arrying is debarred to me by the fact that it is just the sphere that is most yours. Sometimes I imagine the map of the world spread out and you stretched across it. And then I feel that only those areas exist as possibilities for my life which are not covered by you nor within your reach. And, in keeping with my idea of your size, those areas are not many nor do they afford much comfort, and above all marriage is not one of them.[17]

that cannot in the end be blamed on his father's shutting him out of the world.

The painful confusion in Kafka's understanding of himself lies in his feeling that his solitary existence as a writer was forced on him by his father; and in his feeling at the same time that writing was his own deepest choice, so that his lonely bachelor's life of exile from the world was something he was responsible for, an affirmation of himself. His affirmative sense of his writer's calling is obscurely indicated in the fact that the friend in Russia is also Georg's ally; they are both struggling against the father to affirm themselves and they both go down to defeat together, the one by direct condemnation and the other by exposure to Russian revolutions.*

Like so many writers of the modern age, like the modern age itself, Kafka starts out from a feeling of filial grievance. But to push his grievance to the point where he even blames his father for his writer's destiny, although his writing was everything to him, shows a baffled self-understanding. At this point the mythopoeic power of *The Judgment* declines into obscure ingenuity.

Although *The Judgment* aims primarily at psychological truth, it trembles on the point of saying all those other things which we find in Kafka's later works. In the subjective depths in which his stories swim, everything is spiritualized so that there is nothing, not even the most humble object or gesture, that does not become charged with ultimate meaning. Only consider the father's

* Kafka perhaps indicates this affirmative meaning in his opaque comment on the story: "The friend is the bond between father and son, he is the most important thing they have in common. . . . What they have in common [i.e. the bond of the friend] is built up entirely around the father, Georg can feel it only as something foreign, something that has become independent, that he has never given enough protection to, that is exposed to Russian revolutions, and only because he himself no longer has eyes for anyone else but his father does the judgment, which seals his father off from him completely, have so strong an effect." [18] That is, Georg (Kafka the man) has failed to protect the friend (Kafka the writer), has failed to draw him to him, away from the father.

dirty underwear. As an "objective" fact it indicates the old man's fustiness and incapacity to take care of himself any longer; to Georg, who has been intent on marriage and independence, it is a reproach that works to draw him back into his father's orbit. But it also suggests something else. As Walter Benjamin notes, the element in which Kafka's bureaucrats live is dirt [19]: the filth of the inhuman, the prehuman, and the all too human. That is also Bendemann Sr.'s element, who is about to swell out into the officialdom of *The Trial* and *The Castle;* he is pregnant with that meaning. With mythopoeic breadth he reaches from the prehistoric primitive past to the immediate present: the embodiment of a universal arbitrariness which opposes itself to life and freedom, the paternal idea on the point of being raised to a general principle of tyranny.

And yet if one reads the story as a tale of tyranny and victimization one has read only a part. Even in this early story, with its primarily psychological emphasis, his imagination strives to go beyond the ultimately futile reproaches and self-justifications which make up the argument between the generations and find a truth underlying the psychological one of oppressor-fathers and victim-sons. In the end—but only in the end—it does not matter where the "fault" [20] lies as between father and son because the "fault" goes back endlessly and forward endlessly through the generations. Somewhere inside the arbitrary inhuman authority of the father sticks the idea of something against which Georg Bendemann has indeed offended. Somewhere within himself the father incorporates the "law"—the unreasonable law of life which Georg violates just by being defeated in his life. In truth Georg is innocent and his father robs him of his life. As one of Kafka's aphorisms puts it:

> Why do we lament over the fall of man? We were not driven out of Paradise because of it, but because of the Tree of Life, that we might not eat of it.[21]

"God," the supreme bureaucrat, hates life and denies it to man; man does not fall, "God" turns him out of the house of life. But in truth, too, Georg is sinful (*aside* from all questions of guilt and innocence), for he sins against his life by failing to live it. As the very next aphorism puts it:

> We are sinful not merely because we have eaten of the Tree of Knowledge, but also because we have not yet eaten of the Tree of Life. The state in which we find ourselves is sinful, quite independent of guilt.[22]

Georg sins, but against himself, by failing to live, by failing to be human.

The atmosphere of surcharged significance peculiar to Kafka's stories most immediately expresses their character as dream narratives. Like dreams, their surface hides shadowy depths of meaning; inside their explicit content latent contents lurk. But another way to put this is to say that Kafka's words demand to be interpreted—significance in Kafka is a matter of the word and the interpretation thereof. Put thus, we can see how his stories are old as well as new and belong to a tradition of writing that goes back to the Bible. He describes this kind of writing himself in *Investigations of a Dog,* in which the narrator-dog can

> only see decline everywhere, in saying which, however, I do not mean that earlier generations were essentially better than ours, but only younger; that was their great advantage, their memory was not so overburdened as ours today, it was easier to get them to speak out, and even if nobody actually succeeded in doing that, the possibility of it was greater, and it is indeed this greater sense of possibility that moves us so deeply when we listen to those old and strangely simple stories. Here and there we catch a curiously significant phrase and we would almost like to leap to our feet, if we did not feel the weight of centuries upon us. . . . [T]he true word . . . was there, was very near at least, on the tip of everybody's tongue, anyone might have hit upon it.[23]

Kafka's work, too, has something of the quality of "those old and strangely simple stories" with their "curiously significant phrases" which "move us so deeply" because of the "greater possibility" of "the true word" coming to expression in them. Eric Auerbach, comparing Homeric and Biblical narrative, points out that the latter is "oriented toward truth," which the interpreter must search for in the shadows cast by every word, whereas the Greek poems aim to enchant us by the magic of their fictive reality.

> The oft-repeated reproach that Homer is a liar takes nothing from his effectiveness, he does not need to base his story on historical reality, his reality is powerful enough in itself; it ensnares us, weaving its web around us, and that suffices him. And this "real" world into which we are lured, exists for itself, contains nothing but itself; the Homeric poems conceal nothing, they contain no teaching and no secret second meaning. Homer can be analyzed . . . but he cannot be interpreted. . . .
> It is all very different in the Biblical stories. . . . Doctrine and promise are incarnate in them and inseparable from them; for that very reason they are fraught with "background" and mysterious, containing a second, concealed meaning. . . . Since so much in the story [of the sacrifice of Isaac] is dark and incomplete, and since the reader knows that God is a hidden God, his effort to interpret it constantly finds something new to feed upon.[24]

Homeric narrative, which "exists for itself," is literature; Biblical narrative is something else.

Like Biblical narrative, Kafka's narratives reveal a perspective that, beginning with the few words on the surface of the page, extends downward or backward into an indefinite depth. They are literature trying to be revelation. The stark and homely details of *The Judgment,* glowing with the dark luminosity of things seen in a dream, portend revelation. It is as dream narrative that the story has something of a Biblical quality, which is the quality of any piece of writing that in aiming at truth tries to be more than literature. Of course only something of this quality, because *The Judgment* is literature after all. Nevertheless it tries to transcend art and "hit upon" the "true word." How every object and gesture in the story is trying to speak! How mysterious it remains in spite of all elucidation! I mentioned *Death in Ven-*

ice earlier. I feel about it that everything in the story was put there by Mann's great art. He made it; he was a great maker. About *The Judgment* I feel, with Kafka, that it was born out of a visionary effort, unfolding, as he puts it in the diary entry which describes its nocturnal composition, "before me as if I were advancing over water." [25] I do not mean to say by this that the art that struggles to transcend art is better than art—not at all. But it is different.

4 GREGOR SAMSA AND MODERN SPIRITUALITY

The Metamorphosis is peculiar as a narrative in having its climax in the very first sentence: "As Gregor Samsa awoke one morning from uneasy dreams he found himself transformed in his bed into a gigantic insect." The rest of the novella falls away from this high point of astonishment in one long expiring sigh, punctuated by three subclimaxes (the three eruptions of the bug from the bedroom). How is it possible, one may ask, for a story to start at the climax and then merely subside? What kind of story is that? The answer to this question is, I think: A story for which the traditional Aristotelian form of narrative (complication and dénouement) has lost any intrinsic necessity and which has therefore evolved its own peculiar form out of the very matter it

69

seeks to tell. *The Metamorphosis* produces its form out of itself. The traditional kind of narrative based on the drama of dénouement—on the "unknotting" of complications and the coming to a conclusion—could not serve Kafka because it is just exactly the absence of dénouement and conclusions that is his subject matter. His story is about death, but death that is without dénouement, death that is merely a spiritually inconclusive petering out.

The first sentence of *The Metamorphosis* announces Gregor Samsa's death and the rest of the story is his slow dying. In its movement as an inexorable march toward death it resembles Tolstoy's *Death of Ivan Ilyich.** As Ivan Ilyich struggles against the knowledge of his own death, so does Gregor Samsa. But Tolstoy's work is about death literally and existentially; Kafka's is about death in life. Until Ivan Ilyich stops defending his life to himself as a good one and recognizes that it has not been what it ought to have been, he cannot accept the knowledge that he is dying; finally he embraces the truth of his life, which is at the same time the truth of death, and discovers spiritual light and life as he dies. Kafka's protagonist also struggles against "the truths of life and death"; in Gregor Samsa's case, however, his life is his death and there is no salvation. For a moment, it is true, near the end of his long dying, while listening to his sister play the violin, he feels "as if the way were opening before him to the unknown nourishment he craved"; but the nourishment remains unknown, he is locked into his room for the last time and he expires.

What Gregor awakens to on the morning of his metamorphosis is the truth of his life. His ordinary consciousness has lied to him about himself; the explosive first sentence pitches him out

* Tolstoy's short novel was a "great favorite" of Kafka's, so Max Brod reports in a note to the second volume of the *Diaries*.[1] Philip Rahv makes a detailed comparison of *The Trial* with Tolstoy's work in "The Death of Ivan Ilyich and Joseph K." [2] Both stories, he writes, "echo with the Augustinian imprecation, 'Woe unto thee, thou stream of human custom!' "

of the lie of his habitual self-understanding into the nightmare of truth. "The dream reveals the reality" of his abasement and self-abasement by a terrible metaphor; he is vermin (*Ungeziefer*), a disgusting creature (or rather un-creature) shut out from "the human circle." [3] The poetic of the Kafka story, based on the dream, requires the literal assertion of metaphor; Gregor must literally *be* vermin. This gives Kafka's representation of the subjective reality its convincing vividness. Anything less than metaphor, such as a simile comparing Gregor to vermin, would diminish the reality of what he is trying to represent.* Gregor's thinking "What has happened to me? . . . It was no dream," is no contradiction of his metamorphosis' being a dream but a literal-ironical confirmation of it. Of course it is no dream—to the dreamer. The dreamer, while he is dreaming, takes his dream as real; Gregor's thought is therefore literally true to the circumstances in which he finds himself. However, it is also true ironically, since his metamorphosis is indeed no dream (meaning something unreal) but a revelation of the truth.

What, then, is the truth of Gregor's life? There is first of all his soul-destroying job, which keeps him on the move and cuts him off from the possibility of real human associations:

> Oh God, he thought, what an exhausting job I've picked on! Traveling about day in, day out. It's much more irritating work than doing the actual business in the office, and on top of that there's the trouble of constant traveling, of worrying about train connections, the bad and irregular meals, the human associations that are no sooner struck up than they are ended without ever becoming intimate. The devil take it all!

* In the early fragment "Wedding Preparations in the Country," Raban compares himself to a beetle (the idea of vermin is not yet explicit). Kafka uses the vermin simile in the long accusatory letter he wrote his father in 1919: In a rebuttal speech that he puts into the latter's mouth, Hermann Kafka compares his son's way of fighting him to that "of vermin, which not only bite but suck blood at the same time to get their sustenance. . . . You're unfit for life." [4] But of course the letter, in spite of its peculiarities, is a letter and not *Dichtung,* not a story.

Not only is his work lonely and exhausting, it is also degrading. Gregor fails to report to work once in five years and the chief clerk is at his home at a quarter past seven in the morning accusing him of neglect of his business duties, poor work in general and stealing company funds, and threatening him with dismissal. In the guilt-world that Gregor inhabits, his missing his train on this one morning retroactively changes his excellent work record at one stroke into the very opposite.

> What a fate, to be condemned to work for a firm where the smallest omission at once gave rise to the gravest suspicion! Were all employees in a body nothing but scoundrels . . . ?

He has been sacrificing himself by working at his meaningless, degrading job so as to pay off an old debt of his parents' to his employer. Otherwise "I'd have given notice long ago, I'd have gone to the chief and told him exactly what I think of him." But even now, with the truth of his self-betrayal pinning him on his back to his bed, he is unable to claim himself for himself and decide to quit—he must wait "another five or six years":

> . . . [O]nce I've saved enough money to pay back my parents' debts to him—that should take another five or six years—I'll do it without fail. I'll cut myself completely loose then. For the moment, though, I'd better get up, since my train goes at five.

He pretends that he will get up and resume his old life. He will get dressed "and above all eat his breakfast," after which the "morning's delusions" will infallibly be dissipated. But the human self whose claims he always postponed and continues to postpone, is past being put off, having declared itself negatively by changing him from a human being into an insect. His metamorphosis is a judgment on himself by his defeated humanity.

Gregor's humanity has been defeated in his private life as much as in his working life. His mother succinctly describes its deathly aridity as she pleads with the chief clerk:

> ". . . [H]e's not well, sir, believe me. What else would make him miss a train! The boy thinks about nothing but his work. It makes

me almost cross the way he never goes out in the evenings; he's been here the last eight days and has stayed at home every single evening. He just sits there quietly at the table reading a newspaper or looking through railway timetables. The only amusement he gets is doing fretwork. For instance, he spent two or three evenings cutting out a little picture frame; you would be surprised to see how pretty it is; it's hanging in his room; you'll see it in a minute when Gregor opens the door. . . ."

The picture in the little frame shows a woman in furs "holding out to the spectator a huge fur muff into which the whole of her forearm had vanished"; it is the second object that Gregor's eye encounters when he surveys his room on waking (the first was his collection of samples). Later in the story, when his sister and mother empty his room of its furniture, he defends his "human past" by making his stand on this picture, pressing "himself to the glass, which was a good surface to hold on to and comforted his hot belly." That is about what Gregor's "human past" amounts to: a pin-up.

For most of the story, Gregor struggles with comic-terrible pathos against the metaphor fastened on him. His first hope is that it is all "nonsense." But he cannot tell; the last thing he knows about is himself. So he works himself into an upright position in order to unlock the door, show himself to the chief clerk and his family, and let them decide for him, as he has always let others decide for him:

> If they were horrified then the responsibility was no longer his and he could stay quiet. But if they took it calmly, then he had no reason either to be upset, and could really get to the station for the eight o'clock train if he hurried.

The answer that he gets is his mother's swoon, the chief clerk's hurried departure, in silent-movie style, with a loud "Ugh!" and his father's driving him back "pitilessly," with a newspaper and a walking stick that menaces his life, into his room—"from behind his father gave him a strong push which was literally a deliverance and he flew far into the room, bleeding freely. The door was slammed behind him with the stick, and then at last there was silence."

This is the first repulse the metamorphosed Gregor suffers in his efforts to reenter "the human circle." The fact that his voice has altered so that the others can no longer understand what he says, but he can understand them as well as ever, perfectly expresses the pathos of one who is condemned to stand on the outside looking in. Although he must now accept the fact that he has been changed into a monster, he clings to the illusion that his new state is a temporary one: "he must lie low for the present and, by exercising patience and the utmost consideration, help the family to bear the inconvenience he was bound to cause them in his present condition." Like Ivan Ilyich, he wants to believe that his mortal illness is only a "condition."

In Part II we learn about Gregor's all-important relations with his family. An unambiguous indication already given in Part I is the fact that he locks his bedroom doors at night "even at home" —a "prudent habit he had acquired in traveling." Although he is a dutiful, self-sacrificing son, just such a dutiful son as Georg Bendemann, he is as much a stranger to his family as he is to the world and shuts them out of his life—he locks them out as much as they lock him in. Concealment, mistrust, and denial mark the relations in the Samsa family. It now turns out, as Gregor listens at his bedroom door, that some investments had survived the wreck of Samsa Sr.'s business five years before and had even increased since then, though he thought his father had been left with nothing, "at least his father had never said anything to the contrary, and of course he had not asked him directly." Moreover, this sum had been increased by the unexpended residue of Gregor's earnings, who "kept only a few dollars for himself." But he buries the rage he feels at this evidence of the needlessness of his self-sacrifice, as he has always buried his real feelings:

Gregor nodded his head eagerly, rejoiced at this evidence of unexpected thrift and foresight. True, he could really have paid off some more of his father's debts to the chief with this extra money, and so brought much nearer the day on which he could quit his job, but doubtless it was better the way his father had arranged it.

His parents liked to think that his slaving at his job to support the family represented no sacrifice of himself—"they had convinced themselves in the course of years that Gregor was settled for life in this firm." But they were able to convince themselves of this only because he himself cooperated eagerly with them to deny himself. Deception and self-deception, denial and self-denial now "end in horror." To cap it all, it turns out that his family did not even need his sacrifice for another reason: When Gregor ceases to be the breadwinner, father, mother, and sister all turn to and provide for themselves and the old man is even rescued in this way from a premature dotage.

The decisive figure in the family for Gregor is his father. He sees him something like Georg Bendemann saw his—as an old man, almost a doddering old man, and yet strong. This combination of weakness and strength is signaled in the story's very first words about Samsa Sr.: "at one of the side doors his father was knocking, gently [schwach: weakly], yet with his fist." The combination is present in the description of the father's response to Gregor's first breaking out of his bedroom—a "knotted fist" and "fierce expression" go along with tears of helplessness and humiliation:

> His father knotted his fist with a fierce expression on his face as if he meant to knock Gregor back into his room, then looked uncertainly round the living room, covered his eyes with his hands and wept till his great chest [mächtige Brust] heaved.

But in spite of his "great chest," in spite of his voice's sounding "no longer like the voice of one single father" when he drives his son back into his room, in spite of Gregor's being "dumbfounded at the enormous size of his shoe soles," the second time his father chases him back into his room, the elder Samsa, unlike the elder Bendemann, does not loom large like a Titanic figure. He is powerful, irascible and petulant, but not mythically powerful. His shoe soles seem "enormous" to his son because of his insect angle of vision—not because the old man is superhuman but because the son is less than human. Everything in the story is seen from Gregor's point of view, the point of view of somebody who has fallen below the human level.

The father's strength is the ordinary strength of human life, which has been temporarily dimmed by his business failure and his son's unnatural ascendancy as the breadwinner of the family. He does not battle his son to recover his ascendancy as Bendemann Sr. does in *The Judgment*. There is no battle; Gregor cannot "risk standing up to him." [5] The unnatural state of affairs in the Samsa home corrects itself so to speak naturally, by the son's showing forth as what he really is—a parasite that saps the father's and the family's life. A fundamental incompatibility exists between the son and the family, between sickliness and parasitism on the one hand and vigor and independence on the other, between death and life. As the son's life wanes the family's revives; especially the father's flourishes with renewed vigor and he becomes a blustering, energetic, rather ridiculous man—a regular Kafka papa.

From the start Gregor's father deals brutally with him:

> . . . [F]rom the very first day of his new life . . . his father believed only the severest measures suitable for dealing with him.

Indeed he threatens his life: the first time he shoos Gregor back into his room he menaces him with a "fatal blow" from his stick; at his son's second outbreak he gives him a wound from which he never recovers. But though Samsa Sr. throws his son back into his room two out of the three times he breaks out of it, Gregor's banishment from "the human circle" is not a sentence passed on him by his father. Unlike the father in *The Judgment*, Samsa Sr. does not stand at the center of the story confronting his son as the lord and judge of his life. He stands with the mother and the sister, opposite the son but to the side; the center of the story is completely occupied by the son. The father affirms the judgment passed on Gregor—that he is "unfit for life" [6]—but the judgment is not his; it is Gregor's. At the beginning of the novella, before he is locked in his room by the family as a metamorphosed monster, we see how he has already locked himself in as a defeated human being. Gregor is self-condemned.

At the side of the father stands the mother, gentle ("That gentle voice!"), yet "in complete union with him" against her son. Gregor's monstrousness horrifies her no less than the others and she faints at the sight of him. For the first two weeks she prefers, with the father, not to know how or even if Gregor is fed. "Not that they would have wanted him to starve, of course, but perhaps they could not have borne to know more about his feeding than from hearsay. . . ."—Gregor's struggle, in these words, against the truth is a pathetically ironical statement of it. Frau Samsa pities her son—"he is my unfortunate son"—and understands his plight as illness; the morning of the metamorphosis she sends the daughter for the doctor, while Herr Samsa, characteristically (his son is a recalcitrant creature bent on causing him a maximum of annoyance), sends the maid for the locksmith. (Gregor, feeling "himself drawn once more into the human circle" by these steps, "hoped for great and remarkable results from both the doctor and the locksmith, without really distinguishing precisely between them"—agreeing with both parents, he is unable to distinguish between the element of recalcitrance and refusal and the element of illness in his withdrawal into inhuman isolation.) Shame and horror, however, overwhelm the mother's compassion—we learn from Gregor's reflections that the doctor was sent away on some pretext. She protests against Grete's clearing the furniture out of Gregor's room—". . . doesn't it look as if we were showing him, by taking away his furniture, that we have given up hope of his ever getting better . . . ?"—but then acquiesces weakly in it and even helps to move the heavy pieces. At the end, when Grete says that the bug must be got rid of:

"He must go," cried Gregor's sister, "that's the only solution, Father. You must just try to get rid of the idea that this is Gregor. . . . If this were Gregor, he would have realized long ago that human beings can't live with such a creature, and he'd have gone away on his own accord. . . ."

the mother, with a terrible silence, acquiesces again in her daughter's determination, which this time is a condemnation of her son to death.

Gregor cherishes his sister most of all. She in turn shows the most awareness of his needs after his metamorphosis into vermin and he is grateful to her for it. But he notices that she avoids touching anything that has come into contact with him and he is forced to "realize how repulsive the sight of him still was to her, and that it was bound to go on being repulsive." For her, too, he is a pariah, a monster shut out of the human circle, and at the end she is the one who voices the thought, which has hung unexpressed over the family since the morning of the metamorphosis, that Gregor must be got rid of.

This, then, is the situation in the Samsa family revealed by the metamorphosis: on the surface, the official sentiments of the parents and the sister toward Gregor, and of Gregor toward them and toward himself; underneath, the horror and disgust, and self-disgust: ". . . family duty required the suppression of disgust and the exercise of patience, nothing but patience."

Gregor breaks out of his room the first time hoping that his transformation will turn out to be "nonsense"; the second time, in the course of defending at least his hope of returning to his "human past." His third eruption, in Part III, has quite a different aim. The final section of the story discovers a Gregor who tries to dream again, after a long interval, of resuming his old place at the head of the family, but the figures from the past that now appear to him—his boss, the chief clerk, traveling salesmen, a chambermaid ("a sweet and fleeting memory"), and so on—cannot help him, "they were one and all unapproachable and he was glad when they vanished." Defeated, he finally gives up all hope of returning to the human community. Now his existence slopes steeply toward death. The wound in his back, made by the apple his father threw at him in driving Gregor back into his room after his second outbreak, has begun to fester again; his room is now the place in which all the household's dirty old decayed things are thrown, along with Gregor, a dirty old decayed thing; and he has just about stopped eating.

At first he had thought he was unable to eat out of "chagrin over the state of his room"—his mood at that stage of his dying, like Ivan Ilyich's at a corresponding stage, was one of hatred toward his family for neglecting him; he hissed at them all in rage. But then he discovered that he got "increasing enjoyment" from crawling about the filth and junk—it was not the filthiness of his room that was preventing him from eating. On the last evening of his life, watching from his room the lodgers whom his family have taken in putting away a good supper, he comes to a crucial realization:

> "I'm hungry enough," said Gregor sadly to himself, "but not for that kind of food. How these lodgers are stuffing themselves, and here am I dying of starvation!"

In giving up at last all hope of reentering the human circle, Gregor finally understands the truth about his life; which is to say he accepts the knowledge of his death, for the truth about his life is his death-in-life by his banishment and self-banishment from the human community. But having finally accepted the truth, having finally bowed to the yoke of the metaphor that he has been trying to shake off, he begins to sense a possibility that exists for him *only* in his outcast state. He is hungry enough, he realizes, but not for the world's fare, "not for that kind of food." He feels a hunger that can only be felt in full acceptance of his outcast state. Like Ivan Ilyich when he accepts his death at last and plunges into the black sack's hole, he perceives a glimmer of light; in the degradation, in the utter negativity of his outcastness, he begins to apprehend a positive possibility.[7]

He has already had a hint or two that the meaning of his metamorphosis contains some sort of positive possibility. At the beginning of the story, when he is lying in bed and worrying about not reporting to work, he thinks of saying he is sick, but knows that the sick-insurance doctor will come down on him as a malingerer. "And would he be so far from wrong on this occasion? Gregor really felt quite well . . . and he was even unusually hungry." He has just been changed into a huge bug and he is afraid of pleading sick because he will be accused of malingering! And the accusation would after all be correct because he felt quite well and was even unusually hungry! "Of course," the reader says, "he means quite well *as an insect!*"—which is a joke, but a joke that points right to the positive meaning of his metamorphosis.

A second hint soon follows. After Gregor unlocks the bedroom door with his jaws and drops down on his legs for the first time, he experiences "a sense of physical comfort; his legs had firm ground under them; . . . they even strove to carry him forward in whatever direction he chose; and he was inclined to believe that a final relief from all his sufferings was at hand." The first meaning here is ironical and comic: Gregor, unable to accept his transformation into a bug and automatically trying to walk like a man, inadvertently falls down on his insect legs and feels an instantaneous sense of comfort which he takes as a promise of future relief from his sufferings. With supreme illogic he derives a hope of release from his animal condition from the very comfort he gets by adapting himself to that condition—so divided is his self-consciousness from his true self. But there is a second meaning, which piles irony upon the irony: *precisely* as a noisome outcast from the human world Gregor feels the possibility of relief, of *final* relief. *Only* as an outcast does he sense the possibility of an ultimate salvation rather than just a restoration of the *status quo*.

As a bug, too, his wounds heal a lot faster than did his old cut finger: the vitality possible to him in his pariah state (if he can only find the food he needs to feed his spiritual hunger on, for he is "unusually hungry") is in sharp contrast with his human debility. And he finds a kind of freedom in crawling around the walls and ceiling of his room instead of going to work each morning—Kafka dwells so much in the first part on the horror of Samsa's job that we feel his metamorphosis as something of a liberation, although in the end he is only delivered from the humiliation and death of his job into the humiliation and death of his outcast state.

When Gregor breaks out of his room the third and last time, he is no longer trying to deceive himself about himself and get back to his old life with its illusions about belonging to the human community. He is trying to find that "final relief" which lies beyond "the last earthly frontier," [8] a frontier which is to be approached only through exile and solitude. What draws him out of his room the last night of his life is his sister's violin playing. Although he had never cared for music in his human state, now the notes of the violin attract him surprisingly. Indifferent to "his growing lack of consideration for the others"—at last he has the courage to think about himself—trailing "fluff and hair and remnants of food" which he no longer bothers to scrape off himself, the filthy starving underground creature advances onto "the spotless floor of the living room" where his sister is playing for the three lodgers.

> Was he an animal, that music had such an effect upon him? He felt as if the way were opening before him to the unknown nourishment he craved.

It is a familiar Romantic idea that Kafka is making use of here: that music expresses the inexpressible, that it points to a hidden sphere of spiritual power and meaning.* It is only in his

* Thus Kleist, to cite a source of influence near to Kafka, describes the notes of the music score in "St. Cecilia, or the Power of Music" as "the unknown magical signs by which a terrible spirit seemed mysteriously to mark out its sphere." And Coleridge says brilliantly: "Every human feeling is greater and larger than the exciting cause—a proof, I think, that man is designed for a higher state of existence; and this is deeply implied in music, in which there is always something more and beyond the immediate expression."—"On Poesy or Art"

extremity, as "an animal," an outcast from human life who finally accepts his being cast out, that Gregor's ears are opened to music. Yet in spite of all the hints he has had, Gregor still hesitates to grasp the positive possibility contained in the truth about himself and his death in life—the possibility of life in death, of spiritual life through outcastness. All along he has understood the wellbeing he feels as an insect as an indication of his bestialization. "Am I less sensitive now?" he asks himself after marveling at his recuperative powers as a bug; he accuses himself of a growing lack of consideration for others, and so on. Now he does the same thing: "Was he an animal, that music had such an effect upon him?" This time, however, his understanding of himself is clearly a misunderstanding; it is nonsensical to associate music and bestiality, music is at the opposite pole from bestiality. His metamorphosis is a path to the spiritual rather than the bestial. The violin notes that move him so build a way through his death in life to the salvation for which he blindly hungers.

Or they only seem to. Certainly the unknown nourishment exists; the goal of his hunger exists. But the music merely draws him toward his sister with the jealous intention of capturing her for himself and immuring her in his cell with him; it only leads him out into the same old living room of his death as a private person, which with the three indignant lodgers staring down at him is the same old public world of bullying businessmen he knew as a traveling salesman.[9] "There is a goal, but no way," Kafka says in one of his aphorisms; "what we call a way is only wavering." [10]

His final repulse follows, with his sister demanding that "he must go. . . . If this were Gregor, he would have realized long ago that human beings can't live with such a creature. . . ." Painfully turning around, Gregor crawls back into his room without his father's having to chase him back and surrenders his life to this demand:

"And what now?" said Gregor to himself, looking round in the darkness. . . . He thought of his family with tenderness and love.

The decision that he must disappear was one that he held to even more strongly than his sister, if that were possible. In this state of vacant and peaceful meditation he remained until the tower clock struck three in the morning. The first broadening of light in the world outside the window entered his consciousness once more. Then his head sank to the floor of its own accord and from his nostrils came the last faint flicker of his breath.

Both Georg Bendemann and Gregor Samsa die reconciled with their families in a tenderness of self-condemnation. But Georg is sentenced to death by his father; nobody sentences Gregor to his death in life except himself. His ultimate death, however, his death without redemption, is from hunger for the unknown nourishment he needs. What kills Gregor is spiritual starvation —"Man cannot live without a permanent trust in something indestructible in himself, and at the same time that indestructible something as well as his trust in it may remain permanently concealed from him."

Although the story does not end with Gregor's death, it is still from his point of view that the last few pages are narrated. The family are of course glad to be freed of the burden and scandal he has been to them but dare not say so openly. When the tough old charwoman who has survived "the worst a long life could offer" spares them the embarrassment of getting "rid of the thing," their thanks is to fire her. However the tide of life, now flooding in, soon sweeps them beyond bad conscience and troubled reflections. They make a holiday of Gregor's death day and take a trolley ride into the country. Spring is in the air; a review of their prospects shows them to be "not at all bad." Mother and father notice how their daughter, in spite of everything, has

bloomed into a pretty girl with a good figure. They grew quieter and half unconsciously exchanged glances of complete agreement, having come to the conclusion that it would soon be time to find a good husband for her. And it was like a confirmation of their new dreams and excellent intentions that at the end of their journey their daughter sprang to her feet first and stretched her young body.

Life triumphs blatantly, not only over Gregor's unlife but over his posthumous irony—these last lines are entirely without irony. Or if they are ironical it is at Gregor's expense: his moral condemnation of his family here turns into a condemnation of himself. Kafka got his peroration from a description of Ivan Ilyich's daughter in Tolstoy's story, only he twists its meaning right around:

> His daughter came in all dressed up, with much of her young body naked, making a show of it, while his body was causing him such torture. She was strong and healthy, evidently very much in love, and annoyed that his illness and suffering and death should cast a shadow upon her happiness.

Tolstoy's condemnation of the living, with their vulgar bursting vitality and impatience to get on with their business of living forever, in Kafka's hands becomes life's impatient condemnation of the dead that is the novella's last word: "We are sinful not merely because we have eaten of the Tree of Knowledge, but also because we have not yet eaten of the Tree of Life. The state in which we find ourselves is sinful, quite independent of guilt."

Tolstoy's story is dramatic, with a reversal (peripety) and a dénouement at the end in which the dying man finds salvation and death is no more. In Kafka's story there is the beginning of a reversal when Gregor thinks the way to unknown nourishment is opening before him, but it fails to take place and the novella sinks to the conclusion that has been implicit in it from the start. Kafka's story has little drama; a climax that occurs in the first sentence is no real climax. At the beginning of the chapter I described this nondramatic movement of *The Metamorphosis* as a dying fall, a sinking, an ebbing. *The Trial* and *The Castle* too have more or less the same movement, and in his diary entry of December 13, 1914, Kafka remarks on this dying movement of his best work:

> . . . [T]he best things I have written have their basis in this capacity of mine to die contentedly. All these fine and very convincing passages always deal with the fact that somebody is dying,

that it is hard for him to do, that it seems unjust to him or at least cruel, and the reader finds this moving or at least I think he should. For me, however, who believe that I'll be able to lie contentedly on my deathbed, such descriptions are secretly a game, I positively enjoy my own death in the dying person's, therefore I calculatingly exploit the attention that the reader concentrates on death, understand it a lot more clearly than he, who I assume will complain on his deathbed, and for these reasons my complaining [*Klage*, lament] is as perfect as can be, doesn't suddenly break off in the way real complaining is likely to do, but dies away beautifully and purely. It is the same thing as my always complaining to my mother about pains that weren't nearly as bad as my complaints made one think.[11]

The passage is a characteristically ambivalent appreciation and depreciation of his art for the very same reasons. On the side of depreciation, he suggests that his stories aren't real stories at all, with the dramatic conflict of real stories, but a "game" he plays with the reader: behind the apparent struggle of his protagonists to live, undermining and betraying it from the start, is his own secret embrace of death. And just because the struggle is a fake one he is able to prolong it artfully into a sort of swan song, a swan song which at the end of the diary entry he compares to his hypochondriacal complainings to his mother, to his constant whinings about aches and pains. In this Kafka seems to be agreeing with those critics who find him a pusillanimous neurotic, lacking in any force or fight. Edmund Wilson thinks he is "at his most characteristic when he is assimilating men to beasts—dogs, insects, mice, and apes—which can neither dare nor know. . . . the denationalized, discouraged, disaffected, disabled Kafka . . . can in the end only let us down." [12] A psychoanalytic critic concludes that "the striving for synthesis, for integration and harmony which are the marks of a healthy ego and a healthy art are lacking in Kafka's life and in his writings. The conflict is weak in Kafka's stories because the ego is submissive; the unequal forces within the Kafka psyche create no tension within the reader, only a fraternal sadness. . . ." [13]

But on the side of appreciation, Kafka sees his understanding of death as being responsible for his "best things." Thanks to his underlying acceptance of death, the selfsame story that he is always telling about somebody who finds it hard to die is "as perfect as can be" and "dies away beautifully and purely."

Which is it then? Is *The Metamorphosis* unhealthy art—the artfully prolonged whine of a disaffected neurotic with a submissive ego? Or is it a lament (*Klage*) that is perfect, beautiful, pure? Does Kafka let us down in the end or does he try to lift us up "into the pure, the true, the unchangeable"? [14] The two opposing characterizations, "neurotic whine" and "beautiful lament," which I have drawn from Kafka's diary entry express very different judgments, but they agree in pointing to something lyrical about the form of his "best things," something in the nature of a crying-out, rather than a narrative of action with complication and dénouement. Doubtless Kafka's critics would find him depressing in any case. Yet in taxing his stories with lack of tension they misunderstand their form and ask them to be what they are not and do not try to be—representations of action. And in missing their form they miss the meaning—these stories do not mean the unmanliness and discouragement of their protagonists; they mean the courage to see the unmanliness and discouragement which live like an infection at the heart of modern spirituality, perhaps even, as Kafka wrote to Milena Jesenská, at the heart of "all faith since the beginning of time." [15]

The Metamorphosis does not unfold an action but a metaphor; it is the spelling out of a metaphor. It does not end in an Aristotelian dénouement, but draws the metaphor out to its ultimate conclusion which is death. I called the movement of the story a dying fall. But visual terms serve better than auditory ones. The movement is a seeing more and more: waking up, the metamorphosed Gregor sees his insect belly, then his helplessly waving legs, then his room, cloth samples, picture, alarm clock, furniture, key, living room, family, chief clerk—on and on and on in a relentless march of ever deeper seeing till he sees his own death. Everything he sees is a building stone added to the structure of the metaphor of his banishment from the human circle, capped by the stone of his death. In a story of this kind there is no question of tension or of any of the specifically dramatic qualities: it is a vision.

Of course Gregor Samsa "can neither dare nor know." Neither can Hamlet, his ultimate literary ancestor and the earliest protagonist of the modern theme of doubt and despair in face of the threat of universal meaninglessness.* That is just the point of the story: Gregor can neither dare nor know, neither live in the world nor find the unknown truth he craves. The final words of Dostoyevsky's Underground Man, commenting on his own *Notes*, are very apposite here:

> . . . [A] novel needs a hero, and all the traits for an antihero are *expressly* gathered together here, and, what matters most, it all produces a most unpleasant impression, for we are all divorced

---

*
                . . . O God, God,
How weary, stale, flat and unprofitable
Seem to me all the uses of this world!

When Hamlet says the question is, to be or not to be, not only suicide is the question but also Being itself—he calls being into question. That is how he has been understood since the beginning of the nineteenth century, when Coleridge called him a "philosopher or meditator." The view of him as a protagonist of philosophical disillusion and despair goes hand in hand with the exaltation of the play from its old position side by side with Shakespeare's other tragedies to a unique height of reputation in the modern age. For us the play is intensely, archetypally modern; we *interpret* it that way. With *Hamlet* (as we interpret it) imagination turns inward, out of the world and away from action, away from drama, to search inside Wordsworth's "Poet's Mind" (*The Prelude; or, Growth of a Poet's Mind*) and Yeats's "blind, stupefied heart" for a ground of being; imagination labors with unhappy sophistication to discover within the self what formerly it had received from the world in naïve trust. Tragedy, action, drama itself are impossible in such an atmosphere of radical spiritual questioning—then "enterprises of great pitch and moment . . . lose the name of action" and enterprisers lose themselves in morbid introspection. Do we not read *Hamlet* as a vision, a frightening vision of nonbeing, rather than see it as a play? Certainly, with its episodic plot made up of a series of accidents, it reads better than it acts. The metaphysical abyss it discloses to the reader becomes on the stage that gap between the actors' efforts and our idea of the play which makes all productions of *Hamlet* seem more or less of a disappointment.

from life, we are all cripples, every one of us, more or less. . . . "Speak for yourself," you say, "and for your miseries in your underground hole, but don't dare to say 'all of us.' " Excuse me, gentlemen, I am not justifying myself with that "all of us." As for what concerns me in particular, I have only carried to an extreme in my life what you have not dared to carry halfway, and, what's more, you have taken your cowardice for good sense, and have found comfort in deceiving yourselves. So that perhaps, after all, there is more life in me than in you. Look into it more carefully! Why, we don't even know what living means now, what it is, and what it is called! Leave us alone without books and we shall be lost and in confusion at once. We shall not know what to join onto, what to cling to, what to love and what to hate, what to respect and what to despise.

What the Underground Man is saying, what he says all along in his *Notes*, is that action and awareness, daring and knowledge, world and spirit are no longer united but split. To act in the world requires life-confidence based on knowledge; but the Underground Man's "overacute consciousness" exposes doubts which undermine his confidence—self-awareness turns him into a "mouse" who is incapable of avenging an affront, a nasty "babbler" who can only sit with folded hands. On the other hand, "all 'direct' persons and men of action are active just because they are stupid and limited." The man of action and the man of consciousness, the man of the world and the man of the spirit are equally failures, equally cripples; the one because he is stupid, and the other because he is ignominious. Neither knows "what living means now, what it is, and what it is called."

Gregor Samsa, not even a mouse but a bug, finds that his sister's violin music draws him with the promise of that knowledge of "what to love and what to hate, what to respect and what to despise" which would make it possible to realize the union of world and spirit. But his effort to penetrate the mystery of such knowledge fails and he surrenders to the impossibility of living.

Does the Underground Man, Dostoyevsky's and Kafka's, make

his misery out to be the *summum bonum*? Does he end up morbidly affirming his unlife as the highest life? So Lionel Trilling thinks. He finds in the hissings and spittings of the Russian writer's "antihero" a fundamental rejection of the pleasure principle—meaning by pleasure sensual gratification first of all and after that the health of the entire human being as expressed in the energetic use of his powers for the attainment of life-success. Instead the Underground Man chooses suffering and impotence and failure; he perversely prefers a spirituality that turns away from life toward death. Professor Trilling explains his perversity as a refusal "to admit and consent to the *conditioned* nature of man," to bow his neck to modern rationality: "If pleasure is indeed the principle of his being, he is as *known* as the sum of 2 and 2; he is a mere object of reason, of that rationality of the Revolution which is established upon the primacy of the principle of pleasure." [16]

Now of course human life is lived under and through all kinds of conditions; we are not absolutely free, insouciant spirits. The Underground Man would really be crazy if he refused to admit or consent to this. But what drives him nearly crazy is the possibility that we are *nothing but* the product of conditions. His perversity and unreasonableness consist in refusing to accept what he cannot refute: the reasoning of scientific determinism, what he calls "the laws of nature." The painful issue for him is not the conditioned nature of man, but the *absolutely* conditioned nature of man, the scientific arguments for which *he cannot refute.* At one point in his argument Professor Trilling applies the Freudian term "drive" to the pleasure principle—the Underground Man fights against being "driven" absolutely.* In his ravings, it is true, he sometimes seems to be lashing out against all conditions. But that is because Dostoyevsky is portraying a frightened living person and not just an argument; *Notes from the Under-*

---

* The first sentence of *Beyond the Pleasure Principle* asserts the absolute rule of drives: "In the theory of psychoanalysis we have no hesitation in assuming that the course taken by mental events is automatically regulated by the pleasure principle."

ground is after all a story. Helpless to refute the rationality of the "Crystal Palace" and the "nineteenth century" and hang onto his freedom, he falls back like a child on mere defiance and perversity, the only freedom left him: "Of course I cannot break through the wall [of deterministic law] by battering my head against it if I really have not the strength to knock it down, but I am not going to be reconciled to it simply because it is a stone wall and I have not the strength." An ignorant, contrary child and also a spiteful devil,* he is the modern poet-hero, a notorious adolescent who refuses to accept reality—the exiguous reality of a scientism which "excludes value from the essence of matter of fact" (to quote Whitehead again) and exiles the human freedom to choose the good into the unreal realm of modern spirit.

The Underground Man rejects not pleasure in principle, but the pleasure principle, the *Lustprinzip,* because it operates with automatic compulsion, uncontrolled by any idea of what is good. He is a modern poet, which is to say a poet-philosopher; he rejects *modern* pleasure, which is poisoned for him by its inability to justify itself except on grounds of brute necessity, on the grounds that it is necessarily what it is; and by its *indifference* to the question of justifying itself. He does not, with perverted pride, choose unpleasure, as Professor Trilling has it; his plight is that he does not know what pleasure, *true* pleasure, is anymore.† He does not know. And because he does not know, he is powerless to act like a man—for how should a man act?—falling into a void of unlife. But in facing this he is a man.

In Gregor Samsa there is no trace of pride or vanity about himself as a superior suffering spiritual being. The Kafka artist-hero is a genuine hunger artist who fasts because he must, be-

* Professor Trilling compares him aptly to Thersites. But this ignominious Thersites reviles an Achilles who is a beefy football player, a dumb cluck.

† Milena Jesenská wrote to Brod about Kafka: "I know that he does not oppose *life,* but only *this kind of life:* that is what he opposes." [17]

cause the diet of the world cannot satisfy his spiritual hunger, and not because he has made hunger into the supreme good. "Forgive me, everybody," the Hunger Artist whispers in the story of that name when he is dying in his cage. "Of course we forgive you," replies the circus overseer.

"I always wanted you to admire my fasting," said the hunger artist. "We do admire it," said the overseer, affably. "But you shouldn't admire it," said the hunger artist. "Well then we don't admire it," said the overseer, "but why shouldn't we admire it?" "Because I have to fast, I can't help it," said the hunger artist. "What a fellow you are," said the overseer, "and why can't you help it?" "Because," said the hunger artist, lifting his head a little and speaking, with his lips pursed, as if for a kiss, right into the overseer's ear, so that no syllable might be lost, "because I couldn't find the food I liked. If I had found it, believe me, I should have made no fuss and eaten my fill like you or anyone else."

5

THE FAILURE
TO BE
SUBJECTIVE

> . . . [T]o make the external internal, the inter-
> nal external, to make nature thought and
> thought nature,—this is the mystery of genius
> in the Fine Arts.
>
> —COLERIDGE

Amerika

Amerika differs from most of Kafka's other works in describing
an actual milieu with an historical name and a geographical loca-
tion. We see everything through Karl Rossmann's eyes just as we
do through Georg Bendemann's eyes and Gregor Samsa's eyes;
the difference is that what we see is out "there," the customary
real world of the novel, rather than a world reflected in the
depths of the protagonist's subjectivity. Although the features of
the America that Kafka shows us are highly distorted and the
novel makes no claim to verisimilitude, it is still the actual
America, perceived as being objectively there, which it portrays.
In this respect it is his most traditional work.

When Kafka first sat down to write the novel early in 1912 he had not yet hit upon the dream-narrative form. That happened when he wrote *The Judgment* in September of that year. And even though the largest part of *Amerika* was written after that story and has the finished style of Kafka's literary maturity, the novel as a whole remained stuck in its original, pre-*Judgment* narrative method. This was a method which did not really suit his abilities. His own comment on *Amerika* (as I take it to be) in the first flush of elation following his writing of *The Judgment* was: "The conviction confirmed that with my novel writing I am in the shameful lowlands of writing." [1]

There is a fundamental incompatibility between the form of the work and the intentions he tried to realize in it. In its form *Amerika* belongs to the genre of novel, deriving directly from the picaresque novel, which narrates the experiences of an innocent youth who is cast out into the world to make his own way in it—*Oliver Twist* and *David Copperfield* are examples of the type. Kafka himself connects his novel with this genre of writing in a diary entry:

> Dickens' *Copperfield*. "The Stoker" [Chapter One of *Amerika*] a sheer imitation of Dickens, the projected novel even more so. The story of the box, the boy who delights and charms everybody, the menial work, his sweetheart in the country house, the grimy tenements (among other things), *but above all the method*.[2]

The method to which he refers is that of the episodic narrative with its loosely strung together scenes of adventure among the great and the humble, rich and poor, working people and vagabonds. Like the old picaresque novel indeed, *Amerika* even has a chapter ("The Road to Rameses") which takes place on the open road; and there is the pair of rogues, Delamarche and Robinson. Karl himself is the opposite of a rogue: he is an innocent. His very innocence, however, makes him a social outsider like the rogue, for the world in which he finds himself violently rejects innocence. He is a kind of upside-down *picaro*. The work-shy *picaro* made his way by his wits in a world of honest simpletons who labored at a job for their bread. The simple youth Karl Rossmann stumbles from mishap to mishap looking for nothing better than "a job in which he could achieve something, and be appreciated for his achievement." [3] But the workaday world that he is trying to break into, not out of, is an overpowering antihuman modern mechanism in which the interests of "discipline" override the interests of "justice." [4] The result is that Karl, with his thirst for justice, finds himself being continually expelled from it. And like the picaresque novel and the Dickensian novel with its Dick Whittington plot which sprang from the picaresque novel, *Amerika* has an ending in which the opposition between the hero and the world is resolved with sentimental implausibility.

Now this kind of narrative places a premium on knowledge of the world and the lively observation of actual scenes; it demands a multiplicity of shrewdly noted psychological and social types and vivacity and variety of incident. Kafka however had never been to America and knew it at second hand only—it is no wonder that the novel, in spite of some wonderfully comic scenes, remains wooden. But even if Kafka had been acquainted with America at first hand it is doubtful if he would have been able to bring off the work. The nature of the form, with its commitment to the actual world, clashes with Kafka's talents and intentions. His talents, as he remarked in his diary on August 6, 1914, were "for portraying my dreamlike inner life" [5] and discovering reality through subjectivity. And his intentions were the same symbolical intentions that we find in *The Castle*, if less clearly apprehended: to show the struggle of a protagonist to find a human place in an inhuman world of abstract automatisms. The actuality demanded by the novel's method pulls one way, the subjective character of Kafka's art pulls another; the empirical form of *Amerika* is at odds with its symbolical intentions.

Symbolical intention and narrative form split wide open in the fragmentary last chapter, "The Nature Theater of Oklahoma," where Kafka abandons realism entirely to impose a happy ending, in the shape of an elaborate philosophical fantasy, on a course of events that had seemed to be leading to the destruction of the hero. As a milder discrepancy, however, the split runs right through the book. On the opening page Karl Rossmann sees the Statue of Liberty in New York Harbor holding aloft not its actual torch, but the Archangel Michael's sword of judgment which in the Bible "keeps the way to the Tree of Life." The actual furniture of America lends itself uncomfortably to such distortion and one wonders whether Kafka simply made a mistake or is indeed telling us that the New Eden of righteousness will be revealed as still another Paradise Lost.[6] I believe he did not make a mistake and that is what he meant. But the thing does not quite work.

When Karl goes below deck to retrieve his umbrella and encounters the stoker, there is this passage:

> "You're all alone? Without anyone to look after you?"—"Yes, all alone."—"Perhaps I should join up with this man," the thought came into Karl's head, "where am I likely to find a better friend?"

All this is told perfectly respectably in the realistic mode. However, when he is claimed by his uncle and has to part from the stoker after having defended him before the captain, Karl "burst out crying and kissed the stoker's hand, taking that seamed, almost nerveless hand and pressing it to his cheek like a treasure which he would soon have to give up." The difference in emotional intensity between the two passages is inexplicable—what has taken place between the boy and the stoker in the intervening pages cannot account for it. The uncle throws a veil of realistic psychological explanation over Karl's anomalous behavior by saying that "the stoker seems to have bewitched you. . . . You felt lonely, then you found the stoker, and you're grateful to him now. . . ." But this is no explanation at all. What accounts for Karl's emotion is the lurking presence of an absolute idea of loneliness which the author has been unable to realize in the empirical narrative mode.

The discrepancy between narrative form and intention shows up even more inexplicably in a later parting. Karl tells the motherly Head Cook of the Hotel Occidental that he has separated from his two companions Delamarche and Robinson on bad terms.

> The Head Cook seemed to construe this as excellent news. "So then you're free?" she said.
> "Yes, I'm free," said Karl, *and nothing seemed more worthless than his freedom.*

As he was mistrustful of the pair from the start, and has been bullied and taken advantage of by them ever since in confirmation of his misgivings, Karl's despairing thought about the worthlessness of his freedom must strike the reader as senseless. What Kafka is trying to realize here, unsuccessfully, is a symbolical intention; he wishes the narrative to convey the emptiness of a freedom which merely leaves Karl to himself, freedom as sheer negativity. But the actual circumstances of the novel—Karl's concrete relation to the two men in the concrete situation in which he finds himself—defeat his intention. The failure becomes quite clear if we compare this passage with a passage at the end of Chapter Eight of *The Castle,* where something like the same intention is realized with magnificent effect. K. has just been left standing alone in the snow-covered emptiness of the courtyard of the Herrenhof:

> . . . [A]nd now as all the electric lights went out too—for whom should they remain on?—and only up above the slit in the wooden gallery still remained bright, holding one's wandering gaze for a little, it seemed to K. as if at last every connection he had with anybody had been broken and as if now in reality he were freer than he had ever been, and at liberty to wait here in this place, usually forbidden to him, as long as he desired, and had won a freedom such as hardly anybody else had ever succeeded in winning, and as if nobody could dare to touch him or drive him away, or even speak to him; but—this conviction was at least equally strong—as if at the same time there was nothing more senseless, nothing more hopeless, than this freedom, this waiting, this inviolability.

96

K. is free to freeze to death in the desolate courtyard—indeed there is nothing more hopeless than his freedom. But Karl's freedom from Delamarche and Robinson makes it possible for him to accept the Head Cook's kindnesses and have what he so much wants—a job. Why, then, should this freedom seem worthless to him?

When Karl is given a piano by his Uncle Jacob in the second chapter, we are told that "at first [he] set great hopes on his piano playing and sometimes unashamedly dreamed, at least before falling asleep, of the possibility that it might exert a direct influence upon American conditions" [7] (*und schämte sich nicht . . . an die Möglichkeit einer unmittelbaren Beeinflussung der amerikanischen Verhältnisse durch dieses Klavierspiel zu denken*). In the literal circumstances of the novel this is a bizarre, absolutely senseless hope—how can a boy's piano playing change the American world?* Wilhelm Emrich comments that in this sentence "there rings unmistakably . . . Kafka's conception of purposeless childish existence, of the saving function of music and play." [8] He is perfectly right—except that the conception exists there as an obscure intention, not as a meaning carried out in the narrative.

The three great organizations of the novel (leaving aside the Nature Theater)—the ship, Uncle Jacob's "commission and despatch agency," and the hotel—teeter more or less uncertainly between the realistic and the symbolical. Limited to a time and place, and only partly merged with their official representatives who still possess traces of a human character and personal history outside their organizational functions,[9] they lack the absoluteness, and so the symbolical force, of the bureaucracies of *The Trial* and *The Castle*. We learn, for example, that the Head Cook, like Karl, hails from Prague; on her bureau stand framed photographs that "probably came from Europe." Thus she possesses attributes that lie outside her function in the hotel organization. The Head Waiter has been an elevator boy: "it was he

* So the translator, Edwin Muir, apparently thought and substituted "his life in America" for "American conditions."

who first organized the elevator boys"—he is not a Head Waiter absolute, nothing and never but a Head Waiter. But the tendency of the figures in the novel, against its realistic grain, is to merge wholly with their functions, to become absolute. Theresa rises from a kitchen maid because she is called out one day by the Head Cook to arrange napkins for a banquet: ". . . [W]ell [Theresa says], I gave her great satisfaction, for I have always been very good at arranging table napkins." Napkin arranger is on the point of turning into something ultimate, a fundamental category of being, which is what functions are in the later novels.

The court and the castle exist outside of a historical time and place and tend to embrace the whole world. They are universals, with an absence of specific attributes which might seem to echo the "empty" typicality of classical art. Kafka's emptiness, however, is that of a shadowy void and not of classical generalization; the court and the castle lack specification because they are wrapped in mystery, beyond ken—their emptiness, their universality is Romantic. Except for the Nature Theater, the big apparatuses of *Amerika* are too ensnared in their realistic setting to achieve this quality—but the effect of the Nature Theater chapter is to jerk the novel onto a different plane entirely and arbitrarily cancel the previous action.

A similar difference separates Karl from the two K.'s and also from Georg Bendemann and Gregor Samsa. Although *The Judgment* and *The Metamorphosis* are basically psychological stories, Georg and Gregor are not whole figures, existing in the psychological round, with "the old stable ego of the character," as Lawrence put it.[10] Like the K.'s they are empty, null, fragmentary; they move below the level of ego-personality in a terrain that is their own subjectivity written large. In the two novelle that terrain of subjectivity has a more or less psychoanalytic groundplan. In *The Trial* and *The Castle* the psychoanalytic groundplan remains, but deepened beyond the psychological. Karl Rossmann however is a whole figure, a character rather than a figure, even if a rather wooden one, furnished with a personality and moving in the actual world. When the Head Waiter puts him on trial, it is the Head Waiter who accuses him, not his divided self, and with his whole self he repudiates the accusation. Karl lacks the universal possibilities which the later Kafka figures owe to their "emptiness."

Kafka fails in *Amerika* because he tells the story of an outcast's search for a "place . . . in the great city" [11] of the modern world in terms of an idea rather than through an image—producing an intellectual construction rather than the living form of his dream narrative. He had no talent for ideas per se, only for images. He needed to seize his material in a metaphor and tell his story through it. His best work never touches ideas directly; ideas are there, in the images, but Kafka as a storyteller is indifferent to them.

What, then, is the idea of *Amerika*? The idea of America itself: the great, traditional idea of America as the New World, as the refuge and rebirthplace of European mankind wherein it is afforded a second chance, unencumbered by the ruins of the past, to enact a history free of injustice and unrighteousness.* Goethe expressed the idea in his poem "To America" in which he congratulates the New World on its freedom from the past and from a morbid Romantic preoccupation with it:

> *Amerika, du hast es besser*
> *Als unser Kontinent, das alte,*
> *Hast keine verfallene Schlösser*
> *Und keine Basalte.*
> *Dich stört nicht im Innern,*
> *Zu lebendiger Zeit,*
> *Unnützes Erinnern*
> *Und vergeblicher Streit.*
> *Benutzt die Gegenwart mit Glück!*

* In a conversation with Gustav Janouch, Kafka touched on this idea of America, remarking, apropos of constructivist pictures: "They are merely dreams of a marvelous America, of a wonderland of unlimited possibilities. That is perfectly understandable, because Europe is becoming more and more a land of impossible limitations." [12]

Und wenn nun eure Kinder dichten,
Bewahre sie ein gut Geschick
Vor Ritter-, Räuber- und Gespenstergeschichten. *

Kafka, however, treats the idea of America negatively, showing in every episode of his hero's career how the American reality contradicts and denies it—only to reaffirm the idea at the end of the novel, in a more transcendent form, in the grandiose Nature Theater of Oklahoma.

The actual America that Karl Rossmann finds himself adrift in is torn by "futile strife" and is in no way "better off" than the Old World. It is a capitalistic America divided between the swollen rich in their great houses and hotels and the suffering poor crammed in tenement rooms. The story of the death of Theresa's homeless mother—one of the strongest passages in the book—is excruciatingly pitiful. It is an America of huge opposing impersonal forces; when the striking metal workers demonstrate in the streets, they shuffle past mounted policemen in an endless "moving mass . . . whose singing was more homogeneous than any single human voice." In the trial scene in the Captain's cabin of the German ship that has brought Karl to America, Karl's uncle, although an American Senator, enunciates the "European" principle that discipline must take precedence over justice; and subsequently when Karl is abruptly cast off by his uncle, and then fired from his job in the Hotel Occidental, he learns that this same principle of giving second place to justice rules in America as well.

At first, however, America seems a fairyland of "unlimited possibilities" to Karl: a humble steerage immigrant, "the poor lad [so his uncle says], but for the signs and wonders which still happen in America, if nowhere else, would have come to a

* "America, you are better off than our old continent, you have no ruined castles, no basalt. You are not inwardly disturbed, right up to the present day, by useless memories and futile strife. I wish you luck in making the most of your present! And when your children turn to writing poetry, may a happy destiny keep them from tales about knights, brigands and ghosts."

wretched end in New York"—if the Senator had not recognized him and installed him, with a wave of his wand, in his own house, Karl would have perished. But Karl's new state is not one of freedom but of servitude to the jealous affection of his relative, whom he soon finds occasion to offend. Disowned by a letter delivered to him at the stroke of midnight, Karl's pumpkin becomes a pumpkin again and no coach, his mice mice, his old cap is clapped back on his head, and his box of humble European effects is thrust into his hands. He had been sent packing by his parents in Europe because in his innocence "a servant girl had seduced him and got herself a child by him"—his American relative sends him packing for an equally innocent offense.

Thereafter Karl's path, with some interruptions, leads downward. The last we see of him before his translation from an actual America to the Nature Theater of Oklahoma is as a slavey to that primitive-Venus figure, Brunelda.* And Kafka apparently sketched or at least planned further stages in his descent into bottom-dog anonymity, for when the boy is asked his name at the Nature Theater's Bureau for Intermediate Students, "he gave the nickname he had had in his last post: 'Negro.'" Thus Karl, instead of finding America a haven of justice for the oppressed, finds a restless world of "movement without end" in which "helpless human beings" are violently thrown about[13] and destroyed with cruel indifference; instead of making his way in the New World like a latter-day Dick Whittington, he becomes more and more lost in it.†

Throughout the novel its idea tends to show through the thinly fleshed covering. When Mr. Pollunder drives Karl out to the country in the third chapter, the boy finds that the banker's

* In the untranslated fragment *"Ausreise Bruneldas"* he is more her keeper than her servant.

† *Amerika* is Brod's title, not Kafka's. Once only he gave the novel a name, in the diary entry of December 31, 1915, in which he called it *"Der Verschollene"* (translated, clumsily, by some such phrase as "The Missing Person," "The Boy Who Was Lost and Never Heard from Again," and so on); otherwise he called it his "American novel." Brod has been criticized for using his own title instead of Kafka's. Nevertheless his has its aptness.

house, "like the country houses of most rich people in the neighborhood of New York, was larger and taller than a country house designed for only one family has any need to be." It is an old mansion: a seat of power and wealth, a "fortress," Karl calls it when he appreciates the immense length of its corridors, rather than a habitation of righteousness—as it were, one of those "ruined castles" (refurbished for new rulers, for Mr. Pollunder is in the middle of remodeling the mansion) which Goethe had said America was better off for not having. Karl says to the banker's daughter:

> "So you have actually old houses in America too."
> "Of course," said Clara with a laugh, pulling him along. "You have some queer ideas about America."

The actual America is "old," not new. Where, then, does the New World lie? Ever westward, in a mythopoeic Oklahoma that does not figure on any map, in the Nature Theater in which "Everyone is welcome!"

> Everyone is welcome! If you want to be an artist, join our company! Our Theater can find employment for everyone, a place for everyone!

The Nature Theater—a theater of the natural—is "the biggest theater in the world"; it is a "true 'theater of the world' in the old cosmic sense of the Baroque period," as Emrich says,[14] and expresses the Whitmanesque idea of an all-embracing, all-accepting American immensity. By combining the two ideas of a theater (i.e., "playing") and a hospitable American immensity in which everyone is welcome, Kafka attempts, for the first and last time, to render concretely his idea of Paradise—only to break off in the middle of the chapter, apparently finding it an impossible attempt. His image of a Theater of the New World, in spite of its ingenuity, fails him, for it is less an image than a contrivance. The Nature Theater wipes out everything that has gone before in the novel by a mechanical reversal:

> "Everyone is welcome," [the placard] said. Everyone, that meant Karl too. All that he had done till now was ignored; it was not

going to be made a reproach to him. He was entitled to apply for a job of which he need not be ashamed, which, on the contrary, was a matter of public advertisement. And just as public was the promise that he too would find acceptance.

The Nature Theater is a Kafka bureaucracy stood on its head, and it stands the story on its head. The old authorities and organizations of the novel were full of malign suspicion and cast Karl out in spite of his innocence, *because* of his innocence, which affronts their certainty of universal guilt—Karl's crucial realization is that "it's impossible to defend oneself where there is no good will. . . ." [15] But the Nature Theater benevolently takes Karl in in spite of his fibs and faults, because he is an innocent human being. The Head Waiter of the Hotel Occidental cross-examined Karl pitilessly, discovering nothing but wrongdoing in him. But the gentleman of the Nature Theater who interrogates Karl after he has been engaged asks questions that are "very simple and direct, nor did he check Karl's replies by cross-examining him at all." The contrast could not be clearer.

What is strikingly absent from the novel is a conception of freedom. The play-freedom suggested by the idea of a theater remains pale and abstract; what the Nature Theater radiates is the glare of bureaucratic power. Instead of finding freedom at the end of his road Karl finds an unreal paternalistic bureaucracy that saves him from destruction by sentimental magic.* When Kafka tried to imagine human freedom concretely in writing his American novel, he could only dream of a father who finally turns kind. "He feels imprisoned on this earth," he said in an autobiographical aphorism, "he feels constricted; the melancholy, the impotence, the sicknesses, the feverish fancies of the captive afflict him; no comfort can comfort him, since it is merely comfort, gentle head-splitting comfort glozing the brutal fact of imprisonment. But if he is asked what he actually wants

---

* "In enigmatic language Kafka used to hint smilingly," Max Brod reports in the Afterword, "that within this 'almost limitless' theater his young hero was going to find again a profession, a stand-by, his freedom, even his old home and his parents, as if by some paradisal magic."

he cannot reply, for—that is one of his strongest proofs—he has no conception of freedom." [16]

Amerika lacks the coherent poetic structure and the concentrated poetic force of Kafka's dream narratives. There are vivid images in the novel—the lumpish stoker with his pathos of the inferior, the animated scene of New York Harbor, the New York streets, Mr. Green with his monstrous appetite and monstrous cigar, the Head Waiter and the Head Porter, the grotesque Brunelda, the election mob writhing in the glare of headlights—but these images are vivid separately, being joined together only by an idea; they do not make part of a unitary, overwhelming metaphor in the way that is the case with Kafka's successful narratives. On the other hand, considered as a traditional narrative, *Amerika* is episodic to the point of being a chaos of fragments; it has neither the modern unity of image nor the traditional unity of action.

In the Penal Colony

Kafka failed in *Amerika* for lack of a suitable narrative mode, the subjective mode of the dream story. In the short novel *In the Penal Colony*, which he wrote in the fall of 1914, about the same time he began *The Trial*, again he seems to me to fail to master his material. Now, however, the failure is not due to artistic immaturity—now it is the failure of the mature artist to stick with sure instinct to the formal requirements of his own vision. Failure however is too strong a word here. One cannot call such a powerful story a failure. But neither is it a success.

Ideas obtrude in the story with unusual distinctness and in the end the reader is confronted with an intellectual dilemma rather than a living mystery—but not for want of a unitary image through which to tell the story. The image is there, and a very powerful one it is, in the shape of the penal island with its dreadful execution machine squatting in the middle of it—the image of a world under the judgment of the law. Nevertheless, as Austin Warren observes, "this story [is] pretty persistently and consistently allegorical";[17] that is, it refers one *directly* to ideas. If we examine what the allegory consists in and how it is presented, I think we shall find that the power of the story to disturb is not only due to its artistic power.

The world discovered in the story is in a state of schism, a world divided between the Old and the New. That is the essential allegory. On one side stands the traditional machine of judgment under the law, invented and built by the patriarchal old Commandant, now dead. By an ingenious mechanism of vibrating needles it writes a condemned man's sentence deeper and deeper into his flesh till at the sixth hour "enlightenment comes even to the most dull-witted"; at the twelfth hour he dies. The priest of this cruel rite is the officer-judge, a disciple of the old Commandant; he describes the workings of the machine with enthusiastic pedantry to the visiting explorer. On the other side stands the new Commandant, "always looking for an excuse to attack [the] old way of doing things"; his "new, mild doctrine" prefers humane judicial methods, but he hesitates to affront a venerable institution directly and therefore tries to subvert it by harassment and deliberate neglect.

The old law judged according to the principle that "guilt is never to be doubted"—the guilt of mankind was never to be doubted. Therefore no trial needed to take place. "Other courts cannot follow that principle, for they consist of various opinions and on top of that have higher courts over them." [18] The old court then was absolute—the highest court.[19] In the new, liberal order there is no highest court, only "various opinions."

The old law aimed at being eternal law: "We who were [the old Commandant's] friends," says the officer, "knew even before he died that the organization of the colony was so perfect that his successor, even with a thousand new schemes in his head, would find it impossible to alter anything, at least for many years to come." But the new Commandant cares nothing about eternity; what he cares about, as a man of progress and the

times, is "harbor works, nothing but harbor works!" A woman-
izer, he swims in the atmosphere of a crowd of admiring fe-
males; through the "women who influence him" the world is
womanized. The old Commandant had "his ladies" too, but there
was no petticoat government.

The condemned man vomits when he is strapped down in the
machine and takes the felt gag in his mouth, because "the
[new] Commandant's ladies stuff the man with sugar candy before he's led off. He has lived on stinking fish his whole life long
and now he has to eat sugar candy!" The "new, mild doctrine" is
effeminate and, by causing the condemned man to vomit over
himself, degrading. But the condemned man vomits too because
the felt gag has been chewed by hundreds rather than being
changed for every execution as it used to be. So the new regime
is callous as well as sentimental.

"How different an execution was in the old days!" exclaimed
the officer-judge. Then the whole island gathered together in the
true ceremony of belief and the Commandant himself laid the
condemned man under the Harrow.

> "No discordant noise spoilt the working of the machine. Many did
> not care to watch it but lay with closed eyes in the sand; they all
> knew: Now Justice is being done. In the silence one heard nothing
> but the condemned man's sighs, half muffled by the felt gag.
> Nowadays the machine can no longer wring from anyone a sigh
> louder than the felt gag can stifle; but in those days the writing
> needles let drop an acid fluid, which we're no longer permitted to
> use. Well, and then came the sixth hour! It was impossible to grant
> all the requests to be allowed to watch it from near by. The Com-
> mandant in his wisdom ordained that the children should have the
> preference . . . often enough I would be squatting there with a
> small child in either arm. How we all absorbed the look of trans-
> figuration on the face of the sufferer, how we bathed our cheeks
> in the radiance of that justice, achieved at last and fading so
> quickly! What times there were, my comrade!"

Under the old law, *Justice was done.* All shared ritually in the
redemption which the condemned man found under the law in

death. All stood under the same law and could look forward to the same redemption. Death redeemed. Of course, all this is according to the officer's point of view. But the point is that his is the point of view that excludes "points of view"—he lives the conviction of absolute justice.

That is how things were in the old days. Now, however, the sea of faith has ebbed. When the officer is unable to persuade the explorer, who remains convinced "that the injustice of the procedure and the inhumanity of the execution were undeniable," to side with him against the new Commandant, he lies down with devout determination in the judgment machine to execute himself. But execution according to the old law is no longer possible, a new dispensation has succeeded; the machine can no longer "do Justice." Negated, it spits out its parts and goes to pieces, murdering the officer indecently instead of executing him: ". . . [T]his was no [ceremonial] torture such as the officer desired, this was plain murder." Death no longer redeems:

> [The face of the corpse] was as it had been in life; no sign was visible of the promised redemption; what the others had found in the machine the officer had not found; the lips were firmly pressed together, the eyes were open, with the same expression as in life, the look was calm and convinced, through the forehead went the point of the great iron spike.

As Professor Emrich comments, "The age of redemption is no more. The dead man remains stuck in life. He no longer can cross the boundary into the liberating Beyond. Man is consigned entirely to the earth." * [20]

* The sketch "The Hunter Gracchus" is devoted to this theme:

[The Burgomaster asks:] "Are you dead?"
"Yes," said the hunter, "as you see. Many years ago, yes, it must be a great many years ago, I fell from a precipice in the Black Forest—that is in Germany—when I was hunting a chamois. Since then I have been dead."
"But you are alive too," said the Burgomaster.
"In a certain sense," said the hunter, "in a certain sense I am alive too. My death ship lost its way; a wrong turn of the wheel, a

Lawless sentimentality takes the place of implacable judgment, turning the liberated prisoner and his guard into guffawing clowns. The former observes with satisfaction how the officer takes his place in the machine:

> So this was revenge. Although he himself had not suffered to the end, he was to be revenged to the end. A broad, silent grin now appeared on his face and stayed there all the rest of the time.

Justice no longer holds sway, but revenge—an internecine warfare of each against each, in a never-ending pursuit of the upper hand.[22]

In the cavernous, blackened interior of the teahouse, which makes on the explorer "the impression of some historical memory or other," so that he feels "the power of past times," the old Commandant lies buried. All that remains of the old order is a prophecy, written on his gravestone, that he "will rise again and lead his adherents from this house to recover the colony. Have faith and wait!"

In the Penal Colony takes place in historical time—the colony is a more or less recognizable possession of a European power of the late-nineteenth or early-twentieth century—rather than in the timeless subjective dimension into which the protagonists of Kafka's dream narratives awaken out of historical time. Its subject matter is the religious history of the world, which it recapitulates in terms of the old times and the new times of a penal colony. Like most of Kafka's stories, it is concerned with spiritual need, but it treats this subject in historical terms rather than through an individual who experiences the despair of spiritual darkness in the timelessness of his soul. It is an historical allegory.

It would be a mistake, however, to read too-specific references

---

moment's absence of mind on the pilot's part, a longing to turn aside towards my lovely native country, I cannot tell what it was; I only know this, that I remained on earth and that ever since my ship has sailed earthly waters. . . . [I am] still stranded forlornly in some earthly sea or other." [21]

into the allegory. The old regime of the old Commandant does not, for example, pointedly refer to Old Testament days, it only embraces them in its meaning, along with all the other old regimes that based their authority on a transcendent religious absolute.* As an ancient idol which is at the same time a piece of modern machinery, the execution machine reaches from the present all the way back to the most barbarous times of Dagon and the other stocks and stones in whose name our worshiping fathers did absolute justice. The old ends and the new begins at the point at which justice based on supreme authority yields to justice based on "various opinions."

So far I have said little about the explorer, yet as the one through whose eyes the story is narrated and the embodiment of its moral point of view, his role is crucial for the way in which the allegory is presented. A dispassionate observer of the "peculiarities of many peoples," an enlightened modern relativist and naturalist, from first to last he condemns the injustice and the inhumanity of the old law—so much so indeed that he is moved to abandon his attitude of scientific neutrality for once and intervene against the execution. Mixed, however, with his disapproval of the old judicial procedure is a growing admiration for the officer, even though he cannot but deplore his narrow-mindedness. Touched in the end by the officer's "sincere conviction," the explorer decides to do nothing to hinder the operation of the old law, although, by refusing the officer's plea to join forces with him against the new Commandant, he will do nothing to help it either. When the officer lies down under the Harrow to execute himself, he can only approve his decision: "the officer was doing the right thing; in his place the explorer would not have acted otherwise."

What the explorer is confronted with on the penal island is a

* Nor is the labyrinthine script that regulates the workings of the execution machine a reference to the Hebrew Scriptures but to Scripture-in-general. The fact that the explorer finds the script very "artistic" (*kunstvoll*) but cannot understand it, shows that he is a modern man who can "appreciate" scripture as literature but cannot understand it as truth.

moral choice between the old law and the new—the story arranges itself as a kind of contest between the two regimes to win his concurrence. The old law is primitive and cruel, yet the explorer must admire the spiritual unity and conviction it begets in its adherents; a conviction which is able to attain ultimate spiritual knowledge in redemption through final judgment under the law. On the other hand, it is just precisely ultimateness that the new law lacks. He despises its effeminate sentimentality, laxity and shallow worldliness. Nevertheless, he must approve its superior humanity: "The injustice of the [old] procedure and the inhumanity of the execution were undeniable." So actually it is not a moral choice that the explorer is faced with, since there is never any question of what his moral judgment is. The choice he faces is between morality and spirituality. The two have come apart. Before this conflict between the moral and the spiritual, the explorer retreats into a neutrality which has nothing to do with his old scientific detachment. His neutrality now expresses the troubled state of mind of someone who has had a glimpse into hitherto undiscerned depths.

And yet the glimpse he gains is historical rather than religious. It is not insight into religious truth but into the religious past. The explorer does not and cannot believe in the truth of the old law; what he sees is the way it was when mankind was ruled by the idea of supreme truth. The execution machine is an historical demonstration to him of the primitive unity of absolute justice and human society, spirit and the world. But that unity explodes under his very eyes when the officer dies unredeemed ("murdered") in the disintegrating machine—redemption under the old law is an exploded (literally exploded!) religious idea. What the explorer feels toward the old law is a mixture of horror and nostalgia: horror at its cruelty, nostalgia for its spirituality. The story is painfully divided between the moral and the religious (or rather between the moral and the religious regarded nostalgically) and in the end the explorer must flee the dilemma the colony presents him with in dismayed haste.*

* Emrich interprets the allegory as follows: "For the sake of redemption, the old order sacrificed the human person. For the sake

In the Penal Colony is not *about* the conflict between the moral and the religious; it falls victim to that conflict. The explorer's dilemma is only a dilemma because the question of the old law's truth has been left aside. Leaving aside the question of truth casts an obscurantist shadow over the whole story, introduces a moral and intellectual equivocation. When the question of truth is not left aside there can be only one choice: we can only choose to be modern and go on from there. There is no going back to the old law, even if only to the extent of choosing to be neutral toward it as the explorer does. One of the reasons why the story is disturbing is this negative one: because it is morally and intellectually equivocal. The allegory teeters on the edge of a familiar snobbery, which was so strong in Prague among the sons of the Jewish middle class at the beginning of the century—the snobbery, as Werfel puts it in a quotation already cited, of "those . . . who run around as mystics and orthodox believers only because every tailor, schoolteacher and journalist is a believing atheist." [24] But working against the impression of snobbish obscurantism is the mute, unpalliated horror of the execution machine. Never do we lose sight of the fact that "the injustice of the procedure and the inhumanity of the execution were undeniable." The positive power of the story to disturb is owing to the image of the execution machine; its finicky details testify incontrovertibly to injustice. The authentic power of the story lies in its image of a religiosity which is as wicked and destructive as it is spiritual.

In the more or less historical framework of the story, on its level of rational consciousness, the old Commandant's religion, as a relic of the past, can only move the explorer nostalgically, it

---

of the human person, the new order sacrificed redemption. Both orders are barbaric." [23] But the old order, no more than the new, possessed the power of redemption, true redemption—the historical time in which the story is placed forces us as modern men to judge the old order historically, as based on superstition. And the new order is not barbaric. Whatever it is, however shallow it is, it is not barbaric. That is just the point: barbarism has been left behind— at the cost of spirituality.

cannot compel him at the center of his being. An outside observer, an onlooker rather than a participant, he is impressed by the old law's spiritual appearance—aesthetically. The explorer does not face a true dilemma in the penal colony, he is spectator at an allegorical confrontation.

The failure of the story is a failure to be subjective—and through subjectivity to reach the truth. In Kafka's dream narrative of the inner self there is no outside observer to whose detached judgment rival historical conceptions are submitted and between which he is challenged to choose. The protagonist in Kafka's dream stories is not confronted with a choice he must intellectually consider; his whole *being* is caught in a situation in which it is impossible for him to *live*. The injustice of the court in *The Trial* is also "undeniable," but its law is established in Joseph K.'s innermost self, not on an island he can sail away from. Joseph K. is caught in the living mystery of concrete existence, he does not stand there weighing modern relative ideas against ancient absolute ones. It is impossible for men to live without a trust in ultimate justice ("something indestructible"), and at the same time ultimate justice is impossible in a world where one must not accept as true what the law says is true, "one must only accept it as necessary"—to quote the priest's last comment to Joseph K. on the parable of the law.[25] In his dream narrative of the inner self, Kafka is able to unite within the one breast of Joseph K. the subservient primitive soul of the condemned man, for whom the authority of the old law is absolute, and the skeptical, yearning modern consciousness of the explorer, for whom the injustice of the old law is undeniable. In the court he is able to unite the cruel mythic absoluteness of the penal colony's old law with the hollowness of its new law. Out of that unity is born the truth of *The Trial*.

6   *UNJUST*

TRIBUNAL

Then suddenly the scene
Changed, and the unbroken dream entangled
me
In long orations, which I strove to plead
Before unjust tribunals—with a voice
Labouring, a brain confounded, and a sense,
Death-like, of treacherous desertion, felt
In the last place of refuge—my own soul.
—WORDSWORTH

Life, as we find it, is too hard for us; it brings
us too many . . . impossible tasks.
—FREUD

Only our concept of Time makes it possible
for us to speak of the Day of Judgment by that
name; in reality it is a summary court in per-
petual session.
—KAFKA

Every day Joseph K. woke up in the morning, ate the breakfast his landlady's cook brought him at eight o'clock, and went off to his job as chief clerk of a bank. But now, on his thirtieth birthday, in the middle of his life's journey, his system suddenly breaks down: when Anna fails to make her customary appearance and he rings for her, strangers answer instead and arrest him in his bed.

Like Gregor Samsa, Joseph K. wakes into a dream in which he finds himself seized by the truth of his life, which he had managed so far to avoid. The unwelcome truth forced on him is that his life stands under judgment: he is an accused man on trial. The unwelcome truth that Gregor Samsa woke up to was a personal one: his exclusion from the "human circle," his individual failure to be human. The truth that seizes K., however, although just as personal, is more than personal: he stands accused in his life not only because of personal culpability, not only because it is *his* life, but also because it is a human life. K. is guilty of all sorts of sins, including the misuse of his whole life, which is summed up in the first chapter with terrible succinctness:

> That spring K. had been accustomed to pass his evenings in this way: after work whenever possible—he was usually in his office until nine—he would take a short walk, alone or with some of his colleagues, and then go to a beer hall, where until eleven he sat at a table patronized mostly by elderly men. But there were exceptions to this routine, when, for instance, the Manager of the Bank, who highly valued his diligence and reliability, invited him for a drive or for dinner at his villa. And once a week K. visited a girl called Elsa, who was on duty all night till early morning as a waitress in a cabaret and during the day received her visitors in bed.[1]

But it is not only the knowledge of *how* he has misused his life that seizes hold of him, it is also the knowledge of his responsibility for his life, *however* he has used it. What overwhelms K. in the split second of awakening—"the riskiest moment of the day,"[2] when "one is so unprepared"[3]—before his habitual consciousness has mounted its routine guard over his self, is the knowledge that he is accountable for his every act and failure to act before "a summary court in perpetual session":[4] he is "arrested" by the knowledge of good and evil.

"Nobody," Kafka says in one of his aphorisms, "can remain content with just the knowledge of good and evil alone, he must also strive to act in accordance with it." But as a human being "he is not endowed with the strength" for doing good and shunning evil, so inevitably he "must destroy himself" in the attempt to do so; "yet there remains nothing for him but this last attempt." Compelled always to make a last attempt to do what always exceeds his strength, "man is filled with fear; he prefers to unlearn his knowledge of good and evil (the term 'the Fall of Man' may be traced back to that fear)." But the knowledge of good and evil cannot be unlearned, "it can only be obscured."

Man darkens and obscures his knowledge that he is under judgment for his every act and failure to act, by elaborating "reasons" (*Motivationen*) to account for himself and his life. Modern man rationalizes his life in both senses of the word: he explains it rationally (scientifically) in terms of cause and effect; and he also (thereby) explains away his own responsibility for it—he shifts the responsibility from himself to an infinity of "reasons." "The whole world is full of them, indeed the whole visible world is perhaps nothing more than a rationalization of man's wish to find peace for a moment" from his knowledge of good and evil and the obligation it lays on him. The whole visible life of man in the world is nothing more perhaps than an elaborate construction of reasons endlessly leading on to further reasons whose sole purpose is to obscure the fact of his responsibility, beyond all reasons, for himself. The life of modern man is "an attempt to falsify the fact of the knowledge" of good and evil, "to turn the knowledge," which we already possess (or rather which possesses us), into a "goal" still to be possessed at some time in the future.[5]

Kafka plays in the aphorism on the double meaning of the word knowledge as knowledge of good and evil (ethical consciousness) and as science (knowledge of the conditions shaping human life and behavior). The latter kind of knowledge is infinite. Therefore final knowledge in the scientific sense is an unattainable "goal"—man can never know finally all the "reasons" why he is what he is and does what he does. Modern man, Kafka is saying, deliberately confuses knowledge of his *responsibility* for his actions, which he possesses from the first, with knowledge of the reasons for his actions, which he can never fully possess. ("An attempt to falsify the fact of the knowledge [of good and evil], to turn knowledge into a goal.") By means of this confusion he tries to "find peace for a moment" from his responsibility for himself—for by making responsibility wait upon scientific knowledge, which can *never* become complete, he guarantees eternal innocence for himself.*

* Dostoyevsky's Underground Man, attacking with furious disgust "the ordinary human consciousness" of modern times, the "stupid

The aphorism is highly relevant to *The Trial*.[6] Joseph K., too, "prefers to unlearn his knowledge of good and evil." In the very first sentence of the novel he pleads innocent of any wrongdoing and blames his being accused on the malice of others, on the world: "Someone must have slandered Joseph K., for without having done anything wrong he was arrested one fine morning." [7] True, the court never specifies what the charge against him is, and that is manifestly unjust. But the manifest injustice of the court (which is the manifest injustice of the world) does not relieve K. of his own responsibility, it only makes his own responsibility manifest. The fact that the charge against him has been left open leaves it open to K. to judge himself. But he prefers to "make an outcry about [his] feeling innocent." [8] His argument in his own defense culminates, in the cathedral, in a declaration of human innocence *in general*, of universal exemption from culpability: the priest having told him that his "guilt is supposed, for the present, at least, to have been proved," K. says he is not guilty, "it's a mistake. *For how in general can a man be guilty?* Yet we are all men here, one as much as the other." * To which the priest drily replies: "That is true . . . but that's how all guilty men talk." [9]

Against the modern affirmation of human innocence Kafka does not set the traditional religious affirmation of man's fallen

---

and limited" contemporary man who does not doubt that he is an "*homme de la nature et de la vérité*," attributes to him this same disavowal of responsibility for himself:

> . . . [T]hen, you say, science itself will teach man . . . that he never has really had any caprice or will of his own, and that he himself is something in the nature of a piano key or the stop of an organ, and that there are, besides, things called the laws of nature; so that everything he does is not done by his willing it, but is done of itself, by the laws of nature, and man will no longer have to answer for his actions and life will become exceedingly easy for him.

* "*Wie kann denn ein Mensch überhaupt schuldig sein? Wir sind hier doch alle Menschen, einer wie der andere.*" I believe the German text conveys what I say it conveys, but it does so in an unstressed way, under a mask of colloquial words and phrases. My literal translation stresses what in the German is colloquially slid over.

nature; any identification of his conceptions with traditional ones is always mistaken. The term "the Fall of Man," he says, can be traced back, not to man's disobeying God and eating the apple of knowledge, but to a thoroughly naturalistic origin: to the "fear" man feels when he confronts the necessity of acting in accordance with his knowledge of good and evil, because he lacks the "strength" for such action; which fear makes him try to unlearn his knowledge and claim innocence for himself. The Fall of Man is not the getting the knowledge of good and evil through disobedience of God, it is the forgetting it through fear of human weakness. Original sin is not a fall into knowledge, but a falling away from it, a defection from the ethical task imposed on us by our nature, out of fear because our nature lacks the strength for the task. Original sin, "the ancient wrong committed by man," is our claiming to be innocent, not our loss of innocence:

> The original sin, the ancient wrong committed by man, consists in the complaint, which man makes and never ceases making, that a wrong has been done to him, that the original sin was once committed upon him.[10]

Joseph K.'s wrongdoing consists in the complaint, which he never ceases making until just before his end, that a wrong has been done to him.

But of course *The Trial* is not only about the wrongdoing of Joseph K.; it is also about the wrong done to Joseph K.

The Trial is a metaphysical novel because it aims at showing what is most general—the court is a representation of what is most general. *Amerika* is full of metaphysical tendency, but it is not a metaphysical novel (except, inconsistently and implausibly, in the Nature Theater chapter); the more or less realistic narrative form will not allow it. Although the ship, Uncle Jacob's business, and the Hotel Occidental have a tendency to swell out into something ultimate, the most-general, this is checked by the novel's actuality of scene. In the actual world every organization no matter how big it is can only be a particular organization and never the world itself; the particulars of the actual world can represent typicality and they can give rise to metaphysical reflections, but they cannot represent metaphysicality. When Karl runs away from the hotel he is really able to run away from it; getting out of the taxi cab in another part of the city, he does not find the hotel staring him in the face. In *The Trial* Joseph K. can never escape the court. He encounters its representatives in his room, on the street, at work, in the cathedral—everywhere. At his first interrogation he finds the offices of the court in a tenement attic, but he also finds them clear across the city in the tenement attic in which the painter has his room. Titorelli, commenting on his surprise, says: "There are Law Court offices in almost every attic, why should this be an exception?" [11] Behind every door, around every corner—behind all the appearances of waking consciousness—K. finds "a summary court in perpetual session." In *The Trial*, what is most-general is summary judgment.

The metaphysical character of K.'s arrest is directly alluded to by his landlady. Frau Grubach sees that it is not an ordinary arrest, but something quite abstruse, something "learned." She says: "It gives me the feeling of something very learned, forgive me if what I say is stupid, it gives me the feeling of something learned which I don't understand, but which there is no need to understand." [12] A few lines earlier she had remarked that the arrest concerned his "happiness"—it is something abstruse, yet at the same time something that touches him directly, intimately, bodily. (When K. disclaims knowledge of the law by virtue of which he is arrested to the warder Willem, the latter says [in literal translation]: "You'll get to feel it yet." [13]) K.'s guilt is metaphysical, but his metaphysical guilt embraces bed and board and job and Fräulein Bürstner, whose white blouse dangles from the window latch with provoking privateness as he is questioned by the Inspector in her bedroom—embraces his entire concrete existence.

Nevertheless, Frau Grubach thinks that something so abstruse as K.'s arrest should not be taken too seriously—it is not as if he had been arrested for theft. Her view betrays the poverty of common sense. But K.'s view betrays the desperation of common sense. He thinks his arrest is "not even something learned, it is nothing at all. I was taken by surprise, that was all. If immediately on wakening . . . I had behaved sensibly, nothing further would have happened, all this would have been nipped in the bud. But one is so unprepared. In the Bank, for instance, I am always prepared, nothing of that kind could possibly happen to me there, I have my own attendant, the general telephone and the office telephone stand before me on my desk, people keep coming in to see me, clients and clerks, and above all, I am always intent on my work and therefore in possession of my presence of mind [*geistesgegenwärtig*], it would be an actual pleasure to me if a situation like that cropped up in the Bank." [14] K. believes his arrest is "nothing at all"; he blames it on a momentary failure in vigilance. When his mind is "present" and not absent, when his waking workaday consciousness is in command, unwelcome metaphysical intruders from the depths of his self are promptly sent about their business.

Nevertheless K. wonders if Frau Grubach will take his hand when he offers it to her in sign of their agreement about the insignificance of the morning's events:

> "Will she take my hand? The Inspector wouldn't do it," he thought, gazing at the woman with a different, a considering eye. She stood up because he had stood up, she was a little embarrassed, for she had not understood all that he had said. And because of her embarrassment she said something which she had not intended to say and which was, moreover, rather out of place. "Don't take it too seriously, Herr K.," she said with tears in her voice, forgetting, naturally, to shake his hand. "I had no idea that I was taking it seriously," said K., suddenly tired and seeing how little it mattered whether she agreed with him or not. [15]

And in fact she forgets, "naturally, to shake his hand," confirming his conviction that he is a criminal, which he has tried to outface by blustering to her about his self-control when he is concentrated on his work. The fatigue of trying to maintain a lie overwhelms him. The masterly scene concludes with K.'s suddenly crying out the truth, which he has denied all along and goes on denying afterward, at the top of his lungs. The landlady having said that she must speak to Fräulein Bürstner about her late hours and her gentlemen friends, for she tries to keep her house "respectable" (*rein:* clean, pure), K. shouts: "Respectable! [*Die Reinheit*] . . . if you want to keep your house respectable you'll have to begin by giving me notice."

The whole scene is a triumph of "psychoanalytic" narrative. A surface movement of conventionally abstract words aims at reaffirming the innocuous common-sense world, but the literal truth hidden within the conventional abstractions and expressed mutely in gesture strains in the opposite direction toward a sinister metaphysical ("learned") realm of meaning, till the tension explodes in K.'s outcry.

Throughout, the novel is concerned to indicate unobtrusively that K.'s trial is subjective—that the venue of the court which sits on his case is his own head. Kafka cannot simply say straight out that *The Trial* takes place in Joseph K.'s mind. That would change the story from a metaphor into a simile, detach us from our identification with K.'s viewpoint and weaken the novel's assertion of its reality. He can only suggest it within the metaphor. He does so by establishing the authority of the court in the private, intimate area of K.'s life, as something distinct from the conventional legal authorities. The scene of K.'s arrest is his own bed. He is examined by the Inspector in Fräulein Bürstner's bedroom. The arresting officials are employed by a judicial organization that conducts its interrogations on Sundays. This court inhabits remote attics and not marble halls. "Who could these men be? K. lived in a country with a legal constitution, there was universal peace, all the laws were in force, who dared seize him in his own dwelling?" [16] All this points inward. *The Trial* swims in a turgid atmosphere of mind.

K. searches for identification papers: *Legitimationspapiere,* papers which would attest his legitimacy and justify his existence; he finds his bicycle license but discards it as too trivial; finally he turns up his birth certificate which he presents to the warders. From first to last his argument remains the same: born of woman he is a man and therefore innocent, "for how in general can a man be guilty?" [17] But the warders, "who probably stand closer to [K.] than any other people in the world" [18]—so Kafka slyly has one of them say—push his papers aside. There can be no mistake, because the court officials never search out crime on their initiative, "but, as the law decrees, are drawn toward the guilty and must then send out us warders. That is the law." K. himself has summoned—"drawn"—the warders to him. The law is his own conscience. But " 'I don't know this law,' said K. 'All the worse for you,' replied the Warder." K. does not know the law because his conscience is alienated from him; he has tried to unlearn the knowledge of good and evil. With the obtuseness of common sense, K., divining the spiritual nature of this law, thinks he can impugn it by sneering at its subjectivity. "It probably exists nowhere but in your own heads," he says to the warders.[19] This is a piece of Kafka wit, for most certainly the law exists nowhere but in heads, K.'s included—and for that very reason it is powerful. Subsequently in Fräulein Bürstner's bedroom he looks at the Inspector, the two warders, and the three young clerks from his bank and "it seemed to him for the moment as if he were responsible for all of them [als trage er alle auf seinen Schultern]" [20]—they are all creatures of his inwardness.

On one occasion at least Kafka is too clever in insinuating the subjectivity of his protagonist's struggle. When K. arrives at the tenement building in the second chapter and looks for the Court of Inquiry, he sees four separate staircases plus a little passageway and is "annoyed that he had not been given more definite information about the room, these people showed a strange negligence or indifference in their treatment of him, he intended to tell them so very positively and clearly." He arbitrarily chooses the first stairs "and his mind played in retrospect with the saying of the warder Willem that an attraction existed between the law and guilt, from which it should really follow that the Court of Inquiry must abut on the particular flight of stairs which K. happened to choose." [21] And eventually indeed he finds the court in this way, at the top of the particular flight of stairs he happened to choose. But this is too much; it is precious. The machinery of the dream narrative creaks here, calling attention to itself as machinery. Among the "Passages Deleted by the Author" in the Appendix there are several which were perhaps struck out for just this reason.[22]

The court lies along a dream dimension that is at a tangent to K.'s workaday existence. It exercises its authority over him when his mind is not "on his work": at night, early in the morning in his bed and on Sunday. As K.'s preoccupation with the court—that is, its hold on him—increases, his ability to do his job at the Bank declines;[23] when his routine existence in the ordinary world loses its anaesthetic power to protect him, the jurisdiction of the court over K.'s life becomes complete and he is executed. The novel is thus divided between a subjective metaphysical sphere and an objective sphere of common sense; K. struggles, with less and less success, to shake off the hold of the one and resume his old place in the other. There is a certain clumsiness, a patched-together quality, in *The Trial* because of this dodging back and forth between two dimensions. This is not because episodes are patched together into an action which is not a true unified action—Aristotelian ideas of unity do not apply here; the novel is not, as has often been said, episodic—but because of the patching together of two dimensions. In *The Castle*, K. plunges into the dream-metaphysical in the very first sentence and never retreats from it. *The Castle* has the purity of being on purely metaphysical ground. In all of Kafka's work there is a struggle to achieve unity—that besetting problem of modern literature. He achieves it in *The Metamorphosis,* in any number of shorter pieces—"A Hunger Artist" is a notable instance—and on the largest scale in *The Castle*. In *The Trial* he is less successful. But more about this later.

At the very beginning of Joseph K.'s case it occurs to him to put an end to it at once by committing suicide: "K. was surprised, at least he was surprised, looking at it from the warder's point of view, that they had sent him to his room and left him alone there, where he had abundant opportunities to take his life." [24] But then he finds the idea "senseless." One year later to the day, after having ceaselessly protested his innocence, he realizes "the futility of resistance" and lets himself be led off by the executioners without a struggle, admonishing himself in part as follows: "Are people to say of me after I am gone that at the beginning of my case I wanted to finish it, and at the end of it I wanted to begin it again?" [25] In the last moment of his life, however, when K. realizes that self-judgment is expected of him, that he is supposed to seize the knife as it is handed back and forth between the executioners and stick it in himself, he cannot do it. He still cannot do at the end of his case what it flashed through his head to do at the beginning.

At the beginning of his trial K. is seized momentarily by the knowledge of his responsibility for his life, but he lacks the strength to execute the death sentence on himself that follows from that knowledge*—the whole long year of his trial only

* Why must K execute himself? In a world in which man lacks the strength to carry out the ethical task imposed on him by his nature, "he must destroy himself in trying to do so"—that is, death is the inevitable consequence of man's trying to live in the world in accordance with his nature. (This, says Kafka in the aphorism already quoted from, is "the meaning of the threat of death attached to the eating of the Tree of Knowledge; perhaps too it was the original meaning of natural death.") Man destroys himself in the inevitable failure of his effort to live up to himself. Either he is conscious of his responsibility for his failure or he is ignorant of it. To be ignorant of his responsibility is to think he is "done" to death. To accept his responsibility is to accept responsibility for the fact that he destroys himself. "To be responsible for one's own destruction" is the definition of suicide. Or, put another way, to judge oneself is to execute oneself in a world where man must necessarily commit the capital crime of failing to live in accordance with his essential nature. But such self-judgment is too much for our strength. The novel lies in the death grip of an ultimate ethical rigor.

brings him back to that same knowledge and that same impotence. Everything that K. learns as chapter after chapter unfolds he already knows in the first chapter. What happens in the course of the novel is that the knowledge which he tries to fend off, to keep from feeling ("You'll get to feel it yet" [26]), to keep in a state of disassociation, penetrates his being, in something like the way that the sentence inscribed in the prisoner's flesh by the moving needles of the judgment machine in *In the Penal Colony* penetrates the body, till "enlightenment comes to the most dull-witted." [27] The progress of the novel is from the abstract to the literal: from abstract comprehension by K.'s surface consciousness to literal feeling by K.'s whole being. There is no climax or dénouement in *The Trial*, but a steady deepening toward a conclusion already made known at the beginning. If the novel has a climax, it occurs, like that of *The Metamorphosis*, in the very first sentence; everything after that only discloses what is already contained in the first sentence. K.'s execution at the end, which might seem to be the climax of the novel, is only an ultimate perception of what he had already seen a year before when he was arrested in his bed.

The deadly meaning of his trial is indicated to K. in still another passage of the first chapter, which follows hard upon his thought of suicide. Summoned to see the Inspector, K. starts for the door in his shirt-sleeves. The warders shout at him to put a coat on. He lifts one from a chair but they shake their heads. " 'It must be a black coat,' they said. Thereupon K. flung the coat on the floor and said—he did not himself know in what sense he meant the words—'But this isn't the trial yet.' The warders smiled, but stuck to their: 'It must be a black coat.' " [28] Indeed this is the trial. The "trial" began and ended in his bed, in the novel's first sentence, for accusation is a sentence to death "in a court where as a rule all . . . cases are foregone conclusions." [29] This is why K., already a condemned man, must don a black suit, the same black suit he wears in the last chapter as he waits for the executioners to come for him.

If K. is already condemned, legal assistance is pointless.

Therefore, when he asks the Inspector's permission to telephone his lawyer, although it is given instantly, the official says, "I don't see what sense there would be in that, unless you have some private business of your own to consult him about."

> "What sense would there be in that?" cried K., more in amazement than in exasperation. "What kind of man are you, then? You ask me to be sensible and you carry on in the most senseless way imaginable yourself! It's enough to melt a stone! [*Ist es nicht zum Steinerweichen?*] People first fall upon me in my own house and then lounge about the room and put me through my paces for your benefit. What sense would there be in telephoning to a lawyer when I'm supposed to be under arrest? All right, I won't telephone." "But do telephone if you want to," replied the Inspector, waving an arm toward the entrance hall, where the telephone was, "please do telephone." "No, I don't want to now," said K.[30]

What is sensible in the metaphysical world is senseless in the world of common sense—K. finds the Inspector's remark so "senseless" that it is "enough to melt a stone." And in fact the stone that K. has been for many years is melted: he does not make the phone call. He does not make the phone call because he understands at the moment that lawyers—all mediators and mediating agencies that come between the self and its knowledge of its guilt so as to relieve it of the onus of its responsibility—are worse than useless.* But this knowledge that K. gains in the first chapter is dissociated knowledge; it rules him in the present instance (he does not call his lawyer), but he does not acknowledge it to himself and integrate it with all else that he knows. Therefore he allows his uncle in a subsequent chapter to carry him off to the lawyer Huld, whom he engages for his defense.† It needs a year for him to feel fully the knowledge of

---

*". . . [T]he authorities . . . wanted to eliminate defending counsel as much as possible; the whole onus of the matter must be laid on the accused himself."[31]

† Huld promises each client to "lift him on his shoulders" and "carry him bodily without once letting him down until the verdict is reached, and even beyond it."[32] He not only offers to carry his clients through their earthly trial, but to go on supporting them after judg-

the futility of intercessors: a year of exasperation with Huld's method of discouraging and encouraging his hopes in the same breath with a tortuous, inexhaustible flow of hair-splitting argument, in the course of which however Huld tells him plainly enough (as plainly as one has the right to expect from a lawyer) that "none of the lawyers for the defense was recognized by the court";[36] and of learning from every side (but especially from Titorelli) that once the court has brought a charge against somebody "it can never be dislodged from that conviction. If I were to paint all the judges in a row on one canvas and you were to plead your case before it, you would have more hope of success than before the actual court." [37] Finally in the incomplete eighth chapter (which is probably placed too early and should immediately precede the last chapter) K. resolves to dismiss Huld. Thus he returns to the decision that he made in the first chapter when he did not telephone his lawyer, only now he is acting on knowledge grasped with full awareness rather than gesturing like a sleepwalker in dumb incomprehension of the meaning of his own actions.

From beginning to end, K. is given the same piece of advice by the court officials. The advice is expressed in varying accents, according to the speaker, but always with a note of familiarity because the officials are condescending to speak to him unoffici-

---

ment has been passed—that is, to secure for them what his name promises, "clemency, grace." To K.'s complaint about his case getting on so slowly, Huld "retorted that it was not getting on slowly at all, although they would have been much further on by now had K. come to the lawyer in time. Unfortunately he had neglected to do so and that omission was likely to keep him at a disadvantage, and not merely a temporal disadvantage, either." [33] Huld is only a man like any other, and yet he presumes to control the mystery of grace.[34] He presumptuously claims to be able to do what only the great intercessors, "the really great lawyers," are said to be able to do—"our lawyer [says Block the tradesman to K.] and his colleagues rank only among the small lawyers, while the really great lawyers, whom I have merely heard of and never seen, stand as high above the small lawyers as these above the despised pettifogging lawyers." But about these great intercessors one can only dream—"I know of no single instance," says Block, "in which it could be definitely asserted that they had intervened." [35]

ally—the officials are not without condescension. When he is arrested in the first chapter and importunes the warders with his questions and his demands to see their warrant, one of them interrupts his greedy swallowing down of K.'s breakfast to say: "Oh, good Lord. . . . If you would only realize your position, and if you wouldn't insist on uselessly annoying us two, who probably mean better by you and stand closer to you than any other people in the world." [38] He is told this with coarse familiarity. Soon thereafter he is told the same thing by the Inspector, in the easy condescending tone of a higher official:

> "You are under arrest, certainly, more than that I do not know. . . . However if I can't answer your questions, I can at least give you a piece of advice; think less about us and what is going to happen to you, think more about yourself instead. And don't make such an outcry about your feeling innocent, it spoils the not unfavorable impression you make in other respects." [39]

Later on in the narrative, when the priest in the cathedral asks K. what he intends to do next and K. says he is going to get more help, the former advises him with solemn earnestness. " 'You cast about too much for outside help,' said the priest disapprovingly, 'especially from women. Don't you see that it isn't the right kind of help?' " But K. thinks that if he could only get some women he knows to join together and work for him, he would be bound to win his case.

> "Especially before this court, which consists almost entirely of petticoat-hunters. Show the Examining Magistrate a woman in the distance and he knocks down his desk and the defendant in his eagerness to get at her." The priest leaned over the balustrade, apparently feeling for the first time the oppressiveness of the canopy above his head. What awful weather there must be outside! There was no longer even a murky daylight, black night had set in. . . . "Are you angry with me?" asked K. of the priest. "It may be that you don't know the kind of court you are serving." He got no answer. "These are only my personal experiences," said K. There was still no answer from above. "I wasn't trying to insult you," said K. And at that the priest shrieked from the pulpit: "Can't you

see an inch in front of your nose?" It was an angry shriek, but at the same time sounded as if it came from one who sees another fall and because he is frightened out of his senses involuntarily cries out, without thinking.[40]

The advice is always the same: K. should try to realize his position instead of demanding to see official warrants; he should think less about the court and what is going to happen to him, and more about himself; he should look for help within himself rather than casting about for outside help. What changes is the concern with which the advice is given. The warders are callous; the Inspector is nonchalant; the priest is full of pastoral solicitude.

The final revelation to K. of the futility of his resistance occurs in the last chapter. On the way to his execution, he thinks about his life and admonishes himself not to leave the world an obtuse, stubborn man who has learned nothing from his trial.

> "Are people to say of me after I am gone that at the beginning of my case I wanted to finish it, and at the end of it I wanted to begin again? I don't want that to be said. I am grateful for the fact that these half-dumb, senseless creatures have been sent to accompany me on this journey, *and that it has been left to me to say to myself all that is needed.*" [41]

It has been left to him to say to himself all that is needed—this is what K. finally understands at the end of his year; it is up to him to judge himself. And yet he understood something like this at the very beginning; at the beginning he gave himself the same advice. When the warders urged him in the first chapter to give his clothes to them rather than into the uncertain keeping of the depot, "K. paid hardly any attention to this advice. Any right to dispose of his own things which he might possess he did not prize very highly; far more important to him was the necessity to understand his situation clearly. . . ." At the very start he realizes that he needs to understand his own situation, that he needs to examine himself and judge himself, rather than defend himself blindly against the examination and judgment of the court.

But he cannot: ". . . [B]ut with these people [the warders] beside him he could not even think." [42] K. sees at the end what he saw at the beginning, only he sees it with apocalyptic clarity, with his whole being.

K.'s final comprehension comes as a sudden realization which overtakes him while he is being marched along the streets in the grip of the two executioners and he sees or thinks he sees Fräulein Bürstner.

> And then before them Fräulein Bürstner appeared, mounting a small flight of steps leading into the square from a low-lying side-street. It was not quite certain that it was she, but the resemblance was close enough. Whether it were really Fräulein Bürstner or not, however, did not matter to K.; the important thing was that he suddenly realized the futility of resistance. There would be nothing heroic in it were he to resist, to make difficulties for his companions, to snatch at the last appearance of life by struggling. He set himself in motion, and the relief his warders felt was transmitted to some extent even to himself. They suffered him now to lead the way, and he followed the direction taken by the girl ahead of him, not that he wanted to overtake her or to keep her in sight as long as possible, *but only that he might not forget the lesson she had brought into his mind.*[43]

The lesson that Fräulein Bürstner teaches him is acceptance of responsibility for himself, her shadowy figure points in the direction of self-judgment. But *how* does she teach that, point to that?—she appears and disappears in the last scene like a spectre, without saying a word. Again we find that last things have already come first: the lesson has already been taught in the first chapter, if quite obscurely.

On the evening of his arrest K. waits up for Fräulein Bürstner, whom he had defended hotly to Frau Grubach, and has a whispered midnight conversation with her in her room. He apologizes for the liberty that was taken with her quarters during the day and asks her help with his case; "it is too trifling to need a lawyer, but I could do very well with an adviser." In their conversation she remarks that law courts interest her "particularly"; "the

129

court," she says, "has a curious power of attraction, hasn't it?"—using words that recall the warder's about how the officials are attracted toward the guilty: only now it is the court that does the attracting. But if she is to be his adviser she must know what his case is all about. " 'That's just the trouble,' said K. 'I don't know that myself.' 'Then you've simply been making fun of me,' said Fräulein Bürstner, extravagantly disappointed, 'it was surely unnecessary to choose this late hour for doing so.' And she walked away from the photographs, where they had been standing united [*vereinigt*] for a long time." [44]

Fräulein Bürstner is disappointed (and breaks their "union" by walking off) because, as the type of "the free and independent women," [45] the type of the sovereign person who freely accepts responsibility for herself, she expects K. to be the same and to know better than anybody else about his own case. She expects K. to feel "drawn," like herself, to the court of self-judgment, to voluntarily seek it out; but K. is one of the "guilty" who, refusing to judge themselves, draw down upon their heads an alien judgment that withers their souls with its ignominious shamefulness. ("Like a dog!" K. says as he dies; "it was as if the shame of it must outlive him." [46]) Unlike K., Fräulein Bürstner is "shameless" and therefore beyond the reach of the warders of a court of alienated conscience. About her there is an aura of freedom, specifically sexual freedom, which is what brings the landlady, Frau Grubach, down on her; but her sexual freedom is to be sharply distinguished from the sluttishness of the lawyer's nurse Leni, whose only advice, like that of her master, is to submit like a slave to the court. Fräulein Bürstner is master of herself because she takes responsibility for herself. When K., reenacting his arrest for her in her bedroom, rouses her next-door neighbor with his noise, he wants her to let him clear her reputation with Frau Grubach by telling the landlady a story about his having assaulted her. (K. in fact assaults Fräulein Bürstner at the end of their interview.) But she will have none of it.

"I thank you for your offer, but I'm not going to accept it. *I can bear the responsibility for anything that happens in my room, no matter who questions it. I'm surprised you don't see the insult to me that is implied in your suggestion,* together with your good intentions, of course, which I do appreciate." [47]

Throughout the scene she behaves with weary natural dignity in the face of K.'s importunities, even when he grabs her and kisses her all over the face and neck and throat "like a thirsty animal lapping greedily at a spring of long-sought fresh water." [48] What he thirsts for is her freedom. It is a genuine thirst; K. thirsts for this same freedom from the court when he reflects as follows in the cathedral during his colloquy with the priest:

> Yet the priest's good intentions seemed to K. beyond question . . . it was not impossible that K. could obtain decisive and acceptable counsel from him which might, for instance, point the way, not toward some influential manipulation of the case, but toward a circumvention of it, a breaking away from it altogether, *a mode of living completely outside the jurisdiction of the court.** [49]

* Fräulein Bürstner's "mode of living" lies "completely outside the jurisdiction of the court" because she is the master of her own conscience. Her freedom resembles the state that follows from what Titorelli calls a "definite acquittal." "In definite acquittal the documents relating to the case are said to be completely annulled, they simply vanish from sight, not only the charge but also the records of the case and even the acquittal are destroyed." [50] Self-judgment means acquittal because to judge yourself is to "acquit" yourself of the charge of refusing to take responsibility for your own life—the charge that it is the business of this court to bring against K. and all accused persons. Acquittal means taking your case out of the court's hands into your own. Therefore it is not the court's verdict but your own. Therefore the court can never acquit! Like the old law of the penal colony, it can only condemn. *You* can only acquit yourself—by ceasing to plead innocent of the knowledge of good and evil. Then you walk away from the court a free man. You walk into the court yourself and you walk out of the court yourself: "It receives you when you come and it dismisses you when you go." [51]

But Fräulein Bürstner's role in the novel remains an obscure one because she is so little developed. And perhaps she was not developed because she is too positive a figure for the essential feeling of the novel. There would seem to be a contradiction between her freedom through self-judgment, and the self-judgment which would require K. to execute himself. Why should she be exempt from the burden of

But lacking freedom in himself K. tries to take advantage of Fräulein Bürstner's by a greedy sluttish assault. Subsequently in Chapter Four (which should be the second chapter) Fräulein Bürstner refuses through a friend to have anything more to do with him; it would have no "point." Since outside help, especially the help of women, is what K. mistakenly persists in looking for, by turning him down she helps him in the best way she can: she directs him back to himself.[52] The lesson of self-judgment that the sight of her teaches K. at the end of the novel is a lesson already taught him at the beginning.

These passages and scenes illustrate how the entire novel is already contained in some sort in the first chapters. Everything is glimpsed right from the start; what comes after is a cumulation of, an adding to, the vision. The form of the narrative is that of a vision.

There is however a whole side of the novel which my discussion has ignored. I have been talking about the visionary form of the novel in terms of Joseph K.'s wrongdoing. But what about the wrong done to Joseph K.? For two things are indisputable in *The Trial*, where so much is disputable. One is K.'s refusal to admit the possibility that he is guilty. And the other is the court's refusal to admit the possibility that he is innocent. Before this court all accused are guilty, in advance and without exception, and they are executed like dogs—its injustice cries aloud.

So long as K. will not judge himself, he lets the world judge him—and the world's justice is the world's justice. In the court is imaged the justice of this world. It is a sinister comedy. The comic (and sinister) thing about the court is that, though it is the world judging K., it is the world judging K. through himself, through his alienated conscience. The court is K.'s own con-

---

human guilt that weighs on him? Why shouldn't self-judgment be a sentence of death in her case too? Her concrete presentment in the novel as a young woman confident of life and promising to be competent in it, doesn't answer these objections. Kafka's talent was not for solutions. Fräulein Bürstner is abortive in the way all solutions are in the Kafka world.

science, which because it is alienated from him appears to him as something external, set over against him. The fallen world with its great machinery of oppression is only man alienated from himself. This fundamental irony of the novel, this "joke" is thoroughly "psychoanalytic": what K. thinks is being done to him, he is doing to himself.

The court, then, is subjective reality. But the subjective reality mirrors the reality of the world. Kafka is a realist who grasps the objective world subjectively. Like all the great modern writers, he understood that the old opposition between object and subject —a self-sufficient, self-constituted object on the one side, a registering subject on the other—would not do any more and that an art based on it must henceforth be banal. His art shows the world and the mind in closest union—the world as K.'s mind and K.'s mind as the world.

K.'s arrest is a comedy (a "joke," [53] a "comedy," [54] a "farce" [55]— so he calls it at the beginning of the novel) because the court pretends to an authority which it only possesses as long as K. lets it; it is a sinister comedy because K. lets it. All the court's (i.e. the world's) pompous gravity is so much grotesque buffoonery, all its orders naked bullying, its executions plain murder the instant K. refuses to acknowledge the court's authority. But instead of repudiating with indignation the court's authority to judge him and then judging himself, K. keeps protesting to the court that he is innocent—thus acknowledging its authority over him. K. sees the court is a joke, a travesty of justice, but as long as he will not judge himself all his sneers are helpless to hurt the court and only hurt himself by hiding the gravity of his case from him. The court is a joke, but it is a deadly joke as long as K. does not really treat it as a joke and walk away from it a free man. Here we can see how *The Trial* extends and deepens the theme of *The Judgment*. Georg Bendemann sees what a "comedian" his father is ("You comedian!" [56]), a bellowing old man in dirty underwear who, even though he is on his last legs, goes on claiming an authority as absolute as God's, and yet Georg is unable to cast off his father's authority and must drown himself in

133

the river like a cat at the latter's command. The psychological situation of *The Judgment* has been deepened in *The Trial* into a philosophical one, but within the psychoanalytic framework of the dream-narrative form which Kafka discovered in writing the earlier story.

Injustice is the wrong done to K. The course of the novel is a succession of revelations of the comedy of the court's injustice. By not taking responsibility for his own life and judging himself, K. perpetuates the comedy. K. plays along with the comedy of the world, he plays his part in it to the end—"if this was a comedy he would insist on playing it to the end," he says stubbornly at the start of his trial. And at the end he is still playing his part. The last chapter discovers him waiting patiently, dressed in black, for the executioners to come; when the two top-hatted men appear (after going through a "You first, Alphonse," "After you, Pierre" routine of politeness at the front door) K. finds that the court has sent him " 'tenth-rate old actors. . . . They want to finish me off cheaply.' He turned abruptly toward the men and asked: 'What theater are you playing at?' 'Theater?' said one, the corners of his mouth twitching as he looked for advice to the other, who acted as if he were a dumb man struggling to overcome a stubborn disability." [57] It is a comedy played to the bitter end as long as K. will not seize the knife that Alphonse and Pierre politely hand back and forth across his body and "judge" himself. The two actors, in spite of all their exertions and the perfect cooperation of K., the third actor, are unable to lay him down under the knife in a position that isn't "contorted and un-natural-looking"—literally, "forced and unbelievable": *gezwungen und unglaubswürdig*.[58] K. dies sprawled out in his "unbelievable" posture. His death is not a true death but a piece of acting, an unreal scene in the forced, unbelievable comedy of the world.*

The law with which K. wrestles is a comedian that plays the

* *The Death of Ivan Ilyich*, in direct contrast, shows what true dying is: "The expression on the face of the corpse said that what was necessary had been accomplished, and accomplished rightly."

practical joke of its justice on K. as long as he lets it. K. sees that it is a joke right off, but he needs the whole novel to see to the bottom of the joke. The farcicalness of the court, its lack of true legality, its corruption and dirtiness are revealed to K. in the first chapter and then over and over again in the body of the work till the comedy ends with his execution. He is arrested in his bed by two intruders without a warrant. The clownish warders immediately steal his breakfast and start angling for his clothes. An Inspector questions him superciliously, using a nighttable for a desk. Called to his first interrogation, he finds the court domiciled in a dirty tenement attic off a little room in which a young woman is washing children's clothes in a tub. Instead of the solemnity of a hall of justice, K. finds the noisy unjudicial atmosphere of a political meeting in the courtroom.

When he reports to the Examining Magistrate, "a fat little wheezing man," the latter looks at his watch and his first words are an accusation: "You should have been here an hour and five minutes ago"—although K. had not been informed at what time to appear. (He had assumed the interrogation began at nine o'clock: the court is his own assumptions.) K. has been arrested only recently and he is still defiant: " 'Whether I am late or not, I am here now.' A burst of applause followed, once more from the right side of the hall. . . . 'Yes,' said the man, 'but I am no longer obliged to hear you now'—once more the muttering arose, this time unmistakable in its import, for, silencing the audience with a wave of the hand, the man went on: 'yet I shall make an exception for once on this occasion.' " This is another instance of the apparently complaisant but ultimately infernal inconsistency of the court in applying its own rules which K. had first experienced with the warders and the Inspector. The Magistrate is no longer obliged to hear him, but he will make an exception on this occasion. The legal basis of any defense that K. might

---

K.'s death is "unreal," "theatrical," because the truths of life and death have fled from the world. "Death is our salvation," Kafka says in an aphorism, "but not this one." [59]

offer is undermined by the doubt which is thus cast over a hearing that the Magistrate is no longer obliged to hold.

At last the interrogation is about to begin. Though it is a justice conducted in attics and in the atmosphere of a political meeting, and though it is tainted by the suspicion of administrative irregularity, it is all the justice K. is going to get. The Examining Magistrate takes up a notebook "dog-eared from much thumbing. 'Well, then,' said the Examining Magistrate, turning over the leaves and addressing K. with an air of authority, 'you are a house painter?' 'No,' said K., 'I'm the chief clerk of a large bank.' " This is a joke, a huge joke. It evokes "such a hearty outburst of laughter from the Right party that K. had to laugh too. People doubled up with their hands on their knees and shook as if in spasms of coughing." [60] Justice is the broadest kind of joke. As Mr. Bumble says, "The law is a ass, a idiot," but it is an imperturbable and deadly idiot. The Examining Magistrate does not even know who K. is; he thinks he is a house painter; the court has not even got hold of the right man. Yet it does not matter. There is no "right" man. The house painter that "should" have been standing before the Magistrate is guilty, but so is K. Every accused person is guilty at the bar of justice of a world which has unlearned the knowledge of good and evil.

K. submissively returns to the court the following Sunday, for "he assumed that he was tacitly expected to report himself again," [61] and discovers in the empty chamber that the tatterdemalion court does not even have a legal code—or rather its legal code is based on the science of what is, not on the ethics of what should be. What he takes for law tomes lying on the Examining Magistrate's table turn out to be dirty books with dirty illustrations. " 'These are the law books that are studied here,' said K. 'These are the men who are supposed to sit in judgment on me.' " [62] From the usher's wife he learns that the court officials exercise a sort of *droit du seigneur* upon her. It is a court of license, not of law and truth, the court of the world as it is, whose only law is the law of life. The genital heat and sweaty closeness of the teeming life of the world, which spins around forever according to the laws of natural necessity, make the atmosphere of the court offices unbearable for K. and he starts to feel sick.* Two clerks come to his assistance.

> At last he noticed that they were talking to him, but he could not make out what they were saying, he heard nothing but the din that filled the whole place, through which a high-pitched unchanging note like that of a siren seemed to ring. "Louder," he whispered with bowed head, *and he was ashamed,* for he knew that they were speaking loudly enough, though he could not make out what they said.[63]

Amid the oppressive heat and din of the world he hears for a moment a high-pitched unchanging note, the note of the "indestructible," but he cannot make it out and says "louder." He says "louder" to the siren-like sound of the ultimate, but this is an inadvertency committed by his other, true self and he immediately feels "ashamed" of having demanded that a clear ultimate note should penetrate the confusion of life in the world, trans-

---

* More exactly, seasick. "He felt as if he were seasick [*Er war wie seekrank*]. He felt he was on a ship rolling in heavy seas. It was as if the waters were dashing against the wooden walls, as if the roaring of breaking waves came from the end of the passage, as if the passage itself pitched and rolled and the waiting clients on either side rose and fell with it." This passage may contain an allusion to Nietzsche. If so, it is that rarest of things in Kafka, a literary reference. In *Beyond Good and Evil* (Section 23), Nietzsche says that we feel as if seasick at the thought that emotions which morality stigmatizes as bad may be necessary to healthy, flourishing existence, that conscience lames life:

> Suppose, however, a person should regard even the emotions of hatred, envy, greed and thirst for power as necessary to life, as something which must be present, fundamentally and essentially, in the total economy of life and which must therefore be made to thrive more if life is to thrive more—he will suffer from such a view of things as from seasickness [*wie an einer Seekrankheit*].

Joseph K. feels as if seasick in the Nietzschean atmosphere of a court whose only law is the law of life.

At the end of the passage Nietzsche says that thanks to such daring insights psychology is entitled to be recognized again as "the queen of the sciences"—that psychology which Kafka turned away from in revulsion in his thirties, exclaiming, *Zum letztenmal Psychologie!*

forming its feverish theatricality into truth. In the very same sentence, therefore, he switches his demand so as to make it apply to the words of the two court clerks. Because of fear and shame, K. instantly converts a demand which would have brought the walls of the court down, into a submissive plea. Like Gregor Samsa, who hears the same note of the ultimate in his sister's violin playing, K. finds the world unbearable, stifling, but he is ashamed of himself for it. Joseph K. is ashamed before the judgment of the world. His freedom lies in shamelessness, but he lacks the strength for that.

What distinguishes the judges in the comedy of the world's justice is vanity and anger; like the senior Bendemann* they are enraged comedians. The judge's portrait in lawyer Huld's office shows a man seated on "a high thronelike seat," but "the judge did not seem to be sitting in dignified composure . . . it was as if in a moment he must spring up with a violent and probably wrathful gesture to make some decisive observation or even to pronounce sentence." The painted figure is imposing, but the actual man—so Leni, the lawyer's nurse, tells K. before they roll in an embrace on the carpet of the office—is small, "almost a dwarf. Yet in spite of that he had himself drawn out to that length in the portrait for he's madly vain like everybody else here." His throne is fake, "actually he is sitting on a kitchen chair, with an old horse blanket doubled under him." [64]

Subsequently in Titorelli's attic K. finds the painter working on another such portrait of a judge in which the robed magistrate is "rising menacingly from his high seat." When K. cannot identify a large figure hovering above the high back of the judge's chair, the painter tries to help K. see deeper into the nature of the justice of the court by touching up the outline of the figure with a crayon. Still K. cannot identify it.

> "It is Justice," said the painter at last. "Now I can recognize it," said K. "There's the blindfold over the eyes, and here are the scales. But aren't there wings on the figure's heels, and isn't it

* And like the senior Kafka as described by his son in his inordinately long letter to him.

flying?" "Yes," said the painter, "my instructions were to paint it like that; actually it is Justice and the goddess of Victory in one." "Not a very good combination, surely," said K., smiling. "Justice must stand quite still, or else the scales will waver and a just verdict will become impossible."

K.'s criticism is strong enough, but when Titorelli touches up the figure further it ceases to resemble even Justice-as-Victory "but looked exactly like the goddess of the Hunt in full cry." The minatory judges do not even dispense a justice based on victorious might but quite simply harry their prey to death. Their duty is to hunt and destroy, as the whipper's duty is to whip and the painter's duty is to paint. All the judicial trappings shown in the portrait are "inventions" introduced by the painter as part of his commission. The judge himself " 'is by no means a high judge and he has never sat on such a seat in his life.' 'And yet he has himself painted in that solemn posture? Why, he sits there as if he were the actual President of the Court.' 'Yes, they're very vain, these gentlemen,' said the painter." [65]

The judges are vain—which is to say they preen themselves upon an authority they don't possess. They behave like judges of the highest court, although, Titorelli says to K., "the highest court . . . is quite inaccessible to you, to me, and to all of us." [66] In fact they are underlings. "You would lose any respect you have for the judges," Titorelli remarks about the one whose portrait he is painting, "if you could hear the curses that welcome him when he climbs over my bed in the early morning." * [67] The judges are comedians who condemn to death. Their justice cannot justify; at best it may be got to grant an ostensible acquittal which is cancellable the next instant, or to

* Titorelli, the artist, sees deep into the nature of the court which is the world. Art is vision. He has won a certain superiority over the world. But he is a court artist in an age in which the courts of power are without true authority. Because of his association with the gentlemen of the court, he says, "I'm losing a great deal of my *élan* as an artist." [68] He paints only lying portraits and (privately) monotonous, end-of-the-world heathscapes—lies or despair. The modern artist is either a liar or a hunger artist.

postpone the death sentence indefinitely thanks to incessant legal maneuvering. There is no acquittal by this court of murderous clowns; one can only take one's case out of its hands through self-judgment.

The double nature of the court, comic and sinister, infirm and powerful, subordinate and superior,* is the main point of the exegesis of the parable "Before the Law" which the priest and K. conduct together in the ninth chapter. The parable is a résumé of the novel, a little image which resumes the larger one.

The priest tells it to K. as a warning lest he deceive himself about the court, after K. has said that the priest is an exception among those who belong to the court and he can trust him—K., the priest says, must learn to trust himself; K. must learn to trust himself even against the priest. Thus warned by the priest against the deceiving nature of the court, K.'s first thought after hearing the parable is that the doorkeeper (the guardian of the Law, i.e. the court) deceived the man from the country. Again the priest warns K. against relying on the opinion of others: "Don't take over someone else's opinion without testing it"—for K. is only repeating what he thinks the priest said about the court in introducing the parable. The priest's interpretations of the parable are not delivered to K. *de haut en bas* (he had got down from the pulpit after telling K. that his case was going badly), but they put K. in a position to judge the meaning of the parable himself; and in fact the last word on the parable is K.'s, although "it was not his final judgment."

The very figure of the doorkeeper in the parable, with his furred robe, long nose and straggly Tartar beard, is comic and sinister. The priest's first interpretation of the doorkeeper's role shows him as a powerful, implacable servant of the Law, "a precisianist with a stern regard for duty" who is "conscious of the importance of his office, for he says: 'I am powerful,' " and who watches with impersonal superiority at his post before the Law as the man from the country sinks into decrepitude and death beside the entrance. He remains powerful to the end—in-

* The double nature of the court is anticipated in the description of the elder Bendemann and Samsa as both weak and strong.

deed "the difference in size between them has increased very much to the man's disadvantage"—because the right question is asked him too late, the right question which he must answer with the "message of salvation." What is the message of salvation? That the door was meant only for the man from the country all along, who was therefore free to enter just as soon as he realized this—the doorkeeper bars the way only as long as the man from the country believes he needs another's permission to enter. The "right question" thus destroys the power of the doorkeeper [the court], which is only a power to bar the way, not lead the way, into the Law.

The priest's second, counter interpretation of the role of the doorkeeper stresses his subordinate relation to the man from the country. In this interpretation the doorkeeper is a simple-minded, conceited, not entirely unfriendly petty bureaucrat. Far from deceiving anybody, in fact, he is the one deceived. He thinks he is the man's superior when in reality he is his servant, tied to his post where the man from the country is free to come and go, his post moreover being to guard a door that belongs solely to the man. The essence of the doorkeeper's delusion lies in his thinking that he has more "knowledge of the interior" of the Law than the man, when he has less. The priest develops this interpretation by a dazzling casuistry that seems to swing K. completely around from his first opinion:

> "That is well argued," said K., after repeating to himself in a low voice several passages from the priest's exposition. "It is well argued, and I am inclined to agree that the doorkeeper is deceived."

But now K. proves himself an apt pupil of the priest; he has learned to think for himself (at least he has learned to think for himself in parables):

> "But that has not made me abandon my former opinion, *since both conclusions are to some extent compatible*."

He has recognized the dual nature of the court: the court deceives, but is itself deceived. K. argues that if the doorkeeper is deceived, his deception in turn causes the man from the country to be deceived. "That makes the doorkeeper not, indeed, a deceiver, but a creature so simple-minded that he ought to be dismissed at once from his office."

And now the priest tests K.'s new-found power to judge for himself by attacking his interpretation with the ultimate argument of all authority which has nothing but the irrationality of its own power to fall back upon:

> "Many aver that the story confers no right on anyone to pass judgment on the doorkeeper. Whatever he may seem to us, he is yet a servant of the Law; that is, he belongs to the Law *and as such is beyond human judgment.*"

But K. remains unshaken in his opinion.

> "I don't agree with that point of view," said K., shaking his head, "for if one accepts it, one must accept as true everything the doorkeeper says. But you yourself have sufficiently proved how impossible it is to do that." "No," said the priest, "it is not necessary to accept everything as true, one must only accept it as necessary." "A melancholy conclusion," said K. "It makes lies the basis of the world order."

And the priest is silenced, even though "undoubtedly he did not agree with" K.[69] His pupil has grown up to the truth (to be sure, only the truth of parables). The world order is based on necessity, not on truth. The law of the court is the law of the necessity for the world to be the way it is. The image of the court here explicitly unfolds its power to embrace the entire given world. The court is sinister, powerful, superior to the individual who fails to realize the truth of himself as an individual, because it expresses everything that is systematic, impersonal, instrumental rather than ultimate, everything that moves according to laws of nature that absorb and suffocate an individual freedom which would otherwise defeat them as laws.* The court is the system of necessity by which the planets must spin unfailingly

---

* In *Howards End,* a very different kind of novel (to say the least), E. M. Forster treats a similar theme. Helen Schlegel says: "I know that personal relations are the real life, for ever and ever." The Wilcox life of "telegrams and anger" is the unreal life of the world.

in their orbits and K. must roll unfailingly on the carpet with Leni under the portrait of the judge because "she gave out a bitter exciting odor like pepper." [70] What bars the way to the law of the truth of things is the law of the necessity of things. The entire novel is a pun on the double meaning of the word law: law as necessity (life in the world—life without true being) and ethical-ontological law (life in truth).

Yet the court is also comic, infirm, inferior to the individual person who, instead of accepting the world (which is only his alienated self) as necessary and given, realizes himself in his individual truth and through himself realizes the world anew; who redeems the fallen world in the fullness of personal responsibility; who, if he asks the right question, saunters easily past the doorkeeper, now prostrated before him like an oriental slave, into the interior of the Law: out of necessity into freedom. But unfortunately as a human being "he is not endowed with the strength for this."

K., however, has had enough of parables and of "dealing with impalpabilities better suited to a theme for discussion among court officials than for him," [71] even though he has not arrived at a "final judgment." The truth of parables is not the truth of individual life, it only points that way. The knowledge that he has got hold of in his head by reasoning with the priest is still a long way off from the living knowledge that he needs to feel on his body.* He is beginning to acquire this knowledge in the uncompleted eighth chapter in which he calls on the lawyer to dismiss him. K. admits to Huld that he has obtained valuable information about the court from him.

> "But that is hardly adequate assistance for a man who feels this thing secretly encroaching upon him and literally touching him to the quick." [72]

* For this and other reasons it seems to me that the cathedral chapter finds K. at a midpoint in his year's trial. I am therefore inclined to think that it comes too late in the present order of the novel. The sublimity of the end-of-the-world darkness in which the scene in the interior of the cathedral is shrouded is deceptively climactic.

When he was arrested the warder Willem had told him, "You'll get to feel it yet." Now K. feels it. The result is that he fires the lawyer—or is in the middle of doing so as the chapter breaks off.

In this chapter K. witnesses the lawyer's humiliation of Block the tradesman, another accused man, who has been a client of Huld's for more than five years. It is an object lesson in the ignominiousness of looking to others for justification of one's life rather than to oneself. The businessman, with his broad experience of the ways of lawyers and the law, holds him spellbound with his shrewd observations in the first half of the chapter, and K.'s original feeling of contempt for the man changes into one of respect. But Block's knowledge is merely shrewdness; as Huld remarks while he is torturing him, "Block is merely cunning. He has acquired a lot of experience and knows how to keep on postponing the issue. But his ignorance is even greater than his cunning. What do you think he would say if he discovered that his case had actually not begun yet, if he were to be told that the bell marking the start of the proceedings hadn't even been rung?" [73] To go the way of Block, to plead and postpone and hire lawyers by the score, to twist and turn and cringe with religious servility before the "mediator" Huld, is the cunning of ignorance. Huld's domination of Block and Block's subjection to Huld, with the "litanies" [74] he is obliged to recite and the "scriptures" [75] (*Schriften:* papers, scriptures) he must con over, is a parody of all religion which tries to intercede between man and his responsibility for himself.*

In the scene with Block, the lawyer reveals, casually yet explicitly, that the court, although it exercises the ultimate power of life and death, lacks ultimate authority; its power has no sanction, no sanctification. Block having been thrown into a panic by the lawyer's saying that his case perhaps had not even started yet, Huld, disgusted, expatiates as follows:

---

* "Christ suffered for mankind, but mankind must suffer for Christ," Kafka says in an aphorism.[76]

"All that I said was to report a remark made by the judge. You know quite well that *in these matters opinions differ so much that the confusion is impenetrable.* This judge, for instance, assumes that the proceedings begin at one point, and I assume that they begin at another point. *A difference of opinion, nothing more.* At a certain stage of the proceedings there is an old tradition that a bell must be rung. According to the judge, that marks the beginning of the case, I can't tell you now all the arguments against him, you wouldn't understand them, let it be sufficient for you that there are many arguments against his view." * [77]

It is a court of "differing opinions," not a court of indestructible truth, a court behind whose mask of magisterial power lies "impenetrable confusion." The murderous comedy of the court's justice is real only because it is systematically carried out, not because it possesses truth. True justice would dispel the unreal comedy of the world-as-given like a nightmare from which one awakens. But where was the true "Judge whom he had never seen?" K., dying, asks as a window flies open in a house adjoining the quarry and a human figure leans out of it, stretching the arms of mankind toward him in commiseration. "Where was the High Court, to which he had never penetrated?" [78]

"The power to grant a final acquittal . . . is reserved for the Highest Court of all," Titorelli had said, "which is quite inaccessible to you, to me, and to all of us." [79] Only guided by the knowledge of indestructible truth would man's nature be strong enough for him to live in accordance with his knowledge of good and evil. But such knowledge is "permanently concealed from us." In the absence of the High Court there is only the court of

* At the first sign of Block's starting to think about himself and what is happening to him instead of crawling like a dog (so Block literally does) before the interpreter of the power of the world-as-given, he is instantly brought to heel by Huld's assistant Leni:

> In embarrassment Block sat plucking at the hair of the skin rug lying before the lawyer's bed; his terror of the judge's utterance was so great that it ousted for a while his subjection to the lawyer *and he was thinking only of himself,* turning the judge's words round and surveying them from all sides. "Block," said Leni in a tone of warning, catching him by the collar and jerking him upward a little. "Leave the rug alone and listen to the lawyer."

the world-as-it-is, the court of alienated conscience, for which "a single executioner could do all that is needed." [80]

"Though it was not usual for K. to learn from experience" [81]— so it is remarked in the first pages of the novel—nevertheless he has learned a great deal in the course of his trial. Whereas in the corridor of the court offices he instantly felt ashamed for crying "louder" to the sirenlike unchanging note of ultimate justice, now he clamors for it with his dying breath: "Where was the Judge whom he had never seen? Where was the High Court, to which he had never penetrated?" No longer is he ashamed of himself before the judgment of the world; now he is ashamed of the judgment of the world in him, which executes him like a dog. "'Like a dog!' he said; it was as if the shame of it must outlive him!" So ends the comedy of K.'s trial.

"The 'greatness' of literature," T. S. Eliot observed with profound critical tact, "cannot be determined solely by literary standards; though we must remember that whether it is literature or not can be determined only by literary standards." [82] Is *The Trial* literature? The question needs to be asked, seeing how it has been treated as theology, philosophy, psychology, and so on. The question may be asked more specifically: Does *The Trial,* and indeed most of Kafka's work, lack unity? Perhaps it is the most important question *literary* criticism can ask about Kafka.

Kafka is a notorious example of a storyteller whose stories have been swamped in a flood of extra-literary considerations. It is easy to understand how this happened. For one thing, no matter how obscure Kafka seemed, it was obvious that the content of his work had strongly marked psychological, philosophical, and religious features. And then for another a substantial part of his work was not even narrative at all, but thought-stories in which the distance separating imaginative literature from thinking was considerably narrowed. But I believe the most important reason was the obscurity that shrouded the form of his narratives. His form was not clearly apprehended. Without an understanding of his form his stories seemed without aesthetic integrity—the walls of unity protecting his work apparently having great gaps in them, like his own Chinese Wall, it was easy for critics on an unrestrained spiritual hunt to pour through them and overrun his art.

From the very beginning there were protests against treating a *Dichter* as a thinker. But because the form of Kafka's stories was obscure, the first thing criticism seemed obliged to say, when it looked at his major work (the three unfinished novels) as literature, was that it was hopelessly lacking in unity. Thus Eliseo Vivas wrote in 1948 that Kafka's "failure to bring any of his major works to completion . . . may legitimately be taken as the basis for the most devastating criticism that may be leveled against [his] version of reality." [83] More recently Ronald Gray made a similar if more discriminative judgment, which I quote at length because of its trenchancy:

> . . . [W]holes are what Kafka could never achieve except in the short story, the vignette or prose-poem, or the aphorism. None of his novels are complete, and while *The Trial* has an ending, it is one which comes abruptly, without preparation. (The fact that the execution follows immediately on the cathedral scene must not obscure the fact that, as the fragments show, further development between the two scenes was intended.) . . . *The Trial* is really a series of loosely connected or unconnected incidents: Fräulein Bürstner is never heard of again after the first chapter until she is dimly glimpsed in the last; the warders who were to accompany K. everywhere are soon forgotten; the uncle, the advocate, the commercial traveller Block, the painter Titorelli emerge and fade, the prison chaplain supersedes them, and not once does K. or the author reflect on any connection or contrast between them. In addition, if Herman Uyttersprot's investigation of the time sequence in this novel has done nothing else (I doubt whether it is as revealing as he thinks) it has shown how difficult it is on internal evidence even to arrange the chapters in order with any certainty. Should the cathedral scene come before chapter seven or later? Why does K. in fact submit to the authority of the court? How was it that until Charles Neider drew attention to the fact, nobody

noticed that chapter four should have been chapter two? *The Castle*, it is true, is a different matter. . . . [But about *The Trial*] one can only ask with Austin Warren how there can be a logic of composition when one's theme is the irruption of the irrational. The untragic ending is so because tragedy needs to be, for one thing, inevitable, and inevitability implies logic, cause and effect, progression. The decline of Joseph K., though it progresses, is haphazard, sporadic, and arbitrary, and in this last quality it resembles the court which brings it about. The theme of an utterly disconnected justice, incomprehensible to man, is bodied out in the way the novel is built. But if there is really no tragedy, if there is at most pathos or horror, there can be none of the liberation that goes with tragedy.[84]

I hope I have already answered many of the questions raised by Mr. Gray. I cannot answer the charge that *The Trial* is not a tragedy. Indeed it is not. None of the terms of the traditional poetics is able to describe its nature, even when they are stretched as far as possible. If anything, *The Trial* is comedy, or rather tragi-comedy. But to call it a tragi-comedy is to associate it with a form notorious for its equivocalness and nonconformity with orthodox canons. Shakespeare's tragi-comedies also end without a sense of liberation. Kafka's art is not an art of tragic liberation but of terror and dismay. As early as his twentieth year, in 1904, he was able to describe the breakdown quality of the stories he wished to write, even though he had to wait another nine years before he discovered the form in which to write them. In a letter to a friend of his youth he wrote:

I believe that as a rule one should read only those books that sting and prick [the conscience]. If the book we are reading doesn't wake us up with a punch in the head, then why read it? So it'll make us happy, as you write? My God, what would make us happy would be just to have no books at all, the kind of books that make us happy if we have to we can write ourselves. The books we need, however, are those which affect us like a painful misfortune, like the death of somebody dearer to us than ourselves, like our being driven out into the woods away from all people, like a suicide, a book should be the ax for the frozen sea within us.[85]

Kafka is here describing a kind of art in which the despised and uncomprehended spiritual, which has been banished to the dream realm of the unreal, irrupts into awareness as an irrational catastrophe which shatters the frightened and resisting soul of the protagonist. It is an art of awareness, of vision, and not of tragic action; an art of the kind that Henry James practises in *The Beast in the Jungle* and Tolstoy in *The Death of Ivan Ilyich,* except that with Kafka all explanatory distance between the protagonist and the narrator has been eliminated thanks to the dream form so that the narrator and the reader find themselves in the same fix with the protagonist. No superior intelligence, such as we find in James and Tolstoy, seems to guide the story.

The burden of the charge against *The Trial* is that it lacks a logic of cause and effect binding its parts into a whole. That is quite true. Its parts are bound together on a different principle. The unity of Kafka's dream narrative, as I have already remarked, is not a unity of action but of image. The narrative unfolds the image of a case at law, Joseph K.'s spiritual trial. There is a progression, but not a progression of acts having effects leading to further acts; it is a progression which consists in K.'s seeing deeper into—feeling—a situation in which he is already placed at the beginning. The situation does not change; K. just sees more.

The novel is a succession of flashed pictures, a kind of motion picture; but each flashed picture is a picture of the same situation. What changes is the focus, the lighting and the aspect of the situation presented. The principle of progression is one of cumulation.[86] The parts of *The Trial* are therefore not episodes and the novel is not episodic. An episode is an unconnected or loosely connected passage in a plot of action. The parts of *The Trial* are *closely* connected, but it is just the principle of Kafka's dream narrative that the connection—the meaning—should be veiled.* The apparent lack of unity, the apparent senselessness

* "You find my words dark. Darkness is in our souls, do you not think?"—*Ulysses*, p. 49.

is only what is apparent to K. and to the reader standing beside K. The meaning, the unity is there, but K. struggles against seeing it; his constant complaint, which is not really a complaint but a cause he defends, is that the court and all its works are senseless, a ridiculous joke. But as K. is gradually forced to think about himself, to peer into the murk of his own self, the incoherencies of his soul's trial become resolved—the parts of the novel become connected into a unity by an act of perception which consists in K.'s having deeper and deeper insight into the connections of his self. *The Trial* is *about* unity.

The act of perception which creates the unity of the novel under our very eyes is not elucidated logically by the author in the form of connected statements, but is an action of K.'s soul which expresses itself in the form of mute gestures and the taking literally of words and metaphors, as well as in reflections by K. Take the thought of suicide, which occurs to K. at the beginning of his case. It is an idea thrown up into his surface consciousness and seems to have no relation to any realities; therefore he dismisses it as senseless. But it is not senseless. Thanks to what he learns in the course of the year, the idea of suicide deepens into a comprehension, in the last chapter, of the self-judgment that is demanded of him, though he lacks the strength for it.

The cumulative character of the narrative accounts for its intensity, which is inexplicable if the work is judged as scattered and diffuse. It also accounts for the fact that the novel "works" in spite of being incomplete. Completeness, in a beginning-middle-and-end narrative of action, is an all-or-nothing matter: either the action of the narrative is essentially complete or it is not. For the narrative to function at all it must be more or less complete. If it is incomplete it fails as a narrative, however interesting it may be otherwise. But Kafka's dream narrative starts "working" right off by stating an image which implies the whole work; right off, through the initial statement of the image of the work, the narrative acquires a quality of completeness. Theoretically, there is no end to the material which might be included in a dream vision organized on the principle of image cumulation, and in fact we know that Kafka intended to develop further scenes for inclusion in the novel. *The Castle* goes on forever so to speak. *The Trial,* too, might have been prolonged indefinitely if he had not cut it off with the execution scene.

Yet there *is* a defect in the unity of *The Trial.* It seems to me to lie, as I have already said, not in any episodical character of the narrative, but in its division into a subjective metaphysical and an objective common-sensical sphere. A pronounced seam runs down the middle of the work. K. passes back and forth across this seam, stumbling more or less clumsily over it each time. And in addition to the two worlds lying awkwardly along-side each other, there is a third world of "shameless" freedom in which Fräulein Bürstner lives; pale and unrealized, it has no real place in the novel. The spiritual topography of *The Trial* gave Kafka some trouble.

Kafka's dream stories are a vision of how it is impossible for the self to live in the world; his work is all one "proof that it's impossible to live" [87]—*Beweis dessen, dass es unmöglich ist zu leben.* As this general idea, all his work is one. This is its philosophical unity. But aesthetically his works are separate unities. As art his narrative works are each a separate unity according to the particular image they unfold: paternal judgment, bug, execution machine, trial, castle. The German writer Martin Walser, in his firstrate monograph *Beschreibung einer Form,* finds Kafka's basic form to consist in an effort of assertion by the protagonist, followed by its inevitable nullification: impasse, not conflict. But this expresses the formula of Kafka's philosophical unity. The aesthetic unity of his stories rests on "images, only images." [88]

There is of course nothing new about such unity of image, although its adaptation to narrative was the innovation of the modern movement. The image (which was very close to being the percept pure and simple) was the heart of that imagination which the Romantic poets called creative, creative not only of works of art but of the world itself. Unity in modern literature is in general a unity of image. What unites the fragments of Eliot's *Wasteland* is an image; it too is organized on the principle of image cumulation. This is what made it possible for Pound to cut the poem by half so as to give it more concentration. You cannot usually cut away half of something organized on Aristotelian principles without killing it.

The original manuscript of *A Portrait of the Artist as a Young Man* ran to something like a thousand pages. Joyce cut it by two thirds in terms of the image of Daedalus the artificer; nothing remains in the novel that does not bear on Stephen's vocation as an artist of words. In this way a realistic, historically situated growing-up novel was translated into a poem-novel about the modern writer who is seen ultimately in the transhistorical perspective of the eternal archetype of the poet-maker. *Ulysses* is a shapeless naturalistic lump, a heaving Sargasso Sea of mere matter of fact; the reader is plunged into its gross, meaningless empiricism as the Kafka reader is plunged into dream senselessness. But then gradually by dint of repeated reading the chaos of the novel becomes irradiated from within by a shaping meaning hidden in its depths—thanks principally to the Ulyssean image,* which is established by cumulative reference and cross-reference, spirit is laboriously ex-pressed from all the novel's matter. Joyce put it this way in a letter to his brother: "Don't you think there is a certain resemblance between the mystery of the mass and what I am trying to do? I mean that I am trying . . . to give people some kind of intellectual pleasure or spiritual enjoyment by converting the bread of everyday life into something that has a permanent artistic life of its own . . . for their mental, moral and spiritual uplift." [90] In *Ulysses* the bread of the commonplace is converted into spirit by the mystery of the writer's image-making art.

---

* Eliot in his 1923 review of *Ulysses* hailed it for showing the way from the old action unity to the new image unity (or so I interpret him): "Instead of narrative method, we may now use the mythical method. It is, I seriously believe, a step toward making the modern world possible for art, toward . . . order and form. . . ." [89]

Yeats, who sought an image not a book, regretted writing no great long poem, but he hoped that his collected poems, arranged in the right order, united to form a single poem or image. And long before these there is that source work of the modern, *Hamlet*. Episodic and disjointed as an action, bewildering as a tragedy, it is united as an image into a vision of nonbeing.

Having said this, one may perhaps go on to say that there is something inherently less satisfactory in the modern unity of image. Image unity is very intense at the center but fuzzy at the edges. No modern work can compare in unity to most of the great traditional works of the imagination. Action narrative with a beginning, middle, and end *is* better narrative, because it expresses a completer life. Like the life of man which is its subject matter, literature needs to complete itself in action to be truly complete. Schiller wrote: "The idea of poetry . . . is nothing else than that of expressing humanity as completely as possible." [91] Spirit *and* action: they make unity of being. *The Trial* has aesthetic unity; but its aesthetic unity expresses the impossibility of unity of being.

7

A NEW

KABBALAH

Knowledge not purchased by the loss of power.
—WORDSWORTH

K. of *The Castle* differs in an essential respect from Joseph K. of
The Trial. Joseph K., in the characteristic fashion of the dream
narrative, is a passive figure overtaken in his bed by the "senseless" catastrophe of his arrest and made to stand trial in spite of
all his protests. The land-surveyor K., on the other hand, comes
to the castle village voluntarily. The "struggle" he takes up is one
that he himself "had had the hardihood to begin";[1] he fights "for
himself, and moreover, at least at the very beginning, of his own
free will, for he was the attacker," [2] and does not complain about
his hard lot. In "Another Version of the Opening Paragraphs"
published in the Appendix to the novel, we find K. saying quite
explicitly: "I have a difficult task ahead of me and have dedicated

my whole life to it. I do it gladly and ask for nobody's pity." * [3]

The Castle therefore introduces a fundamental modification into the dream story; the culmination of its development in Kafka's masterpiece is at the same time a transformation of it. Heretofore the Kafka protagonist has fought with all his might to avoid the kind of confrontation which K. dedicates his whole life to pursuing. Heretofore he has been the frozen sea passively opposing itself to the ax of truth unsheathed by his dream; but now K. is more the ax than the ice. When Gustav Janouch called *The Metamorphosis* "a terrible dream, a terrible conception," Kafka had said that "the dream reveals the reality, which conception [*Vorstellung*] lags behind." [6] Now at last in *The Castle* "conception" stops lagging behind. The land-surveyor K. is a reasoner, a "conceiver," above all, who advances to grapple rationally with the spiritual reality instead of recoiling from it. Joseph K. was a reasoner too, but his reasoning was mainly a panic effort to prove that his trial was senseless and unreal. Reason has seemed weak and contemptible in the dream narrative because the protagonist uses it to dispute and deny the dream truth even as that truth has him by the throat and is killing him. In K. the land-surveyor, however, reason no longer stands opposed to the dream truth but seeks it out with passionate dedication, convinced of its reality. Although the castle hill is "veiled in mist and darkness" when K. arrives in the village, he stands "for a long time gazing into the *apparent* emptiness above him" [7]—he is convinced the emptiness is only apparent and in spite of all the doubts he discovers and the defeats he encounters he never loses his conviction.

* Though after the Village Head introduces K. into the ambiguous, labyrinthine circumstances of his being summoned by the castle to serve as land-surveyor, he says: "I was enticed here." [4] Once K. begins to appreciate the magnitude of the organization arrayed against him and the extent of the control it exercises over everything that happens, despair tempts him with the thought that what he undertakes from his side is in reality determined from the castle's side. In a diary entry for January 1922, the month in which Kafka started to write *The Castle*, he speaks about his solitary introspective life, his life dedicated wholly to writing, as being partly forced on him and partly his own

As a dream narrative, *The Castle* is K.'s own dream and the castle terrain is the terrain of his own self and of the world as it confronts his self within himself. Unlike his predecessors, K. means to embrace his dream rather than fight against it, and so master its truth rather than being crushed by the truth. The tables have therefore been turned: the despised and disregarded spiritual, which heretofore in the dream story has emerged out of the shadows in some monstrous or terrible image-form to revenge itself on the world of mere fact for its neglect, is no longer the pursuer but the pursued. K. is still another dreaming protagonist of the Kafka dream tale, but he dreams as it were fully awake*—with conscious determination, in rational pursuit of his goal of elucidating the meaning of his dream of the castle, as compared with Joseph K.'s rationalizing flight from the meaning forced on him by his dream of the court. The Inspector had told Joseph K. to think less about the court and more about himself because all his thinking about the court was stubborn self-evasion. K., too, is a stubborn thinker about the great apparatus opposing him, but "thinking about the castle," unlike "thinking about the court," is not an evasion of truth but the determined pursuit of it. Amalia, the scornful, withdrawn daughter of a family scorned by everybody in the village after she had spurned the peremptory sexual command of a castle official, jeeringly says to K. when she overhears a phrase of his conversation with her sister: "Telling castle stories? . . . Do you really concern yourself with such stories? There are people here who live on them, they stick their heads together just like you two and entertain each other by the hour; I didn't think you were one of those people." Joseph K. is always being given pause by his dissuaders, as well he might be, but land-surveyor K. vigorously defends his interest in the castle: "Yes, I am. They are just the people I am

choice—but, he immediately asks, "what else was this [choice] if not compulsion too?" 5

* The animal narrator of *The Burrow* says: "I am privileged, as it were, not only to see the spectres of the night in all the helplessness and blind trust of sleep, but also at the same time to confront them in reality with the calm judgment of the fully awake." 8

one of; whereas people who don't concern themselves with such stories and leave it all to others don't impress me particularly." [9]

All the dream narratives have unfolded a basic image, but *The Castle* unfolds its image by a process of excogitation carried on by K., that dogged student of castle stories. That is, the Kafka dream narrative and the Kafka thought-story have at last come together. K. addresses himself to the castle image as the narrator of *The Great Wall of China* addresses himself to the image of China, as the dog "I" of *Investigations of a Dog* addresses himself to the image of the dog world. He traces this feature and that feature, in as many of their consequences as he can follow, in the course of conversations and reflections, till the image is unfolded: he *thinks* it out. Where *The Castle* differs from the thought-story, which is purely meditative, purely a mulling over and thinking out by the story's mind of the "problem" presented by the image of the story, is in being a narrative: K. does not just think out an image; his individual fate is directly involved in his thinking in that his life is staked on it; whereas the mind that thinks in the thought-story, though it is enclosed in the image it excogitates rather than contemplating it from outside, is thinking out some kind of general truth rather than its own life and death. Perhaps this distinction can be summed up in the statement that the thought-story may or may not have a central figure—"The Hunter Gracchus" and "Josephine the Singer" have one, *The Great Wall of China* does not—but it has no real protagonist; in place of the protagonist is a mind contemplating and considering.

To describe *The Castle*'s form as a union of the dream story and the thought-story immediately suggests why the novel is the culmination of Kafka's literary efforts and his most ambitious work, for it unites *all* of Kafka's art—the reflective side of it as well as the narrative side, which he has hitherto, with some exceptions,* kept more or less apart—in a final endeavor. Of

* In "A Country Doctor" the narrative and reflective elements clash rather than combine, with the latter predominating. In *In the Penal Colony* the explorer stands apart from the narrative, thinking about

course, this is to look at the novel from the side of form alone and says nothing about its substance. But if the form of the novel as it is described here is really an appropriate form, a form appropriate to its content, naming the form should at the same time name the content. And in fact the formal description, "union of dream story and thought-story," of narrative and reflection, tells us what K. is striving for: his effort is to unite being and thinking; concrete life and abstract thinking-about-life; spontaneous, self-evident existence and reflective self-awareness seeking justification; unconsciousness and consciousness; sensual heedlessness and stuporousness and spiritual care and clarity; submission to the automatism of the world as a member of the common life, and freedom from the automatism of the world in the solitariness of introspective seeking.

Professor Emrich describes the duality which constitutes the essence of the novel as follows:

The reaction against [the modern scientific, abstract] way of thinking, which dissolves everything concrete [into mathematical quantities], is as strongly evident in Kafka [as it is in Goethe]. Only from such a point of view is K.'s struggle against the castle authorities explicable. "All that the authorities . . . did was to defend remote, invisible things in the name of remote, invisible masters, while K. fought for something vitally close, for himself." [10] Indeed, this is why K. even derives a certain superiority vis-à-vis the authorities. The officials, for example, find the sight of him unbearable and have to keep to their rooms as long as he remains standing outside [in the corridor of the Herrenhof], the result of which is that K. dominates the battlefield as it were, even though . . . he experiences his very domination of the battlefield as lack of direct contact with the officials and therefore as his own weakness and defeat. It is expressly stated that his superiority lies in the mere "earthly weight" of himself which he opposes to the officials and which forces the official apparatus to work. "He was, after all, by now well able to play on this official apparatus, this

---

it and weighing its opposites in his mind, rather than being in it—at the end, in fact, he literally runs out of the story. In *The Trial* the reflective element is subordinated to the narrative.

delicate instrument always intent on striking some kind of equilibrium. The art of it lay essentially in doing nothing, leaving the apparatus to work by itself and forcing it to work only by one's standing there, irremovable in one's earthly weight." [11] . . . Thus the castle organization is dependent on the concrete earthly. What it is, in fact, is nothing else but life reflected upon and brought into consciousness, including the subconscious life of instincts and dreams. . . . Since the officials represent all the [biological, psychological, sociological, physical, etc., etc.] laws of life [Gesetzmässigkeiten] . . . they are present *everywhere,* even in the most private spheres of the individual, and exercise an unlimited power. However, it is just exactly the *laws* of life that they represent, not life itself. . . . The duality consists in K.'s needing the officials in order to win clarity over himself and his life, in order to "survey land"; and yet through these officials he is involved in endless reflections and contradictions which make a secure life on earth more than ever impossible for him. . . . K. and the officials are basically *a single man,* man himself, the entire man as he is torn by self-conflict. . . . Kafka wrote about himself once: "What else can happen but that the two worlds split apart, and they do split apart, or at least clash horribly. There are various reasons, I'm sure, for the furious tempo of the inner process, the most obvious one is introspection, which won't allow a single idea to sink to rest but must pursue it upwards, only in turn to be pursued itself as an idea by new introspection. . . . The direction this pursuit is taking me is out of mankind." The other world, however, the concrete "outer one, limps along at its usual speed." [12] Both worlds, the world of endless reflection and the world of sensual existence, coexist in every person; without them there would be no human life. But the two worlds clash in Kafka because, in the 20th century, they have grown so far apart.[13]

Kafka's two opposed story forms had expressed the split-up of the self into the two opposing realms of life and thinking-about-life, limping existence in the world and racing reflections about the world. But now in *The Castle,* both dream narrative and thought-story, K. aspires, in the words of E. M. Forster, "to live in fragments no longer."

The world that Kafka imagines in *The Castle* is remarkably simple, or rather simplified. There are the castle, the village, and the stranger K., in the snowy blankness. Apart from these three primary elements there is only blankness—the secondary aspect of things, all the complex, variegated details of actual life, are buried out of sight beneath the snow. Thus the landscape of *The Castle* is metaphysical, a landscape reduced to "first things." By stripping down its world to primary elements, the novel aims at revealing "a clearer meaning than [what] the muddle of every-day life" affords; it wishes to rise above the muddle of everyday life in the same way that K. recollects the church tower in his native town did:

> The church tower, firm in line, tapering straight upwards unfalteringly, broad-roofed and red-tiled, an earthly building—what else can we build?—but with a higher goal than the humble dwelling houses and a clearer meaning than the muddle of everyday life.[14]

This passage helps to make clear in what sense *The Castle* is a religious work. The story that the novel tells is an earthly one, for what else can we tell? Therefore one has no warrant to read it wholly or in part as setting forth the action of a more than earthly agency. God is not in *The Castle*, only man. Only in the sense that it endeavors to reveal a higher goal and a clearer meaning than what the everyday muddle discloses, is the novel religious. In a passage which immediately precedes the one just quoted, Kafka indicates that the novel has nothing at all to do with traditional religious conceptions; he shows us K. deliberately turning his back on the kind of nostalgia for the religious past which caused the explorer in the story *In the Penal Colony* to admire the old law with its terrible judgment machine for its spiritual appearance, even though he was unable to believe in its truth:

> K. had a fleeting recollection of his home town; it was hardly inferior to this so-called castle. *If it was merely a question of enjoying the view, it was a pity to have travelled so far and K. would have done better to revisit his old home where he had not been*

for such a long time. And in his mind he compared the church tower at home with the tower above him.[15]

If it was merely a question of enjoying the appearance of things —if it was merely a question of aesthetic feeling—K. would have done better to return home to the altars of his fathers. Space here means time, going home means returning to past pieties. But since it is a question of truth and not appearance, K. finds himself forced to sacrifice "wife and child" [16] and the tranquillity of a home-keeping existence (being) in order to travel the long introspective way (thinking) to the "ultimate earthly frontier" [17] over which the castle stands guard.

Not only is the imagined world of *The Castle* highly simplified, it is also intensely solitary—the simplification indeed is a result of the solitariness. When K. turns off the main road and crosses the bridge into the village, he leaves behind the ordinary world, warm with its densely packed humanity and wholly preoccupied with the business of living, and arrives at a solitary, freezing outpost of the human spirit, a lonely, ultimate frontier. "Alas," the chambermaid at the inn says to K. in "Another Version of the Opening Paragraphs," "nobody comes, it is as though the world had forgotten us." [18] The peculiarly intense quality of solitariness which pervades the novel is not explained by Kafka's literary skill *tout court*, but by his literary skill working through the dream-story form. For *The Castle* does not just depict a lonely, remote scene; it has the loneliness of complete inwardness, the loneliness of the dreamer alone with his dream. And yet the solitariness, in spite of its origin in dream inwardness, is not psychological but philosophical-religious. It is not a manifestation of K.'s psychological condition, as Gregor Samsa's metamorphosed state, for example, manifests his psychological condition of loneliness and exclusion; what it is is a detachment from "the muddle of everyday life," a disconnection from immediate things which makes it possible for permanent intelligibilities to stand forth from the ruck of existence. I have been anticipating certain words of Whitehead, which I should now like to quote:

The great rational religions are the outcome of the emergence of a religious consciousness which is universal, as distinguished from tribal, or even social. Because it is universal, it introduces the note of solitariness. Religion is what the individual does with his solitariness.

The reason of this connection between universality and solitariness is that universality is a disconnection from immediate surroundings. It is an endeavor to find something permanent and intelligible by which to interpret the confusion of immediate detail.[19]

Solitariness is a quality of all of Kafka's writing. But in *The Castle* it is detached from its origins in Kafka's personal condition of psychological strickenness and becomes the sphere of being (or rather nonbeing) of the modern poet engaged in his universal task. K.'s entry into the domain of the castle is an entry into pure universality. No such line as runs through *The Trial,* dividing the ordinary world from the universal one, mars the unity of *The Castle.* It is a work of unmarred unity.

Using a literary form modeled on a psychological phenomenon, dreams, Kafka writes a novel that is purely philosophical. The work may be described as a dream narrative with metaphysical-religious content, or, more briefly, a dream-metaphysical narrative. The term "dream-metaphysical narrative" reflects the fundamental aesthetic fact that *The Castle* is a union of the dream story and the thought-story.

"Landstreicher" or *"Landvermesser"*

K. arrives in Count Westwest's domain "late in the evening" * and goes to sleep beside the stove of the public room in the Bridge Inn. He is waked up by the son of an under-castellan and

* This is (1) autobiographical—Kafka is no longer the thirty-year-old official Joseph K. in the middle of life's journey, but the land-surveyor K. near its end; (2) historical—"Westwest," recalling the Hotel Occidental of *Amerika,* tells us that the novel is "about" the

asked to show his permit, for "this village belongs to the castle, and whoever lives here or passes the night here does so, in a manner of speaking, in the castle itself. Nobody may do that without the Count's permission." K., apparently still dazed by sleep and not knowing where he is, repeats what he has just been told in the form of questions, "as if he wished to assure himself that what he had heard was not a dream"—like Gregor Samsa in *The Metamorphosis*, K. wakes up into a dream of truth which commences with the assurance that it is no dream.

If he must have a permit, the now fully roused K. says, why, then, he'll just have to go and get one.

"And from whom, pray?" asked the young man.
"From the Count," said K., "that's the only thing to be done."
"A permit from the Count in the middle of the night!" cried the young man, stepping back a pace.
"Is that impossible?" inquired K. coolly. "Then why did you waken me?"
At this the young man flew into a passion. "The manners of a tramp! [*Landstreichermanieren*]" he cried. "I insist on respect for the Count's authority! I woke you up to inform you that you must quit the Count's territory at once." [20]

K.'s disrespect consists, not in his presuming to impose himself upon the Count in the middle of the night, but in his presuming to impose himself upon the Count at all; not in his insouciant tramp's manners, but in his daring to tramp into the Count's territory in the first place—the insignificant question of decorum masks an ultimate question so that the surface of the work presents a ludicrously pedantic appearance. The concealed ultimate question is: Can K. as a concrete individual impose himself upon, directly confront the impersonal automatism of the

West, and moreover about the West at a point where the West has reached its west, its evening; and (3) religious—the comically doubled name is also sinister and points, like the swarms of crows circling around the castle tower when K. views it on his first morning in the village, to death: the castle of the world stands under the sign of death.

world? * Can K. compel the all-determining system of necessity which rules the world to take account of him as a self-determined person? Can K. compel the Count, who is a lord of files and cases —that is, units in a system of control—officially to admit him into his territory as an uncontrolled individuality? K. wishes to live in the world, which is a world of necessity, and yet be free ("I want to be free always" [21])—in that consists his disrespect for the Count's authority. Because he wishes to be a wandering unfixed element *in* a world of fixities and iron determinations, the castellan's son calls him a tramp (*Landstreicher*).

"Enough of this comedy," K. retorts and announces himself as the land-surveyor (*Landvermesser*) whom the Count has sent for.[22] The comedy K. has had enough of is his own pretense of not knowing where he is or what he is up to—his own pretense of not knowing. What he is sick and tired of is Joseph K.'s role: acting the sleeping innocent who refuses to take responsibility for who he is. K. says straight out that he is a land-surveyor and that there is "no sense in acting the sleeper" [23] (*den Schlafenden zu spielen*). In the universal dream landscape of *The Castle* land means life, the spiritual terrain of human life. One who comes to survey land in such a universal world is a life-surveyor, a thinker who tries to grasp the whole of life in the survey of his consciousness. Land-surveyor K. is a knowledge-seeker, a philosopher, or rather a philosopher-poet since he does not address himself to an abstract universal knowledge but to the concrete universal of "castle stories." He is the artist-protagonist of modern literature whose lineage goes back to the philosopher-poet whom Coleridge found under the prince's disguise of Hamlet. One way to state the novel's theme is: Can the poet-as-knower (i.e. the modern poet) live in the world? Can Dostoyevsky's Underground Man, "the man of acute consciousness" who will not submit to the "whole legal system of nature," nevertheless live above ground? To be, and at the same time to survey and understand one's being reflectively—is that possible?

* The automatism of the world is what the Underground Man calls "the whole legal system of nature," the system elucidated by the modern scientific world view.

The young man Schwarzer circumspectly telephones the castle to verify K.'s claim that he is the Count's land-surveyor, reporting how he found K., "a man in his thirties, a really ragged fellow, sleeping calmly on a bag of straw with a tiny rucksack for pillow and a knotty stick within reach." This describes a tramp. And after the castle calls back in reply, Schwarzer hangs up angrily, crying: "Just what I said! Not a trace of a land-surveyor [Landvermesser]. A common, lying tramp [Landstreicher], and probably worse." Schwarzer, peasants, landlord, and landlady seem about to fall on K. together, and he scurries underneath his blanket,* when the phone rings again and he hears Schwarzer say: "A mistake, is it? . . . How am I to explain it all to the land-surveyor?" [24]

For Schwarzer (and for K. too) it is a case of K.'s being either a *Landstreicher* or a *Landvermesser* and he has little doubt which K. is when he telephones the castle. The castle's first thought is to agree with him—after it calls back the first time K. is about to be thrown out of the village as a tramp. But upon second thought the castle acquiesces in his claim and K. is allowed to stay. However, the initial hesitation of the castle casts a shadow over its recognition of K. The ambiguity is deepened by K.'s own attitude toward his being named land-surveyor: it is "unpropitious" for him on the one hand, he reflects, though on the other hand it is "propitious"; and he observes to himself that the castle "was accepting battle with a smile." [25] Recognition does not give K. "rest" [26] (*Ruhe*) and shelter in the bosom of the community, it starts a battle for existence (". . . my existence is at stake, [it] is threatened by a scandalous official bureaucracy . . ." [27]), a frantic "pursuit" [28] (*Jagd*) in which he careers wildly about the village for six days and never reaches a sabbath conclusion. In a deleted passage, an official protocol sums up K.'s early history in the village as follows: "The land-surveyor K.

---

* Having taken his courage in his hands, cast off all pretense and published himself for what he is to the world, at the first sign of opposition K. dives under the blankets to rejoin the "sleeper" Joseph K.!

first of all had to endeavor to establish himself in the village. This was not easy, for no one needed his work. . . . So he roamed about in a seemingly aimless way, doing nothing but disturb the peace of the place." * [29] His later history is no different: ". . . [H]e's always prowling around the Herrenhof, like the foxes around the henhouse, only in reality the secretaries are the foxes and he is the hen." [30] K. has tramped a long distance through life, after renouncing wife and child, to find a regular job as the castle's land-surveyor and he hopes for acceptance into the community of men, but instead he encounters the most exasperating uncertainty about his appointment and each night there is even a problem about where he is to sleep—the foxes have holes and the birds of the air have nests, but land-surveyor K. has nowhere to lay his head.†

What K. does not understand—what he *will* not understand—is that to be a *Landvermesser* is necessarily to be a *Landstreicher:* the two are one. To be a thinker about life is to be cast out of life, a tramp and vagabond. The very word *Vermesser,* which rubs against the words *vermessen* and *Vermessenheit* with all their suggestions of temerity, presumption, overstepping limits,[32] whispers the fate reserved for its bearer: that as a surveyor of life he must forever be a trespasser on it. K. says about himself early in the book: "I don't fit in with the peasants, nor, I imagine, with the castle." [33] He cannot join the peasantry in the village and immerse himself in concrete, unselfconscious, unilluminated being, because what he seeks is just

* K. is directly descended from Michael Kohlhaas, also an assaulter of castles who roams about and violates the public peace.

† *The Castle* belongs to the last period of Kafka's life, after he had been retired from the Workers Accident Insurance Institute on account of tuberculosis. He was free at last of the job he hated, but this freedom, like the ringing of the castle bell on K.'s first morning in the village, "was menacing, too," for "it threatened him with the fulfillment of his uncertain longing" [31] to be a writer and nothing but a writer. Kafka felt mortally "threatened" by his new freedom as a writer because leaving his job meant cutting his only remaining connection with life and surrendering completely to the inhuman solitude of his literary calling and its psychosomatic consequence, tuberculosis.

166

precisely being illuminated by consciousness and consciousness is the castle's business (" 'Nothing here is done without taking thought,' said the Village Head" [34]). On the other hand, he cannot join the "gentlemen" of the castle and give himself entirely to abstract knowledge without forfeiting his earthly weight, his concrete existence.* He cannot be a villager without forfeiting knowledge (the universal); he cannot be an official without forfeiting concreteness. He is and must remain a land-surveyor: somebody who strives to unite concreteness and universality, that is, the poet. For "concrete universal" defines art. K. is an artist whose "high, unfulfillable demands" [35] are only fulfillable in art, not in life. *The Castle* is the fruit of K.'s land-surveying, an imagined concrete universal about striving for an impossible real concrete universality. In this sense Kafka's religious goal is to aestheticize life, to make the concrete universal real. Underneath their unfinished exteriors his works are complete aesthetically; it is only as religious efforts *in life* that they are incomplete. But that was what Kafka cared about most of all—the religious goal of aestheticizing life—and could not stop content at the aesthetic goal of writing works of literature. Hence his testamentary requests to Max Brod to burn whatever of his writings he had.

K. seeks being and consciousness, the innocence of Paradise and the freedom of self which the Tree of Knowledge confers; he wants to have Adam's apple and eat it too. He wants to unite the village and the castle. Now it is true that the village and the castle are already united: as the teacher tells him, "There is no difference between the peasantry and the castle." [36] Peasants and officials are united in abjectness under the yoke of the laws of life. The peasants, "with their open mouths, coarse lips, and literally tortured faces—their heads looked as if they had been beaten flat on top, and their features as if the pain of the beating had twisted them to the present shape—" are beaten flat by the

* Kafka's "gentlemen" have a main source in the "gentlemen" of the *Notes from the Underground,* those modern abstract consciousnesses who "contrive to be some sort of impossible generalized man."

flailing tail of the Leviathan world. And the castle gentlemen are tired with the infinite fatigue of overworked officials dozing at their desks with never a moment's relief from the eternal burden of upholding the world-as-it-is. "He's asleep," Frieda says about Klamm after K. has viewed him through the peep hole of the Herrenhof barroom:

> "Asleep?" cried K. "But when I peeped in he was awake and sitting at the desk." "He always sits like that," said Frieda; "he was sleeping when you saw him. . . . That's how he sleeps, the gentlemen do sleep a great deal. . . ." [37]

The castle and the village are united in their subjection to a world of necessity, a world in which being is enslaved by ignorance to automatism, and knowledge is that automatism become conscious of itself and haughtily elevated above the life it controls. They are united in disjunction—the very image of man's self. But K. wishes to conjoin castle and village so that the two merge into one: to free being through knowledge and to vivify knowledge through being. He wishes to recover innocence through *increased* consciousness—as Kleist put it, he wants to "eat of the Tree of Knowledge a second time in order to fall back into the state of innocence." K.'s "high, unfulfillable demand" is for a second Fall of the fallen world forward out of history back into Paradise.

Much of the surface confusion of the novel is due to the fact that K. strives simultaneously after two contradictory goals—to settle in the village (life) and to penetrate into the castle (thinking-about-life)—without his recognizing the contradiction. He is the man in the joke who rushes out of the house in opposite directions. His failure to recognize the contradiction is ignorance of the world, of reality, which is why the landlady of the Bridge Inn, that expert on reality, calls him "the most ignorant person in the village." [38] But what is confusion, madness, impossibility in the perspective of the world and its reality, is courageous effort in the perspective of the spirit. K.'s worldly confusion (ignorance) is at the same time spiritual effort (awareness). What is senselessness on the surface of the novel, on the level of reality, as the manifest content of K.'s dream, is spiritual purpose in its depths, at the level of symbol, as the latent dream content. In the world, K. is foolish, childish, crazy (*meshuggah**); in the spiritual realm he is a dangerous fox—reality and spirit, in the modern world of mere matter of fact, stand at daggers drawn. The marvelous truth of the art of *The Castle,* of the dream-narrative form at the height of its development, lies in its faithfulness to the protagonist's confusion of life as well as to his spiritual effort. It is not a case of the life-confusion not mattering, spirituality being all. The confusion matters as much as, is as true as, the spiritual meaning: the Kafka nightmare is as true as its interpretation and is not something simply to be worked through. K. the ignorant stranger to life, the ineffectual blunderer about the world who, though "he's been living here among us in the village long enough," is still "capable of getting lost in the three streets there are in the village," is not the price Kafka willingly pays down for K. the poet, the spiritually conscious K. K.'s life-failure is not justified as spiritual distinction; it *is* failure. He does not, thumbing his nose at the world, turn life-failure into spiritual success. "The spirit only becomes free," Kafka aphorized, "when it ceases to be a stay" [39]—a support and consolation. Because spirit without world, knowledge without power, is not spirit or knowledge. And so K. is not a hero and *The Castle* is not an epic if an epic needs a hero; he is a confused man struggling with himself and with the world.

Early in the novel K. recognizes the world's dilemma: in the inconsistencies of Klamm's first letter to him, about his appointment to the Count's service, he perceives a "frankly offered choice" as to "whether he preferred to become a village worker with a distinctive but merely apparent connection with the castle, or an ostensible village worker whose entire job was in reality decided for him by the messages which Barnabas brought" from the castle—the choice is between really settling in

* Kafka Sr.'s Yiddish epithet for his son.

the village and having an apparent connection with the castle, or ostensibly settling in the village and really working for the castle. K. does "not hesitate in his choice" when faced with this clear alternative; with fine decisiveness he chooses—both courses! the village and the castle: "Only as a worker in the village, removed as far as possible from the sphere of the castle, could he hope to reach anything in the castle itself, these village folk who were now so suspicious of him would begin to talk to him once he was, if not exactly their friend, their fellow citizen, and if he were to become indistinguishable from Gerstäcker or Lasemann—and that must happen as soon as possible, everything depended on that—then all kinds of roads would surely be opened to him at one stroke, which would remain not only forever barred to him but quite invisible if it were solely a question of the favor of the gentlemen up above." [40] K.'s life-confusion, his inability to choose between the two realms so that he incoherently rushes off in opposite directions, is at the same time a coherent spiritual effort to unite the two realms. The perplexity and confusion of the reader is K.'s own perplexity and confusion at trying to live impossibly, to reconcile the irreconcilable. What mystifies in *The Castle* is the truth—the truth of a world in which reality and spirit stand opposed—and not an obscurantist art.

K. wants to be a village worker so as to reach the castle. He is aware however of the danger of "sinking to the workman's level": "the pressure of a discouraging environment, of a growing resignation to disappointment, the pressure of the imperceptible influences of every moment . . . but he would have to risk this danger in giving battle." [41] The danger of life in the world, of unreflective being, is spiritual obtuseness and apathy and K. resolves to guard himself against them—which means that he can never become a villager "indistinguishable from Gerstäcker or Lasemann," who are unaware of the dangers of unawareness; his reservations about the life of a village worker cancel his intention to become one. On the other hand he has no desire for an official's post. He is unimpressed when the Bridge Inn landlady describes to him how Momus is twice a village secretary, for Klamm and for another official.

> "Actually twice," said K., nodding to Momus . . . as one nods to a child whom one has just heard being praised. If there was a certain contempt in the gesture, then it was either unobserved or else actually expected. Precisely to K., it seemed, who was not considered worthy even to be seen in passing by Klamm, these people had described in detail the services of a man out of Klamm's sphere with the unconcealed intention of evoking K.'s recognition and admiration. And yet K. had no proper appreciation of it; he who strove with all his might for a single glance from Klamm, valued very little, for example, the post of a Momus who was permitted to live in Klamm's eye, for it was not Klamm's environment in itself that seemed to him worth striving for, but rather that he, K., he only and no one else, with his own and not another's wishes, should get to Klamm, and should get to him not to rest with him, but to go beyond him, farther yet, into the castle.

K. does not want a job in "Klamm's sphere," in the castle bureaucracy; he does not want to be fitted in as a working part of the control mechanism of the automatism of the world. What he wants is to confront Klamm with his own concrete being, with his own individual person, and after Klamm other, remoter forces, so as to compel the castle to acknowledge "his own . . . wishes"—that is, his freedom. When K. asserts the freedom of his self in this way, he becomes superior to the castle's system of necessity so that the "contempt" he evinces for Momus is "actually expected." The castle bureaucrats recoil in dismay from K. whenever he deliberately thrusts his particularity upon their abstractness, whenever he affirms his concrete being consciously. Like Michael Kohlhaas, land-surveyor K. is a threat to the established order of the world—the philosopher-poet threatens the established order with a concreteness which is yet free (i.e. self-aware). But it impossible to live always at such an inhuman pitch of spiritual effort. K. has to return home, he has to live in the world as well as scale the heights: "And he looked at his watch and said: 'But now I must be going home.'" The instant he reenters the system of the world, however, he loses his superiority to it: "Immediately the position changed in Momus' favor. 'Yes, of course,' the latter replied, 'the school work calls. But you must favor me with just a moment of your time. . . .' " [42]

So land-surveyor K., who does not "fit in with the peasants, nor . . . with the castle," wanders lonesomely between being and consciousness with "no fixed abode" * in either, a confirmed tramp and outsider just because he is a confirmed land-surveyor, though not an officially confirmed land-surveyor because "Official Land-Surveyor" is a contradiction in terms: abstract consciousness and concrete being contradict each other. Or as the Village Head informs K., he will *never* be appointed land-surveyor because "there wouldn't be the least use for one here" [44] —this is told to him in the course of the dazzling colloquy of Chapter Five in which the nature of the stronghold he is trying to breach is patiently unfolded for K., the ignorant stranger, for the first time in all its systematic impenetrability. K.'s retort to the village official's reiterated declaration that he can never be engaged as land-surveyor is to say that he is land-surveyor already, in proof of which he displays Klamm's letter to him. After duly considering the letter in consultation with his wife, the Village Head's reply to that is: "This letter is in no sense an official communication, but only a private letter. That can be clearly seen in the very mode of address: 'My dear Sir [*Sehr geehrter Herr!*].' Moreover, there isn't a single word in it showing that you've been taken on as land-surveyor; on the contrary, it's about state service in general, and even that isn't absolutely guaranteed, for you are only taken on 'as you know'—that is, the burden of proving that you are taken on is laid on you. . . .† To

---

* Like Odradek in "The Cares of a Family Man": " 'Well, what's your name?' you ask him. 'Odradek,' he says. 'And where do you live?' 'No fixed abode,' he says. . . ." [43]

† "My dear Sir. As you know, you have been engaged for the Count's service. . . ." [45] The Village Head is only reminding K. of something he has already understood. When K. first received Klamm's letter he reflected: "Nor did the letter pass over the fact that if it should come to a struggle, K. had had the hardihood to make the first

anyone who knows how to read official communications, and consequently knows still better how to read unofficial letters, all this is only too clear. That you, a stranger, don't know it doesn't surprise me." [47] If K. is a land-surveyor he is so only in a private, not an official sense. That is, he is a land-surveyor not because the world-automatism represented by the castle has so decreed, not out of impersonal necessity operating according to inflexible laws, but because he himself has chosen to be it; K. the individual person, and he only, is responsible for his being what he is. Never can the world officially appoint K. to a place in its system, K. privately appoints himself to be himself, because it is of the essence of land-surveying—of the poet's assertion of a concreteness which is yet free (a concreteness united with knowledge of the general laws of life)—that he should appoint himself, rather than be appointed by the lord of the files.

Proof that Klamm's letter is a private one is the mode of address: "*Sehr geehrter Herr!*" Privately we are all *Herren,* the equals of the castle "lords" or "gentlemen," Klamm and his companions; in our nature lives the possibility that as *Herren,* as lords and masters of ourselves, we should freely choose ourselves and through ourselves the world, transforming its necessity into freedom. This is the great Romantic intuition of the infinite—that is, divine—possibilities of the human self, Blake's intuition of the "human form divine." The trouble with the private sphere, however, is that it is only private, only a sphere of possibility, and meanwhile hard necessity continues to rule in the public realm of the real.

Nevertheless, as long as K. struggles to affirm his private person with all its infinite possibilities he can never be driven out of the castle realm, even though it is equally impossible for him to overthrow the Count's power and institute the reign of freedom

---

advances; it was very subtly indicated and only to be sensed by an uneasy conscience—an uneasy conscience, not a bad one. It lay in the three words 'as you know,' referring to his engagement in the Count's service. K. had reported his arrival, and only after that, as the letter pointed out, had he known that he was engaged." [46]

on the basis of private possibility realized publicly and made "official." Thus in Chapter Eight K. finds out from Pepi, the barmaid who replaces Frieda at the Herrenhof, that Klamm's sleigh is waiting in the yard and the official is about to leave for the castle. Like a shot he flies to the courtyard, to catch Klamm as he is leaving and force his concrete presence on the "mighty one's" attention. But then Klamm does not appear. After a while the coachman, huddled on the driver's seat of the sleigh, says, "It might be a long time yet."

> "What might be a long time yet?" asked K., not ungrateful at being disturbed, for the perpetual silence and tension had already become a burden. "Before you go away," said the coachman.[48]

He waits and waits, the coachman unhitches the horses and puts the sleigh away, the electric lights go out—"for whom should they remain on?"—and K. is left alone in the freezing desolation of the snow-covered yard. The field is his, he is the victor, but what a victory!

> . . . [I]t seemed to K. as if at last every connection he had with anybody had been broken and as if now in reality he were freer than he had ever been, and at liberty to wait here in this place, usually forbidden to him, as long as he desired, and had won a freedom such as hardly anybody else had ever succeeded in winning, *as if nobody could dare to touch him or drive him away*, or even speak to him; but—this conviction was at least equally strong —as if at the same time there was nothing more senseless, nothing more hopeless, than this freedom, this waiting, this inviolability.[49]

Finally K. "tore himself away and went back into the house"—he has to tear himself away from a freedom which is inviolable and yet menaces him with an Arctic death—and Klamm is able to depart. K. cannot be expelled from the courtyard, which is "usually forbidden to him," because the abstract castle sphere recoils from his concreteness with alarmed sensitivity. (". . . [I]t's amazing how sensitive the gentleman [Klamm] is," Momus remarks.[50]) But never on the other hand can K. force Klamm to meet him face to face. It is a Mexican standoff: nobody can drive K. out of the castle domain, but on the other hand nobody is ever going to admit him into the castle or officially confirm his appointment as land-surveyor.

The Village Head had already told K. as much. At the end of their talk, when his head was spinning from the complexities and complications which the old man educed from the "question" of his being summoned as land-surveyor, K. had said sardonically: "So the only remaining conclusion . . . is that everything is very uncertain and insoluble, including my being thrown out."

> "Who would take the risk of throwing you out, Land-Surveyor?" asked the Village Head. "The very uncertainty about your summons guarantees you the most courteous treatment, only you're too sensitive, by all appearances. Nobody keeps you here, but that surely doesn't amount to throwing you out." [51]

Nobody (except himself) has invited K. in or wishes to detain him, but that does not mean that anybody would dare to throw him out. K. conquers the world, which is a world enslaved to abstract necessity, by forcing it to give way before his freely (consciously) asserted being, but by giving way before him the world forever eludes K. and with the world his being in it. On the other hand, when K. drops down exhausted from these exertions, to rest and sleep, when he falls back upon the world and recovers his being in it, it is precisely through the repose (unconsciousness) which he so desperately needs that he forfeits his freedom and becomes subject to the castle's necessitarian system.*

This is the story that *The Castle* tells, over and over. Or to put it more exactly: this is a discursive paraphrase of the meaning of the living metaphor of the novel; and though the discursive paraphrase is arrived at only by a laborious effort of interpretation, the metaphor itself shines out as vividly, in all its essential

---

* The repose of life in the world is figured for K. above all by Frieda, whose instinctuality (i.e. submission to the laws of nature) is certain and secure because untroubled by self-reflection.

completeness, in the first pages as in the last. Right off in the very first chapter K. and the castle lock together in the standoff which constitutes the unchanging situation of the novel. On his first morning, in a bold sally, he makes straight for the castle by the main street of the village and tries to assault it head on. But the street "did not lead up to the castle hill, it only made toward it and then, as if deliberately, turned aside, and though it did not lead away from the castle, it led no nearer to it either" [52]—the road does not take him to the castle, but on the other hand it does not take him away from it; rather it leaves him in the neither-nor state which results from the standoff between spirit and world.

K. follows the road, which "came to no end," like an "obsession" through the snow and cold and utter "absence of human beings" till, tired out, he must finally turn into a side lane and seek rest and warmth inside a human habitation. However, the people of the cottage he knocks at are as mistrustful of him as Schwarzer was at the Bridge Inn and admit him reluctantly. ("Are we to let in everybody who wanders about in the street?") Though K. tries "to justify himself before" them as the Count's land-surveyor, his audacious disrespect in accosting the girl from the castle confirms their suspicion that *Landvermesser* is the same as *Landstreicher* and he finds himself pushed out the door and "alone in the falling snow" again. " 'A fine setting for a fit of despair,' it occurred to him, 'if I were only standing here by accident instead of design.' " [53] So there he is again on his lonely, endless land-surveyor's road, and even though he was pushed out of the house he is there, he reflects, by choice and not by accident.

K. runs on and on in pursuit of his goal only to find that he has been running in place all the time,* and the story ends where it began, with this difference that K. becomes not only tired but tired to death. In striving to unite being and consciousness—his "high, unfulfillable demand" [55]—he attempts the im-

* Kafka called his whole life "a marching in place" (*ein stehendes Marschieren*).[54]

possible and his attempt is just as impossible at the end of the story as it is at the beginning. Nothing happens in the novel in the sense of an action narrative, because everything that happens only enacts the same standoff found at the beginning of the work. But this is not to say that nothing at all happens—what happens is that K. sees more and more how unattainable his goal is, without ever giving it up. Although the novel lacks a concluding chapter, we have some idea of how Kafka meant to end it, or at least we know what he once said to Max Brod about how he meant to end it. As Brod recollects it,

> The presumed land-surveyor finds partial satisfaction at least. He doesn't relax in his struggle, but dies worn out by it. Round his deathbed the community assembles and from the castle comes this decision: that K. has no claim to live in the village by right—yet taking certain auxiliary circumstances into account, it is permitted him to live and work there.[56]

The ending is sardonic because the castle's decision about K.'s case arrives only when his file is being closed out and it can no longer do him any good. But this is a mild irony compared with the irony of the fact that the decision gives him no more than what he has had (what he himself has taken) all along—as K. lies dying, he is granted permission to live and work in the village, which is exactly what the second phone call from the castle conceded him at the beginning of the novel, when Schwarzer was about to throw him out of the Bridge Inn and back over the bridge; what Klamm's letter in the second chapter allowed him; what the Village Head assured him when he said, "Nobody keeps you here, but that surely doesn't amount to throwing you out." And K.'s reply to the Village Head was: "I don't want any act of favor from the castle, but my rights." [57] K. gets no more satisfaction at the end than he got at the beginning. What he has wanted all along—the only thing he has wanted all along—is to live and work as land-surveyor by *right*, as an officially recognized land-surveyor. And that is what the castle refuses him, first and last. For "Official Land-Surveyor," as we have seen, is a contradiction in terms. K. struggles impossibly, as a redeemer of the modern soul, at his high endeavor of closing the wound driven in between life and spirit, and dies in the attempt.

Like *The Trial, The Castle* is a vision that progresses by image cumulation: the protagonist sees deeper and deeper into his situation which doesn't change but is impressed upon him over and over in a succession of episodes. However, the progression in the earlier novel is much more psychological and *The Trial* is in general much more literally a dream. Joseph K.'s seeing deeper is a movement from dissociation to integration: from the disjunction of mental surface and depths, of understanding and acts, to their union; from what is dimly glimpsed as other to what is starkly apprehended as self. The parable the priest tells him about the man who seeks admittance into the Law, which offers K. the instruction of an example rather than constituting a psychological experience, is exceptional; it illustrates the narrative rather than being part of it. Whereas *The Castle* transforms the images of the dream-narrative form from symbols acting psychologically on K. to moral-existential symbols with a distinct allegorical cast; progression in the later work is by moral example rather than through psychological experience. The individual episodes are parables that K. (and the reader) must think out; they illustrate paradigmatically the basic contradiction, or an aspect of it, that he struggles against and instruct him in the foolishness of fighting reality. Thus the fact that the village street does not lead K. to the castle (though it does not lead him away from it either—that is the other side of the coin) teaches him a lesson about the infinite distance between the village and the castle which is dinned into him subsequently by the castle telephone, the Bridge Inn landlady, the Village Head, Frieda, the schoolteacher, the example of the Barnabas family, his own experiences—by virtually everyone and everything except the gnomelike Bürgel of Chapter Eighteen, who is just precisely "liaison secretary" (*Verbindungssekretär*), or the one responsible for bridging the distance and establishing a "connection" or "union" (*Verbindung* has both meanings) between castle and village.* [58]

Bürgel reveals to K. the special circumstances in which the impersonal castle bureaucracy must surrender to an applicant's personal wishes; he shows him the way to obtain official recognition as land-surveyor, to be *Landvermesser* without thereby being condemned to be a *Landstreicher*. But K. is too exhausted to grasp the opportunity—"there are sometimes, after all, opportunities that are almost not in accord with the general situation," Bürgel says, "opportunities in which by means of a word, a glance, a sign of trust, more can be achieved than by means of lifelong exhausting efforts. Indeed, that is how it is. But then again, these opportunities are in accord with the general situation in so far as they are never made use of." [60] *The Castle* is a succession of parables (images, symbols, metaphors—the German word for parable, *Gleichnis,* means all these things) adding up to one big parable about the impossibility of uniting the village of life with the castle of thinking-about-life; it is a lesson to K. in the reality of the world.

But at the very same time, and with equal force, K. is a lesson to the world in morality: the novel is a parable about the unavailing struggle of man, which he nevertheless must not and cannot give up, to spiritualize the world-reality and thereby liberate it.

* Bürgel's job used to be more important than it now is. A fragment annexed to the text tells us that the "glory" of Friedrich, the castle official to whom he is specifically responsible, "has greatly declined in recent years. . . .   What is certain, at any rate, is that Friedrich's agenda is today one of the most unimportant far and wide, and what that means to Bürgel, who is not even Friedrich's first secretary, but one rather far down the list, anyone, of course, can see for himself. Anyone, that is, but K." [59] The office concerned with the reconciliation of being and consciousness has very little business "today."

Frieda

"Frieda" means peace. She draws K. to her with the promise of the peace of being, of the comfort and contentment and repose (*Ruhe*) of unself-conscious life. When she comes to live with him in his attic room at the Bridge Inn after their night of love-making on the floor of the Herrenhof barroom, he finds that it is not "really unpleasant to drink at the table the good coffee that Frieda had brought, to warm himself at the stove which Frieda had lit, and to have the assistants racing ten times up and down the stairs in their awkwardness and zeal to fetch him soap and water, comb and mirror, and eventually even a small glass of rum because he had hinted in a low voice his desire for one." [61] Frieda is K.'s one bit of luck. Pursuing a lofty, unattainable goal which leads him farther and farther out of life into a desolation of spiritual effort, he unexpectedly acquires through her a share in life. "If Frieda should leave him"—so he thinks when Klamm, whose mistress she has been, calls out for her from the next room as they are rolling in self-forgetful bliss on the barroom floor—"he would lose all he had." Frieda is all he has in the way of worldly goods, all he will ever have of the world's good. At the same time he is relieved to be roused by Klamm's call from a "state of unconsciousness" in which he feels that he is "losing his way" and being diverted from his goal. "Instead of pursuing his way with the caution befitting the greatness of his enemy and of his ambition, he had spent the whole night wallowing in puddles of beer, the smell of which was now stupefying." [62]

It is impossible for K. to "rest" with Frieda without feeling that he is "losing his way"; it is impossible for him to "pursue his way" without losing Frieda. As far as his high ambition is concerned, Frieda is a burden to him. K. can hardly breathe on the barroom floor, so "suffocating" is the atmosphere of love-making, so "stupefying" the smell of beer; leaving the Herrenhof with her and the assistants and going out into the snowy emptiness,

he is able to "breathe a little more freely" in the rarefied, ultimate air. "So happy was he to be in the open air [*im Freien:*
where he is "free" and not bound by the laws of life, specifically
the biological sex drive] that it made the laboriousness of the
way seem supportable this time; if K. had been alone he would
have got on still better." [63] When he had labored through the
snow first with Barnabas and then with Barnabas' sister Olga, he
had needed to lean on them for support to make any progress
along his "way." As K. is a stranger in the world, so the Barnabas
family, who have been ostracized by the villagers, are pariahs;
there is a natural "alliance aimed at the castle" [64] between K. and
the Barnabases which makes it possible for them to help him
toward his goal. Whereas Frieda only hinders him: "without her
he would have got on still better."

But "without Frieda" he is nothing, a no-body, "a nonentity,
staggering along after silkily shining will-o'-the-wisps [*Irrlich-
tern:* lights that lead astray] of the sort that Barnabas was, or
that girl from the castle." [65] Without Frieda K. does not exist in
the world. She makes for the homeless stranger the only home
he ever has. With her pathetic little store of possessions consist-
ing of an embroidered cloth and a coffee pot, and with her
dauntless spirit, Frieda is able to claim a few square feet of the
world for them in the face of overwhelming difficulties, inspiring
him with a respect and a love for her which he never loses. Coming back to their attic room at the Bridge Inn after his first absence from her, he finds that "the room was improved almost
beyond recognition, so diligently had Frieda worked. It was well
aired, the stove amply stoked, the floor scrubbed, the bed made,
the maids' filthy pile of things and even their photographs
cleared away; the table, which had hit one in the eye before
whichever way one turned with its dust-encrusted top, was covered with a white embroidered cloth. Now one could even have
guests; the fact that K.'s small change of underwear, which
Frieda had apparently washed early in the morning, was hanging up in front of the fire to dry, hardly spoiled the
impression." [66] And she greets K. with a kiss like a regular wife.

Of course the drying underwear does spoil the impression, for it shows that the room is no real home but the temporary billet of a wanderer, a "tramp" who must "pursue his way." Moreover the room is not really K.'s, an undisputed possession, but the inn maids', who come clumping in and out in their heavy boots even while K. and Frieda are making love and leave them little "peace." K. possesses nothing indisputably his own. Still, such as it is, the maids' room of an inn, without walls on two sides to shut it off from the rest of the attic, Frieda has made a home of it. K. now has the self-assurance to retort brusquely to the schoolmaster when the latter refers to him as a stranger—"what K. had submitted to when he felt homeless he did not intend to put up with now here in his room." [67] Brusque, however, as K.'s answer is, nevertheless it is an assent to the teacher's statement: in spite of his room which Frieda's brave housekeeping has made into a home, he is indeed a stranger and must remain one always.

But then K. loses even his poor attic room when the landlady turns him out of the Bridge Inn. At Frieda's earnest plea he consents to accept the job of school janitor so that they might have a place to live, even though "he was not much concerned about his lodgings." [68] The living quarters assigned K. and Frieda in the schoolhouse are no better than the attic room, in fact they are worse. In return for the work he does, the schoolmaster tells K., "you have the right to live in whichever one of the classrooms you like, but when both rooms are not being used at the same time for teaching, and you are in the room that is needed, you must of course move to the other room." [69] It is a Kafka joke: what the teacher slides over, in offering this slapstick-comedy arrangement, is the question of what K. and Frieda shall do when both rooms are being used for teaching!

Life in the schoolhouse is predictably chaotic. On their first morning there, after a night made turbulent by the antics of the assistants, they awake to find themselves surrounded by gaping children. K. and Frieda construct a sort of tent by throwing a blanket over some gymnasium equipment, so as to be able to shelter themselves from the eyes of the children while getting dressed.

> He was not given a minute's peace, however, for the woman teacher began to scold because there was no fresh water in the washbasin—K. had just been thinking of getting the basin for himself and Frieda, but he had at once given up the idea so as not to exasperate the woman teacher too much, but his renunciation was of no avail, for immediately afterwards there was a loud crash; unfortunately, it seemed, they had forgotten to clear away the remains of the supper from the teacher's desk, so she sent it all flying with her ruler and everything fell on the floor; she didn't need to bother about the sardine oil and the remainder of the coffee being spilled and the coffee pot smashed to pieces, the school janitor would of course soon clean that up. Not yet fully clothed, K. and Frieda, leaning on the parallel bars, witnessed the destruction of their few possessions.[70]

In fact K. finds very little peace (*Friede*) with Frieda and their attempt at housekeeping is destroyed under their eyes. It is an impossible task to keep house for a wayfarer for whom all resting places are never more than temporary camps.*

Nevertheless K. never abandons his often stated determination to marry Frieda and settle in the village:

> I came here of my own free will [he tells Olga] and of my own free will I have hung on here, but all that has happened to me since I came, and, above all, any prospects I may have—dark as they are they still exist—I owe entirely to Frieda, and you can't argue that away. True, I was received here as land-surveyor, but only apparently so, they were playing with me, I was driven out of everybody's house, they are playing with me still today . . . yet I already have, however insignificant it may all seem, a home, a position and real work, I have a fiancée who relieves me of my

* Frieda shares the responsibility for the failure of their home life by her indulgence of the zany assistants, who follow every thoughtless childish (and also erotic) inclination and impulse they feel (for that is what they represent: careless, primitive-childish impulses and instincts).

professional duties when I have other business, I'm going to marry her and become a member of the community. . . .[71]

K. is going to marry Frieda and acquire a footing in the world. However, he does not forget that he has "other business" too. At the very same time that he means to marry and join the human community, he also means to press on to his goal in the castle without caring about anything else, not even about Frieda. The two purposes contradict each other, but K. will not see this— wills not to see this.

> The conversation with Hans had raised new hopes in him, admittedly improbable hopes, completely groundless even, but all the same not to be put out of his mind; they almost hid from view Barnabas himself. If he pursued them, and he couldn't do anything else, then he must concentrate all his strength toward that end, care about nothing else, not about food, lodgings, the village authorities, no, not even about Frieda; and basically it all came down to a question of Frieda, for everything else concerned him only because of Frieda. Therefore [!] he must try to keep this post, which gave Frieda a certain degree of security, and he must not regret it if for this purpose he put himself in a position where he had to endure more from the teacher than he would have otherwise had to endure. All that sort of thing wasn't too painful, it belonged to the ordinary continual petty afflictions of life, it was nothing compared with what K. was striving for, and he had not come here to lead a respected, peaceful life [*um ein Leben in Ehren und Frieden zu führen*].[72]

For the sake of his "end" he must not care about food, lodgings, the village authorities who have given him the school janitor's job, or even about Frieda; for the sake of Frieda he must care about his job, which provides them food and lodgings, and therefore too about the village authorities, who provide the job. For the sake of a life of "peace" ("Frieda") he must endure the petty afflictions of the world, which are nothing compared with his goal, which is *not* a life of peace (*"Frieden"*)! Underneath its mask of plausibility, the passage is torn by contradiction. K.

tries to drown a fundamental contradiction in a flow of reasonable-sounding phrases.*

K. absurdly imagines he can pursue two contradictory goals at the same time. However, in a world in which reality and spirit stand opposed (as I have said) what is absurd really, is spiritually true: the cracked mask of plausibility shows forth as a true spiritual countenance. Nevertheless, this true face of the spirit is a negative one, divorced from reality, seamed with contradiction. K.'s great effort is to resolve the contradiction so that knowing and being are united in reality, so that spirit and reality are one. The way he means to do this is by meeting Klamm face to face, hearing his voice and "knowing from him how he stands in relation to our marriage" [73] (von ihm wissen, wie er sich zu unserer Heirat verhält).

Before he marries Frieda, he announces to the Bridge Inn landlady in their first conversation, "there's something I must absolutely do. I must have a talk with Klamm." The landlady's comment on this is:

> "You are strange," said the landlady, and she was intimidating as she now sat more upright, her legs planted apart and her great knees projecting under her thin skirt. "You ask for the impossible." [74]

In wanting to talk to Klamm face to face, to confront personally one of the impersonal and abstract "mighty ones" who run the world, and know from him directly how he stands in relation to his marriage, K. is flying in the face of reality, which causes the Bridge Inn landlady, who is a reality expert with a "broad knowledge of life and men," [75] to draw her massive figure up so that K. is intimidated; K. is momentarily intimidated by a representative of the massive reality he outrages with his "impossible" demand. The landlady tries to dissuade K. from attempting what is impossible (and therefore "shameful" [76]) by reminding him of

* There is a copious use in the passage, as there is generally in Kafka, of logical connectives, but in fact the connectives connect nothing.

185

his ignorance of the world. (His "ignorance," his "childishness" is something K. is reminded of on every side.*)

> . . . [Y]our ignorance of the way things are here is so appalling that it makes one's head spin to listen to you and compare what you say and have in mind with the real situation. It's an ignorance that can't be corrected all at once and perhaps not at all; but it would be a great improvement if you would only believe me a little and always bear in mind your own ignorance. For instance, you would at once be less unjust to me and you would begin to have an inkling of the dismay it caused me—a dismay I still feel the effects of—when I realized that my darling girl [Frieda] had deserted the eagle for the earthworm as it were, only the real disparity is much worse even than that and I have to keep on trying to forget it, otherwise I couldn't say one word to you calmly. . . . Wherever you may be, never forget that you're the most ignorant person of all, and watch out: here among us where Frieda's presence saves you from harm you can drivel on to your heart's content, for instance here you can explain to us how you intend to have a talk with Klamm; only in reality, only in reality, I entreat you, I entreat you, don't do it.[77]

But K., unlike Joseph K., is "shameless" and unafraid before the judgment of the world. Freely admitting his ignorance, nevertheless he sees in it an advantage, the advantage that "the ignoramus dares more, and therefore I am willing to bear with my ignorance and its undoubtedly evil consequences for a little while more, so long as my strength holds out. But these consequences really affect nobody but myself, and that's why I simply can't understand your pleading. . . . So what are you afraid of?" And now K. defies the powers of the world, like a Prometheus speaking for man and flinging his challenge right into their teeth. It is his most heroic moment (though not his bravest; he has no "bravest" moment)—and his most foolish.

> "Surely you're not afraid—an ignoramus thinks everything possible"—here K. was already opening the door—"surely you're not

* Because of his ignorance and childishness the village authorities send him back to school (as a janitor).

afraid for Klamm?" The landlady gazed after him in silence as he
ran down the staircase with the assistants following him.[78]

It is his most foolish moment because, as experience and reflection teach him subsequently, Klamm is not to be laid hold of
by K.'s going up to the Herrenhof and simply collaring him.
Taught by experience and reflection, he comes to realize later on
that "Klamm was far away."

> Klamm was far away. Once the landlady had compared Klamm
> to an eagle and that had seemed laughable to K., but it did not
> seem so now; he thought of Klamm's remoteness, of his impreg-
> nable dwelling, of his muteness, broken perhaps only by cries such
> as K. had never yet heard, of his downward-piercing gaze, which
> could never be demonstrated or disproved, of his wheeling in circles
> which were indestructible from K.'s distance down below, which
> up above he followed according to incomprehensible laws and
> which only for instants were visible—all these things Klamm and
> the eagle had in common.[79]

In striving to obtain official recognition from the castle as
land-surveyor, and to obtain a personal interview with Klamm so
as to "know" exactly in what relation the official stands to his
marriage, K. is striving for the same thing: to make official, legal
(i.e. real) the union of being and knowledge, of the concrete and
the universal. The two endeavors are one; or rather what K.
seeks in marriage is an aspect of his one effort. The whole novel
is a "marching in place" not only in the sense that K. never advances any nearer his goal, but also in the sense that its apparently diverse episodes and occasions and individual histories are
only aspects of the story's one matter.

Why should K. want a personal interview with Klamm in particular? About Klamm Frieda says that it was thanks to "his
work that we found each other under the bar." [80] Klamm's
"work," then, is to tumble people into one another's arms. The
mighty force that drives people together, he is head of the Department of Love. When Frieda and K. are rolling on the bar-

room floor of the Herrenhof "in a state of unconsciousness which K. tried again and again but in vain to master," they are described as "landing with a thud against Klamm's door [*schlugen dumpf an Klamms Tür*], where they lay among the small puddles of beer and other refuse scattered on the floor." [81] The German phrase, which also means "knocked at Klamm's door," tells us that to copulate is "to knock at Klamm's door." K., however, strives to "master" orgasmic unconsciousness so as not to "lose his way," the way of consciousness leading to knowledge; he strives to confront in personal awareness the impersonal sex drive (Klamm), to know it, and by knowing it converts its coarse instinctual necessitarianism into freedom. Thus Klamm is first of all orgasmic unconsciousness, sexual being; but beyond that he holds out the possibility of reaching through him another kind of love, a sexuality in which the sex drive is illuminated and known so that life and love are no longer driven, are no longer "drives," without ceasing to be life and love. The two kinds of love are explicitly referred to in a deleted passage in which K. rehearses what he wishes to say to Klamm face to face:

> "We, Frieda and I, love each other and want to marry as soon as possible. Yet Frieda loves not only me, but you [Klamm] too, though admittedly in a wholly different way, it is not my fault that language is so poor that it has only one word for both. Frieda herself does not understand how it comes about that there is room in her heart for me too, and *she can only think that it became possible solely by your will. After everything I have heard from Frieda, I can only concur in her opinion. . . ."* [82]

Frieda, who swoons in perfect abandonment in the sexual embrace, loves Klamm, the blind god of swooning love. Yet she also loves K. who seeks a love that sees open-eyed in the midst of swooning; and K. "can only concur in her opinion" that not only their blind rolling in beer puddles under the bar was the will of Klamm, but also her attraction to the K. who is in search of another kind of love. The two kinds of love are clearly figured in the beer and ordinary liquors dispensed at the Herrenhof, and the flask of magical brandy which K. gets out of the side-pocket of Klamm's sleigh at the coachman's invitation after he has ventured inside the vehicle.[83] K.'s and Frieda's embrace under the bar is the ordinary beer of life. But Klamm, a beer drinker ordinarily, has a private stock of brandy "whose perfume was so sweet, so caressing, like praise and good words from someone whom one likes very much, yet one does not know clearly what they are for and has no desire to know and is simply happy in the consciousness that it is one's friend who is saying them." Alas, however, when K. actually tries Klamm's brandy it is changed "in drinking" from a subtle elixir "into a coachman's drink" *—a disillusionment, be it noted, for which K. reproaches *himself:* " 'Can it be?' K. asked himself *as if self-reproachfully,* and took another sip." † [84] Later at the Herrenhof bar K. orders brandy, then pushes it away disgustedly after tasting it and calls it "undrinkable."

> "All the gentlemen drink it," replied Pepi curtly, poured out the remainder, washed the glass, and set it on the rack. "The gentlemen have better stuff as well," said K.[85]

The customary drink of the lords of life is beer and burning rotgut, but they have "better stuff as well."

In pursuit of his goal of a love composed of "better stuff," a marriage relation with Frieda illuminated and clarified by knowledge of Klamm's relation to it, K. is always neglecting Frieda and running off to the Barnabases or the Herrenhof, following any will-o'-the-wisp that promises to lead him to Klamm. But in so doing he loses Frieda and with her love and marriage. Frieda on her side either violently rejects Klamm and all his works and "dreams of a grave, deep and narrow, where we could clasp each other in our arms as with clamps, and I would hide my face in you and you would hide your face in me, and nobody

---

* The Muirs' translation falsifies this passage by introducing the adverb "wonderfully" into the description of the transformation.
† D. H. Lawrence writes in *The Captain's Doll* of "the vulgarity of disillusion."

would ever see us any more"—dreams, in other words, of a love
in which each loses himself in the other and both in death, for
"here on the earth there's no quiet place for our love, neither in
the village nor anywhere else," [86] a love from which every
element of life and body and natural instinct has been drastically expelled; or she surrenders to Klamm's power so completely, with such glad unthinkingness, that K. must say:
"You're still Klamm's sweetheart, you're still a long way from
being my wife" [87]—for she cannot master the spontaneous,
thoughtless delight she takes in those "emissaries of Klamm's," [88]
the two assistants, and must be forever looking and laughing at
them, caressing them, stroking their hair. When she is lying beside the sleeping K. in the middle of the night and fooling with
the assistants, she tells him, "one minute I'm afraid you'll
awaken and it will all be ended, and the next I spring up and
light the candle so that you'll waken at once and protect me." [89]
Frieda alternates between a state of sensual being-with-K. which
is ended by his awakening to consciousness, and an unearthly
love which turns away from life toward death. The effect of all
this on her well-being is disastrous: "A few days of living with
K. . . . and . . . she was withering in his arms." [90]

Try as she may, Frieda cannot understand K.'s efforts to "talk
to Klamm." She quotes to him the Bridge Inn landlady's words
about his not valuing her (Frieda) but only her connection with
the official; she is only an instrument to him by which he hopes
to reach his goal; she is nothing and his goal is everything; his
love is not love but calculation. K.'s reply to this is: in acting for
himself he acts for her[91]—his mission is a universal one. For
Frieda too, as for the landlady, K. "asks for the impossible," [92] for
her, too, his neglecting her and visiting at the Barnabases' is
finally too shameful to endure and she leaves him to return to
her old job of dispensing the common refreshment of the world
as barmaid at the Herrenhof.

K., however, never stops loving Frieda and at the end of the
novel his praise of her qualities is practically a eulogy. In his
long talk with Pepi he says:

". . . [W]hen I compare myself with you something of this kind dawns on me: it is as if we both had tried too hard, too noisily, too childishly, with too little experience, to get something that with Frieda's calm and Frieda's matter-of-factness can be got easily and without any fuss. We have tried to get it by crying, by scratching, by tugging—just as a child tugs at the tablecloth, gaining nothing, but only bringing all the splendid things down on the floor and putting them out of its reach forever. I don't know whether it is like that, but what I am sure of is that it is more likely to be so than the way you describe it as being." [93]

K.'s criticism of himself recalls Joseph K.'s self-reproach, as he is being led off to execution and he thinks he sees Fräulein Bürstner, that he "always wanted to ransack the world with twenty hands." [94] Here chastened spirit bows humbly before life and reproaches itself with the sin of impatience.* Elsewhere K. speaks of Frieda as one who has always "followed her own heart." [96] Frieda is plucky, whole-souled, full of heart, a heart that she follows with calm, unhesitating assurance—she is the only touching female character in all of Kafka's work. Yet Frieda's lifeability is based on an unreflecting heart and K.'s unforswearable goal is to bring the heart under reflection. Therefore, though K. would "be happy if she was to come back to me . . . I should at once begin to neglect her all over again. This is how it is." [97]

K. learns patience at the end: that the castle is not to be conquered in a day, or even at all. He learns to appreciate Frieda's naïve love and courage and matter-of-fact acceptance of the life his impatient spirit wishes to master at one stroke. Yet the novel does not aim at showing such a development; it is not based on a poetic of development. If Frieda came back to him he would *at once begin to neglect her all over again*—The Castle is based on

* As Kafka writes: "There are two cardinal sins from which all the others spring: impatience and laziness. Because of impatience they were driven out of Paradise, because of laziness they don't return. Perhaps, however, there is only one cardinal sin: impatience. Because of impatience they were driven out, because of impatience they don't return." [95]

the ever-defeated, ever-repeated effort of K. to unite Frieda's effortless peace of being with his own reflective effort.

At the Barnabases'

At the middle of the novel stands the story of the Barnabas family, which Olga recounts to K. in the course of a conversation that goes on for some eighty pages. Everything that happens to K. before his talk with Olga is early history; after it, late. One reason for this is Frieda's leaving him during his long absence at the Barnabases'—the setback he suffers in his ambition to marry Frieda, coming on top of his defeated attempts to march straight up to the castle or one of its great officials, writes finis to his early period of overweening hopes. But an equally important reason is the conversation itself.

In his interview with the Village Head early in the novel K. had been told flatly that what he thought were communications between himself and the castle were nothing at all: "You have never really come into contact with the authorities. All these contacts of yours have been illusory, but because of your ignorance of things you take them to be real." [98] This statement, if K. had thought about it, already called into question Barnabas' value to him as a messenger. It is true that Klamm in his first letter to K. had appointed Barnabas messenger between them, but then the Village Head had authoritatively pronounced the letter to be a private one, without official significance. Now, however, K. learns from Olga that her brother himself questions his messengership; he is ridden by the most terrible doubts whether he is really messenger, whether the offices he reports to up above on the castle height are really the castle offices, whether it is really Klamm he speaks to and who speaks to him. Olga's account of Barnabas' ordeal in the castle offices opens K.'s eyes wider to the infinitely ambiguous nature of the castle authority, so that he is able to appreciate how childish his original conceptions were: "Only think, up there is the authority in its inextricable vastness—I imagined that I had an approximate conception of its nature before I came here, but how childish my ideas were. . . ." [99] What in K. had exasperated (and frightened) the Bridge Inn landlady beyond all endurance—his childishness—he now freely acknowledges. K. must always be the ignorant child she called him because he deliberately ignores reality and pursues an impossible goal, yet the K. who has digested Olga's narrative sees a lot deeper into the depths and difficulties of his contest with the castle than did the newcomer to the village who simply barged right into things. Olga's knowledge and wisdom, clearly and modestly expressed, make K. wiser so that he is able to speak wisely to her in turn:

". . . [T]here's something—I don't know what it is—that hinders you from seeing fully how much Barnabas has—I'll not say achieved—but has had bestowed on him. He's permitted to go into the offices or, if you prefer, into an anteroom—well, let it be an anteroom, it has doors that lead on farther, barriers that can be passed if one has the skill. To me, for instance, even this anteroom is utterly inaccessible, for the present at least. Who is it that Barnabas speaks to there I have no idea, perhaps the clerk is the lowest of the whole staff, but even if he is the lowest he can put one in touch with the next man above him, and if he can't do that, he can at least give the other's name, and if he can't even do that, he can refer to somebody who *can* give the name. This so-called Klamm may not have the smallest trait in common with the real one, the resemblance may not exist except in the eyes of Barnabas, blinded by excitement, he may be the lowest of officials, he may not even be an official at all, but all the same he has work of some kind to perform at the desk, he reads something or other in his great book, he whispers something to the clerk, he thinks something when his eye falls on Barnabas once in a while, and even if that isn't true and he and his actions have no significance whatever, he has at least been set there by somebody for some purpose. I mean to say by all this that something is there, something is held out to Barnabas, something or other at the very least, and that it is Barnabas' own fault if he can't get any farther than doubt and anxiety and despair." [100]

These are the accents of the late K.; before his talk with Olga he is still incapable of such speech. This talk and the others which make up so much of the novel are not really dialogues; their character is not dramatic but didactic-visionary. The change that K. undergoes in the course of them takes place, not in the dramatic-psychological mode of realism, but in an old-new mode of narrative that advanced the art of fiction by going back to poetry and rhetoric.

As the hopes K. has set on Barnabas decline, his interest in him as a companion spirit rises: "He was indeed gradually losing all hope in the success of Barnabas' messengership, but the worse it went with Barnabas up above, the nearer he felt drawn to him down here, never would K. have believed that such an unhappy effort as that of Barnabas and his sister could have come out of the village itself." [101] That is, as Barnabas loses significance as an actor in K.'s story, as he drops out of K.'s plot, he and his family acquire significance for K. as actors in a story which parallels his own. Like himself, they are excluded from the life of the village and involved in a desperate effort to reach the castle—they are "people who were, at least externally, in the same situation as himself." [102] Their story illuminates K.'s story analogically much more than it is a part of it intrinsically. Its place in the narrative is therefore "rhetorical"; it is "poetry" rather than "prose"; matter for reflection for K. rather than matter of his experience. Like Joyce, Kafka is a medievalizer who uses rhetorical devices to construct a design; though Kafka's story design is a simple repetitive one in which analogies and paradigms reiterate the novel's one matter, whereas Joyce's has a Daedalian elaborateness. Kafka aims at the simplicity of parable, an antiliterary form dear to such mistrusters of art as Tolstoy; Joyce aims at a complex art-of-all-art employing a superliterary style which expresses the modern everything by being the no-style of all styles.

Along with a peculiar kind of allegory erected on the literalized meanings of word and images, analogy and comparison are

Kafka's main rhetorical means in *The Castle*. (Though the dream-narrative form as a whole is rhetorical, a figure of speech —it is rhetorical-realistic, a point where rhetoric and realism come together, as imagination and reality come together in the dream.) The most extensive analogy in the novel is that between the outcast Barnabas family and the outsider K. But the story of the Bridge Inn landlady; of Pepi; of the woman teacher Gisa and her lover Schwarzer; Amalia's and Olga's individual stories; and Frieda's story too—these also stand in an analogous relation to K.'s story, not to the whole of it but to the erotic part. Their histories illustrate different types of love-attitudes and love-efforts which form a constellation or design around the central love-effort of K. Each of these characters is pulled one way or the other by the antithesis between worldly love and spiritual love; only K. tries to reconcile the two. All of them have a greater or lesser share in K.'s story, yet with the exception of Frieda they are more important for their own stories, as illustrative *exempla* (to use the medieval term), than as participants in K.'s; and in Frieda's case participation and illustration merge indistinguishably.

K. has an eye for analogies. When he tells the Bridge Inn landlady that the blessing was over her and her husband during their courtship, only the failure lay in not knowing how to bring it down, she asks him what the omission was.

> "To ask Klamm," said K.
> "So we're back at your case again," said the landlady.
> "Or at yours," said K. "Our affairs run parallel." [103]

Olga tells him that "it is a matter of life or death for Barnabas whether it's really Klamm he speaks to or not." " 'And for me no less,' said K. and they moved nearer to each other on the settle." [104] K. is surprised, as we have seen, that such a desperate effort as Barnabas and Olga make to reach the castle, an effort which is so much like his own, could have come out of the village itself—that such a struggle for justification before the ultimate powers could have originated in the very midst of self-evident, unquestioning being. Himself an outsider from the start, his existence has always lacked self-evidency so that the position of seeking justification is so to speak a natural one for him. But how did the Barnabases, who were once thriving villagers, get themselves into such a fix? The answer to this question lies in the story of Amalia's rebuff of Sortini's summons, followed by the village's ostracism of the family. K.'s ears prick up, after hearing this long tale, when Olga describes how her father, having lost all hope of getting an official hearing for his petition of forgiveness, decided to try a personal, unofficial approach to the officials.

> "Since he had failed in proving an offense, and consequently could hope for nothing more through official channels, he would have to depend on entreaties alone and try to approach the officials personally. There must certainly be some among them who had good sympathetic hearts, which they daren't give way to in their official capacity, but surely they might extra-officially, if one caught them at the right time."
>
> Here K., who had listened with absorption hitherto, interrupted Olga's narrative with the question: "And you don't think he was right?" His question would surely have answered itself in the course of the narrative, but he wanted to know at once.

K. starts at the mention of a personal approach to the officials because that is just what he has been trying to do: meet Klamm personally. He is impatient to hear Olga's answer because it concerns his own effort as much as her father's—the two are analogues.

> "No," said Olga, "there could be no question of sympathy or anything of the kind. Young and inexperienced as we were, we knew that, and Father knew it too, of course, but he had forgotten it like nearly everything else. The plan he had hit on was to plant himself on the main road near the castle, where the officials pass in their carriages, and seize any opportunity of presenting his plea for forgiveness. To tell the truth, an utterly senseless plan, even if the impossible should have happened and his prayer have really reached an official's ear. For can a single official give a pardon?

. . . What a pass Father must have been in to think of possibly succeeding with his new plan! If there were even the faintest possibility of that kind, that part of the road would be packed with petitioners, but as it's a sheer impossibility, impressed on one by the most elementary education, the road is absolutely empty. But maybe even that strengthened Father in his hopes, he found food for them everywhere. He has to; a sound mind would never have let itself be drawn into such grandiose speculations [*grossen Über-legungen*], it would have recognized right away that the thing was impossible on the face of it." [105]

Olga's view is the Bridge Inn landlady's and the world's: to confront an official personally is "a sheer impossibility, impressed on one by the most elementary education." (The Village Head had sent K. back to school to teach him that.) No "sound mind" would ever let itself be drawn into such "grandiose speculations" about the ultimate powers, only a mind unhinged by the misfortune of finding itself thrust out of life and in need of justification. K., however, does not retort defiantly to Olga as he did to the Bridge Inn landlady, but hears her out with only an occasional question. No longer is he the childish, inexperienced K; nor is Olga for her part a reality expert like the landlady—that is, a mind that knowledge of the world has enslaved to the world —even though their views agree. Ingenuous rather than shrewd, an outcast and a striver with the castle like K. himself, though with a more modest goal, she discloses in her words a depth of knowledge of the castle's workings which makes K.'s own experiences seem small to him: "Olga's story was opening for him such a great and almost incredible world that he could not help setting his own small experiences beside it, as much to convince himself of its existence as of his own." [106]

"Almost incredible," however, as is the castle world which Olga's story opens to him, it differs from the one he knows already only in its greater depth and detail; she does not disclose a different, totally unexpected castle regime to him. And the conclusion of her recital of her father's attempt to accost an official in person describes a situation and a scene which K. has already experienced himself. The old man having posted himself beside the road near the castle entrance, he wears out his days and his health fruitlessly following his "desolate calling" (*öden Beruf*), cowering in the snow and wet and racked by rheumatism.

> "In the night he groaned with pain, and in the morning he was many a time uncertain whether to go or not, but always overcame his reluctance and went. Mother clung to him and didn't want to let him go; he, apparently grown timid because his limbs wouldn't obey him, allowed her to go with him, and so Mother began to get pains too. . . . [H]ow often we found them crouching together, leaning against each other on their narrow seat, huddled up under a thin blanket that scarcely covered them, and round about them nothing but the gray of snow and mist, and far and wide for days at a time not a soul to be seen, not a carriage, a sight that was, K., a sight to be seen!" [107]

This was K.'s own situation in the snow of the Herrenhof yard when he waited fruitlessly to catch Klamm coming out to his sleigh; it is the desolate fate of all those called and compelled for whatever reason to be castle-seekers.

Yet there is an important difference between K.'s striving and the father's. Although both seek to justify themselves before the highest powers, K.'s quest has a universal goal rather than a narrowly personal one; he wants, not forgiveness and reacceptance into the scheme of things-as-they-are, but the transformation of the scheme, a new relation of being and spirit. Barnabas' father, having lost his footing in the world and fallen from it, wishes only to scramble back again with his family to where they were. Of course, the only way back is by the perilous path that leads straight up the castle hill and past the "ultimate barriers" [108] before the last office, and to follow that path to its end is just precisely to transform the scheme of things-as-they-are. So willy-nilly the Barnabases find themselves in K.'s situation, but involuntarily and without his universal awareness. K.'s effort is purer, more religious.

At the heart of the Barnabases' story is Amalia's story, "Amalia's Secret," as the subtitle calls it. It is because Amalia spurns the castle official Sortini that the family becomes pariahs. Something in this act of rejection offends fundamentally against the common life and causes Amalia and all related to her to be cast out of the village. What is Amalia's secret? She betrays it to K. even before he hears her story from Olga's lips.

Toward the end of Chapter Fourteen, having finished his chores at the schoolhouse, K. sets off at a run for Barnabas' house to see if there are any messages for him from the castle. Neither Barnabas nor Olga is at home, only Amalia and her decrepit parents. At Amalia's invitation K. waits for Olga, then says he cannot stay any longer because his fiancée is expecting him at home. Amalia expresses surprise at hearing he is engaged and is sure that Olga will be surprised too. But K. is convinced that Olga already knows about his engagement to Frieda.

> Amalia assured him, however, that Olga knew nothing about it, and that it would make her very unhappy, for she seemed to be in love with K. She had not directly said so, for she was very reserved, but love betrayed itself involuntarily. K. was convinced that Amalia was mistaken. Amalia smiled, and this smile of hers, though sad, lit up her somber, contracted face, made her silence expressive, her strangeness confidential, *and gave away a secret, gave away a hitherto closely guarded possession* which she could indeed take back again, but never completely. Amalia said that she was certainly not mistaken; that in fact she knew more, she knew that K. also had an inclination for Olga, and that his visits, whose pretext was some message or other of Barnabas', were really intended for Olga. But now that Amalia knew all about it he need not be so strict with himself and could visit oftener. That was all she wanted to say. K. shook his head and reminded her of his betrothal. Amalia didn't seem to waste much thought on this betrothal, the direct impression made on her by K., who was after all unaccompanied, was decisive for her. . . .

Olga enters soon after this.

> She . . . greeted K. without embarrassment and asked at once after Frieda. K. looked meaningfully at Amalia, who seemed, however, not to think she had been proven wrong. Irritated a little

by this, K. talked about Frieda at greater length than he would otherwise have done. . . .[109]

Amalia's "secret" is "given away" in this passage. Such revelations are characteristically obscured in Kafka by trivia which are given equal stress, so that the narrative presents a monotonous, unemphatic surface—this is Kafka's "psychoanalytic" imagination of the hidden struggle between depth and surface. The obscurity is increased in this instance by an obvious but insignificant error of fact that Amalia seems to make almost deliberately. The byplay is quite complicated. Amalia asserts two things, a fact and a truth. The asserted fact is that Olga is ignorant of K.'s betrothal to Frieda. The asserted truth is that Olga loves K. and K. Olga, and that that is why he comes to visit them—his interest in "some message or other" Barnabas has for him is a dodge, whether he knows it himself or not. When Olga enters and immediately asks after Frieda, K. looks triumphantly at Amalia, for this is proof that Olga knows about his betrothal. Irritatingly, however, Amalia does not seem the least bit disconcerted by having been proven wrong. K.'s betrothal and the question of whether Olga knew about it or not are insignificant facts about the surface of life on which she does not "waste much thought" because, betrothed or not, K. wants Olga and Olga K. and that is the sole truth of things, not the hullabaloo K. raises about messages and marriages and meeting Klamm face to face. The secret that Amalia's sad, sardonic smile gives away is her knowledge of the nothingness of spirit, of all striving toward the castle; and the omnipotence of gross necessity, of the inexorable life-mechanism which makes Olga want K. and K. Olga. K.'s answer to this is to talk "about Frieda at greater length than he would otherwise have done," in proof of his devotion to her; Olga's greeting him "without embarrassment" is proof that she on her side does not lust for him. But expressions of devotion on the part of K., and Olga's unawareness of the drives at work in her, count for nothing in Amalia's eyes; consciousness is nothing and necessity all—the only true consciousness is the conscious-

ness of necessity, the only spirituality despair about the nothingness of spirit.

Amalia utters her same secret, with sardonic wit, in the passage already quoted from in part in which she mocks K. and Olga
for taking such an interest in castle stories. When K. defends his
interest in them and decries those who do not trouble themselves
about the castle, she answers as follows:

> "Indeed," said Amalia, "well, people's interests are of all kinds, to
> be sure, I heard once of a young man who thought of nothing but
> the castle day and night, he neglected everything else, people
> feared for his good sense because all his wits were up in the castle.
> It turned out at length, however, that it wasn't really the castle
> he had had in mind but the daughter of a woman who cleaned
> the offices up there, so he got the girl and was all right again."
> "I think I should like that man," said K. "As for your liking the
> man, I doubt it," said Amalia, "it's probably his wife you would
> like. . . ." [110]

All spiritual concern is illusion; all the efforts of castle-seekers to
convert necessitarian being into freedom by understanding it,
are delusions, misunderstood manifestations of that same necessity. Amalia sees the truth about life, she stands "face to face
with the truth" [111] that it is ruled by appetite and need, which
infect all spirituality; she sees through life and is unable to live
in the world. As she sees through life and spirit, there is no place
for her on earth, neither in the village nor the castle. There is no
place for K. either, but by striving to unite the two he lives pre-
cariously without a place. At least he lives; Amalia is dead—
hence her "distinguishing mark," her "deadened glance, devoid
of all feeling" [112] (*stumpfer, lieblosen Blick*).

Amalia's secret, then, is the knowledge which disillusions. One
has a right therefore to read the story of her encounter with Sortini, which belongs among such lapidary examples of the Kafka
thought-story as "An Imperial Message" and "Before the Law," as
the explanation of how she acquired such knowledge, and to fit
the episode into the novel's pattern of repetitions and analogies.
Without getting into an extended exegesis of this much debated

episode, it is enough to point out (following Professor Emrich) that it concerns an encounter—collision is a better word—between two highly spiritual types.[113] Sortini—"a small, frail pensive" castle official with a forehead remarkably furrowed by thought, whose character it is to "keep well in the background" for he is "unused to the world"—has been "deputized" to preside over a celebration on the occasion of the presentation of the village Fire Brigade with a new pump-and-hose truck. It is a tumultuous fête in which the villagers get drunk on the sweet castle wine, blow trumpets noisily, and cheer on those taking part in the games and exercises. Sortini deputizes for the castle official regularly in charge of such things—his own work is not Dionysian abandonment but meditation and musing, he runs the Department of Spirit. Amalia, dressed in her finery for the occasion, is universally admired, and her father says, "Today, mark my words, Amalia will find a husband." "She wasn't beautiful by any means," Olga tells K., "but her somber glance, and it has remained that way ever since, was lifted high over us and involuntarily one had almost literally to bow before her" [114]—her somber glance is lifted high above the stir of sensual life around her. Sortini sits apart, bored and indifferent, till his eye lights on Amalia; he leaps over the shaft of the fire engine, "though his legs were stiff from working at desks," [115] to get a nearer look at her. "That was all." It is said later that Sortini has fallen in love with her and that she has "fallen head over heels in love with Sortini." [116]

The next morning a messenger hands Amalia Sortini's peremptory letter, "couched in the vulgarest language," commanding her to come to him at the Herrenhof. "And it wasn't a love letter, there wasn't a flattering word in it, on the contrary Sortini was obviously angry at having been seized by the sight of Amalia and held back from his work. Later we explained it to ourselves that evidently Sortini had intended to go straight to the castle that evening, but on Amalia's account had stayed in the village instead, and in the morning, being angry because even overnight he hadn't succeeded in forgetting her, had written the letter." [117] The erotic "seizes" hold of Sortini, who is "unused" to the sensual world, and "holds him back from his work" in the Department of Spirit. Angered, he tries to discharge the erotic feelings which detain him from his abstract occupations by the brutal exercise of seigneurial *droit*. To recover his pure spirituality Sortini has to be purely, brutally sensual—where world and spirit are divided, spirit is only spirit at the expense of world, and world world at the expense of spirit. Of course, the castle officialdom as a whole, and not only Sortini, represents spirituality, for it stands for life under the aspect of consciousness, life as it is abstracted by thought into ideas; yet where spirit is separated from life, a separate official is needed to represent that very separation, which is called pure spirit.*

Amalia on her side has been seized with love by the sight of Sortini. But looking high above the sensual stir inside herself, repudiating an essential principle of life instead of trying to understand it like K., she sees only Sortini's pure spirituality even as he, flip-flopping into a Klamm-like official, deputizing as the love-force, sees only "the girl with the garnet necklace"—so he addresses her in his letter. Hence the shock of disillusion she experiences when she receives his summons—spirit is proven to be a fraud and she falls from life into an abyss of despair. Because Amalia denies a fundamental human principle, she and her family "were no longer spoken of as human beings, our name was no longer uttered; if they had to refer to us they called us Barnabas' people, after the most innocent one of us, our very cottage acquired an evil odor. . . ." [119]

Amalia's place in the analogical design of the novel is now clearer. If the Bridge Inn landlady is wholly of the world, then balancing her on the other side is Amalia, who is wholly of the spirit, albeit a wholly negative spirit. Between them are Frieda, who alternates between world and spirit, and K., who strives always for their union.

In contrast with Amalia is Olga. Standing like her sister on the

---

* However, since the unity of life can never be completely negated, and since all thought is ultimately hypostatization, "the officials generally deputize for one another and so it's difficult to perceive what this or that official is responsible for." [118]

spiritual side, she however represents a positive spiritual effort. Olga tries to track down the castle servant who delivered Sortini's letter so as to atone to him at least, for Sortini himself has withdrawn into unapproachable regions of the abstract. "For more than two years, at least twice a week," she "spends the night with the servants in the stable" of the Herrenhof—she is flung back and forth among the castle servants, personifications of sensual appetites who are described as "a wild unmanageable lot, ruled by their insatiable impulses instead of by their regulations. Their shamelessness knows no limits, it's lucky for the village that they can't leave the Herrenhof without permission, but in the Herrenhof itself one must try to come to an understanding with them. . . ." Olga, in other words, submits herself to those very sensual powers, the principle of which her sister has offended against, so as to understand them. (High officials represent universal principles or laws, servants the energies obedient to those laws.) She is not a slut but, like K., a castle-seeker, though she does not aim as high as he; her aim is to acknowledge a vital energy, his to master a law. She never finds Sortini's servant; but on the other hand, she says, "what I've achieved in the Herrenhof is a certain connection with the castle; don't despise me when I say that I don't repent what I've done." [120] Her understanding of things shows that she has indeed achieved a certain connection with the castle. Far from despising her, K. esteems her for "her bravery, her breadth of vision, her wisdom, her sacrifices for the family" [121] of man—so he reflects as he finally says goodbye to Olga and passes out into the night.

In the Corridor of the Herrenhof

Now the novel is moving toward its end, a Kafka ending that peters out or breaks off after the intensification by elaboration of the same old impossible situation in which the story starts. The tone of the penultimate chapters is light and in places even dancing; K.'s nocturnal conversation with Bürgel in the latter's room, and his disruptive watching of the distribution of the officials' files, are among Kafka's finest comic inventions.

Olga had told K. that it was out of the question that an official should show sympathy for a petitioner, that an official should listen to a personal plea and shape objective reality (the laws of nature) to an individual's wish. The laws of nature may be as complex as you please, disclosing ever greater depths of complexity, yet they remain inflexible, for otherwise they would not be laws—man is made for the world and not the world for man. But when he blunders accidentally into Bürgel's room in the middle of the night—for "according to an old saying, the secretaries' doors must always be open" [122]—the good-humored "liaison secretary" between the village and the castle, whose gnome-like, contradictory face appropriately combines the laughing childlike and the deeply thoughtful, encourages him to press on in his quest in spite of disappointments, and describes to him the rare, almost unheard of circumstances in which the official apparatus must surrender to an applicant's plea—in which the battlemented and moated world-reality standing over against the individual person must dissolve like frost under the first warm breath of the self's self-utterance, in which "the world will offer itself to you to be unmasked, it has no choice, it will writhe in raptures at your feet." [123]

"The secret lies in the regulations regarding competence. For it is not the case, and in such a large living organization it cannot be the case, that there is only one particular secretary competent to handle each matter. It is rather that one is mainly competent, but many others are also competent to a certain, even though lesser, extent. Who, even if he were the hardest of workers, could keep together on his desk, single-handed, all the connections and relations of even the most minor occurrence? Even what I have been saying about the main competence is saying too much. For is not the whole competence contained even in the smallest? Is not what is decisive here the passion with which the matter is tackled? And is this not always the same, always present in full intensity? In all things there may be distinctions among the secretaries, and there are countless such distinctions, but not in the passion; none of them will be able to restrain himself if it is demanded of him that he shall concern himself with a case in regard to which he is competent if only in the smallest degree. Externally, of course, an orderly operating procedure must be established, and so for every applicant one particular secretary comes forward as the one he must stick to officially. This, however, doesn't have to be the one most competent for the case, what is decisive here is the organization and its particular needs at any moment. That is how things are." [124]

The secretaries are K.'s own thoughts, the instruments of consciousness, reason itself, without which he cannot understand his being. But the essence of reason is to limit, to define; in understanding his own being he curtails and amputates it by confining it within the definitions of reason, which are to the fullness of being as a thimble is to the oceans. ("Who . . . could keep together on his desk . . . all the connections and relations of even the most minor occurrence," not to speak of the human self?) His understanding stands over against his being, serving the objective world-system—the external "organization and its particular needs"—not his own self. His life is constrained, confined, and determined by a necessity which is his own alienated understanding standing over against him, the courts and castles of the world. However, just because a category of reason is never "competent to handle any matter" fully, is never adequate to the fullness of no matter how small a bit of being, other categories must come to its assistance: "others are also competent to a certain, even though lesser, extent." That is, the secretaries must "deputize" for one another: "the officials generally deputize for one another and so it's difficult to perceive what this or that official is responsible for." [125] Conception must come to the aid of conception in order to uphold the whole externalized structure of understanding which is culture and history, because singly they are incapable of holding up even themselves. The external world of man's alienated self leans together like the boards of an old shack which hold one another up. The castle is also an old shack.* And as any bit of reality no matter how small has implicit in it the whole of reality, so, correspondingly, each competence no matter how small has implicit in it the whole or ultimate competence: "For is not the whole competence contained even in the smallest?" This is the chink in the armor of the world: in the limited responsibility of each official is implicit a plenary and final responsibility, in every official lurks a person; in each poor, limited, needy self is implicit the understanding of the whole self, if only it were possible for the self to utter itself wholly. The self passionately longs to understand the *whole* of itself, *universal* being, so as to transcend itself, so as to be and know its own being at the same time: subjectivity and objectivity, person and official. Man searches to reenter Paradise, in Kleist's words, by going all the way around the world and coming in the back door: innocence *and* knowledge, innocence through knowledge ultimate enough to grasp the universal law of the self, the "indestructible something" which redeems being from its fallen state.

What Bürgel discloses to K. is how to make the bureaucratic rational consciousness, which thrives on division of function and limitation of responsibility, behave personally, humanly, that is, take the responsibility for the whole human being; how to make the fixed objective world express—be one with—free subjective being, how to make the officials sit in the applicants' seats without ceasing to be officials, and vice versa.† The trick is for the applicant to catch the official apparatus unawares by coming unannounced into a secretary's room in the middle of the night and uttering his personal plea. The applicant cannot intend to do this because to intend it is to think about it and

* Weak and strong, like all the Kafka fathers, and like the door-keeper before the Law and the court judges.
† ". . . [T]he necessary barrier . . . between the applicants and the officials . . . weakens, and where otherwise, as is right, only questions and answers are bandied back and forth, what sometimes seems to take place is a singular, wholly improper exchanging of places between the persons." [126]

betray it to the official consciousness, which then is able to deal with the applicant with inhuman officialness. It has to happen without premeditation, between waking and sleeping, in the exhaustion and despair such as K. feels when he catches Bürgel unawares by coming unannounced into his room in the middle of the night. And when it does happen, the Leviathan world writhes in raptures at the applicant's feet, thirsting for (as well as fearing) its own transformation.

"And now, Master Land-Surveyor, consider the possibility that through some circumstance or other, in spite of the obstacles already described to you . . . an applicant does nevertheless, in the middle of the night, surprise a secretary who has a certain degree of competence with regard to the given case. I daresay you have never thought of such a possibility? That I will gladly believe . . . for it does, after all, practically never occur. . . .You think it cannot happen at all? You are right, it cannot happen at all. But some night—for who can answer for [bürgen*] everything—it does happen. Admittedly, I don't know anyone among my acquaintances to whom it has ever happened, but that proves very little to be sure . . . and besides it is by no means certain that a secretary to whom such a thing has happened will admit it, as it is, after all, a very personal matter that in a sense touches the official sense of shame. . . . You must only conceive the situation correctly. The never beheld, always expected applicant, truly thirstingly expected and always rationally regarded as out of reach—there this applicant sits. By his dumb presence alone he invites one to enter into his poor life, to look around† there as on one's own ground, and there to suffer with him and his unavailing demands. This invitation in the silent night is seductive. One gives way to it, and now one has actually ceased to function as an official. It is a situation in which it very soon becomes impossible to refuse a plea . . . even if . . . it positively tears the official organization to shreds. . . . Without being able to spare oneself in the slightest, one must show him in detail what has happened and for what reasons this has happened,

* "Bürgel" is the benign little brownie who "answers for" the fact that the castle organization cannot answer for everything.
† Sich umtun also means to apply for something—the official has become the applicant.

how extraordinarily rare and how uniquely great the opportunity is, one must show how the applicant, though he has stumbled into this opportunity in utter helplessness such as no other being is capable of than precisely an applicant, can, however, now, if he wants to, Master [*Herr*] Land-Surveyor, master [*beherrschen*] everything, and to that end has to do nothing but in some way or other utter his plea, for which fulfillment is already prepared, which indeed it is already coming to meet; it is the official's hour of travail. But when one has done as much as that, Master Land-Surveyor, everything essential has been done and then one must resign oneself and wait."

But K. falls asleep.

K. was asleep, impervious [*abge*schloss*en:* locked out of the *Schloss*, the castle] to everything that was happening.[127]

It needed an unheard of combination of consciousness *and* unconsciousness, sleeping *and* waking, thinking *and* being, knowledge *and* innocence. By prodigies of introspective effort K. arrives at the very gates, without knowing it. He does not know it because his very effort to know has stupefied him with fatigue. Thus he fulfills all the preliminary conditions for the breakthrough. But then when he is called upon to utter his plea his strength gives out and he loses the necessary consciousness of self. As Bürgel says to him when he is wakened by knocking on the wall: "One's bodily strength reaches only so far; who can help the fact that precisely this limit is significant in other ways too?" And he cries out irritably for K. to leave.

Once again the failure to reach the castle leaves K. stranded in a scene of desolation: "How indescribably desolate this room [of Bürgel's] now seemed to him." [128] After a curtly official interview with Erlanger, the secretary he had been summoned to the Herrenhof to see in the first place, daybreak finds him standing in the inn corridor, worn out to the point of collapse by two interrogations and no sleep, listening to the happy din of voices arising from the officials' rooms. It is "like the jubilation of children getting ready for a picnic . . . like daybreak in a hen-roost, like the joy of being completely in accord with the awaken-ing day, somewhere a gentleman even imitated the crowing of a cock." [129] K. stands there, not in the midst of awakening life, but in the midst of the "administration" of life starting up its daily operations. When two servants enter, pushing a little cart before them, and begin to distribute the files to the secretaries' rooms, the world-machine has started to operate. K. haunts the corridor, with his poor worn-out personal presence, like a "ghost" of the night, and delays the world's official day from breaking*—that is what the landlord and the landlady of the Herrenhof reproach him with when they hurry up in answer to the violent ringing of the secretaries' bells and hustle K. out of there: "K. [had] planted himself where he was most visible, and if by doing so he had been able to prevent the day from breaking, he would have done so. He could not prevent it, but, alas, he could delay it and make it more difficult. Had he not watched the distribution of the files? Something that nobody was allowed to watch except those directly concerned? Something that neither the landlord nor his wife had been allowed to see in their own house." [130]

Because of physical exhaustion, K. had not been able to grasp the opportunity Bürgel held out to him in his room. Straining to transform existence by uniting world and spirit, he had failed because he fell asleep—the physical limitations of the body have a spiritual significance too. Yet in his failure he has carried the self-searching of the poet (the searching of the modern self which is also the world) to so far a point that in the corridor he threatens, in his paradoxical state of unconsciousness-cum-overstrained consciousness, no longer to transform the world, but to destroy it, if that were at all possible. Though he could not stop the sun from rising, "alas, he could delay it and make it more difficult" by watching the distribution of the files, by ob-

* Gang, corridor, also means the workings, operations of a mech-anism; K. in the "Gang" is a little piece of particularity, an individual grain of sand that has unprecedentedly got into the universal works of the world-machine and threatens to bring it to a halt.

truding his particular being "suddenly and unmediatedly [*plötzlich unvermittelt*], in all its truth to nature," upon the abstract *Herren*. What sort of person would do that? the Herrenhof landlady demands. "Well, yes, it must be a person like K. Someone who rode roughshod over everything, both over the law and over the most ordinary human considerations, with this obtuse stuporousness and sleepiness of his, someone who simply did not care that he was making the distribution of the files almost impossible and damaging the reputation of the house and who brought about something that had never happened before, that the gentlemen, driven to desperation, had begun to defend themselves, and, after a conquest of their own nature inconceivable to ordinary people, had reached for the bell and called for help to drive K. away, upon whom nothing else could make any impression! They, the gentlemen, calling for help!" [131]

Joseph K. had told his landlady that if she wanted to keep up the reputation of her house she would have to throw him out of it—he had accused himself before the world. Now it is the Herrenhof landlady who accuses K. of hurting the reputation of her house—the world accuses K. before himself. Joseph K. had been ashamed before the court employees for whispering "louder" to the unchanging siren note of the ultimate sounding incomprehensibly through the court offices. But now the castle *Herren* shrink ashamed before K.'s "natural truth"; the great world stands accused before the ultimate truth of K.'s individual human self: ". . . [T]he gentlemen had not been able to come forth out of their rooms, since . . . they were too ashamed, too vulnerable, to be able to expose themselves before the gaze of strangers." [132] The impersonal necessitarian world, estranged from the concrete human being over whom it rules, quails and calls for help before the poet K.'s conscious (universal) assertion of his unconscious (concrete) being. The world cannot endure to be examined before the dumbness of being which yet through the poet's power struggles to find the tongue to utter itself, it can only dictate over dumb being from the abstract distance. But at this point of intolerable strain between the world and spirit the world comes to the aid of the world and K. is hustled out of the corridor. At last the sun is able to rise.

It is a kind of victory over the world that K. achieves, yet he no longer wants such victories, if indeed he ever did. He does not want to destroy the world, but to redeem it. K. carries spirituality to a point where it seems to threaten the world with destruction. But since the world is his own self written large, this is only to say that so extreme a spirituality threatens himself with destruction. At the end of the episode we see K. drawing back from this extreme. He apologizes to the landlord and his wife for upsetting their house. He blames his illegal presence in the Herrenhof corridor on excessive fatigue, the result of the unaccustomed strain of two successive nocturnal interrogations. He

> would gladly have done without all the prohibited insight . . . and this all the more readily since in reality he had been quite incapable of seeing anything, for which reason even the most sensitive gentlemen could have shown themselves before him without embarrassment.
>
> The mention of the two interrogations—particularly of that with Erlanger*—and the respect with which K. spoke of the gentleman inclined the landlord favorably toward him." [133]

K. would gladly have done without such insight, all the more so as he had seen nothing because of his extreme fatigue: his overstrained consciousness has repeated its earlier failure in Bürgel's room, only now K. is glad about it instead of desolated. Because in Bürgel's room he had stood at the door† of Paradise, on the point of redeeming the world, whereas in the Herrenhof corridor he seemed about to destroy it. K. does not hate the world, the fallen world. He speaks of the *Herren*—that is, the ruling life-powers—"with respect." This is not so startling a change in the "tramp" (*Landstreicher*) as it might seem. He respected the common life right from the start; it was never his intention to destroy it. One of his purposes in coming to the village was to

---

* Bürgel is not as respectable as Erlanger!
† Kleist's back door.

settle there and become a member of the community. Yet now that his vision reaches so much farther into the castle, so does his respect reach farther, as far as the officials themselves, whom he has learned to appreciate as upholders of the common life. Standing in the corridor, he had watched all the official activity there "not only with curiosity *but also with sympathy*. He almost felt at home in the midst of this bustle." [134] K. learns to respect the officials. But at the same time he does not stop regarding them as antagonists; he still does not feel at home in their midst, only "almost" at home. He will never cease from Mental Fight, he will never cease to be the land-surveyor K.

The last (twentieth) chapter of the novel might seem to be an anticlimax after the serio-comic sublimities of the encounter with Bürgel (Chapter Eighteen) and the scene in the Herrenhof corridor (Chapter Nineteen). However, these sublimities, like the sublime cathedral chapter in *The Trial*, are not climactic but cumulative and repeat the original situation with a more ultimate accent; they are a further "marching in place" (*stehendes Marschieren*), except that by this time K. is beginning to wear a hole in the ground just big enough to be his grave. And if there is no climax there can be no anticlimax. What happens in Chapter Twenty is that the novel, reverting to the erotic theme again, enables K. to review his relations with Frieda in the light of his wiser appreciation of the world. Here it is that he delivers his eulogy of her life-ability,[135] defending her against the foolish denigrations of Pepi, that almost touching embodiment of female shallowness and chagrin. And a new development of the erotic theme seems to be announced when Pepi proposes that K. should come and live secretly with her and her two fellow chambermaids in their little room in the bowels of the Herrenhof—secretly, because everywhere in the inn except the barroom is forbidden ground to K. But this new development, if it is that, is cut short by the breaking off of the novel.

The erotic theme is by no means subsidiary to what one may call the bureaucratic theme; the two are aspects of the novel's single matter. It looms more or less as large in Kafka as it does in Joyce and Yeats, Foster, Pirandello, and the early Eliot and Mann. All the tedious talk between Pepi and K. about dresses and ribbons, underwear and shoes, Frieda's short, thin hair that is not as clean as it might be and Pepi's luxuriant curls that nobody can resist touching, is no decline from high matter but its continuation by other means. And after all, Chapters Eighteen and Nineteen are tedious enough too—as K. himself finds while listening to Bürgel's droning voice: ". . . [B]e-tween the competent secretaries on the one hand and the non-competent on the other, and confronted with the crowd of fully occupied applicants, he would sink into deep sleep and in this way escape everything." [136] The Herrenhof, the shabby village outpost of a shabby castle, is no splendid hostelry but a country inn reserved for humdrum officials with nasty personal habits; according to Pepi's report, they make a filthy sty out of their rooms which it would take another Flood to flush clean. Every-where in Kafka there is the drabness of an undistinguished fallen world; he is, in the words of Edwin Muir's poem, the "sad champion of the drab and half," possessed by

> a famishing passion quick to grab
> Meaning, and read on all the leaves of sin
> Eternity's secret script, the saving proof.

Here again, though their quality is so different, he resembles Joyce.

After an enigmatic exchange, at the end of the chapter, be-tween K. and the touchy, super-refined Herrenhof landlady about her clothes, the novel trails off in a few fragments. The landlady accuses him of not telling the truth when he says he is a land-surveyor, and he accuses her of being more than a land-lady. To which she replies that he is "either a fool or a child, or a very wicked dangerous man" [137] and she orders him to leave, shouting after him, in *The Castle*'s last connected sentence, that perhaps she will send for him the following day to show him a new dress she is getting. It all has a threatening sound, especially as her calling him either a foolish innocent child or else a wicked dangerous man repeats the very same judgment pronounced on Georg Bendemann by his father just before he sentences him to death, in the story that begins Kafka's true career as a writer: "An innocent child, yes, that you were, truly, but still more truly have you been a diabolical man!" [138] Foolish child or wicked man or both—this is the world's judgment on the modern poet trying to redeem the world. The antithesis, conventional enough looking on its abstract face, is full of literal terror. It makes the poet's innocence a reproach and his visionary knowledge a crime, cutting off his escape before and behind and stifling him to death in a "windowless and airless cell." [139] Although experience and reflection have taught K. to be a redoubtable antagonist, we know that he must, not bow to the judgment like Georg, but collapse under it at last.

A New Kabbalah

On January 15, 1922, the month in which Kafka began to write *The Castle,* he noted in a diary entry already quoted from more than once that he had suffered something like a nervous breakdown the week before. It was possible, he wrote, to understand the breakdown in two ways, neither of which excluded the other. The first way was psychological: the near-collapse was the result of the split between his hyperactive inner life of introspection, which raced wildly on at a "fiendish or demonic or anyhow inhuman tempo," and his limping external life. He was afraid his frenzied introspection, which he called a "pursuit" or "chase" (*Jagd*), might end in utter isolation and madness, "the pursuit races right through me and tears me apart." However, if he was able to hang on to his sanity, then the near-breakdown might have a metaphysical-religious result, the "pursuit," when pressed to its limit, ending not in madness but in an "assault against the last earthly frontier."

But if I can—I can?—hold up even the littlest bit and let myself be borne along by the pursuit, then where will I end up? "Pursuit," of course, is only a metaphor, I can also say "assault against the last earthly frontier," an assault moreover from below, from the side of man, and since this is a metaphor too, I can replace it by the metaphor of an assault from above, aimed against me down below.

All this writing [meaning the early pages of *The Castle*] is an assault against the frontiers, and if Zionism hadn't intervened might easily have developed into a new secret doctrine, a Kabbalah. There are beginnings in that direction. Of course, it needs an almost inconceivable genius that would be able to strike root again in the old centuries, or would create the old centuries anew without using itself up in doing so, but would only then begin to flower forth.[140]

A compulsive introspectiveness which threatens to drive the poet mad might be mastered and transformed into the ultimate effort of *The Castle*, the mind's frenzied "pursuit" of itself might be turned into an "assault against the last earthly frontier" hidden in the mind*—the poet can save himself as it were poetically, by a switch of metaphors. Since the mind can never go beyond metaphor and reach anything-in-itself, it has a choice of metaphors. In this choice, which is apparently arbitrary, lies moral freedom; it offers the poet the possibility of a creative-religious transformation of his psychological defeat.

One notices how the diary entry does not distinguish between Kafka's introspection as a general psychological activity and the form it takes in his writing. Life and art have become identical. And in fact the entry expresses his feeling, as he faces the task of writing *The Castle*, that his very sanity depends upon the outcome of his effort to switch metaphors. Having set out to write the novel, having launched himself (or been pushed: imagination may be a psychological mechanism) into the boiling current of his introspective imaginings, he will either drown in his own

---

*Though there was a sneaking suspicion in him, as always, that the attack he thought he was making against the powers of the world was really their attack against him.

psychology or swim along in it to a last shore, beyond psychology. Dream stories of inner breakdown like *The Judgment* and *The Metamorphosis* or even *The Trial* will not do any more, his own life of near-breakdown will not do anymore; either he will go beyond the psychological or break down completely. A largely psychological art will not do anymore; either he will strike root again in the old centuries of the spirit and create a new Kabbalah, or he will lose his mind in a modern wasteland in which one thought endlessly follows another without ever reaching a final conclusion.

One of the most important things Kafka says in the entry is that both ways of understanding his near-breakdown are true, the psychological and the more than psychological, the metaphor of "pursuit" and the metaphor of "assault against the last earthly frontier." In turning back to the past he does not, like some of his colleagues in the modern movement, foolishly deny modern truth. Kafka's imagination is a modern psychoanalytic one from start to finish, but at the finish it is more than psychoanalytic, having turned back to the allegorical old centuries to find help in the great task of imagining modern life, of "making the modern world," as Eliot said about *Ulysses,* "possible for art." [141] His old breakdown stories were an art of "misfortune," [142] of immersion and drowning in the modern; now he needed a form in which K., without ceasing to be immersed in it, could yet struggle with it and try to grasp it as a whole—a form that thrusts K. into the very midst of modernity and yet enables him to survey it as a whole as it were from the outside. Kafka found that form in the allegorical modification of the dream narrative. The more or less psychological symbols of the dream story are charged, in *The Castle,* with a weight of generalizing thought that gives them a peculiar allegorical quality, without their ceasing to be symbols. Thanks to allegory K. is able to survey systematically the concrete existence in which he flounders. The bug in *The Metamorphosis* is a symbol that wells out of ground that our minds, following Kafka's, identify as being more or less psychological. The stranger K. in *The Castle* is just such a psychological symbol too.

But he is also the land-surveyor K. who shoulders a burden of assigned meaning which makes him allegorical as well. The invidious distinction drawn between symbol and allegory, the one living and mysterious and the other cut-and-dried, mechanical, which was stressed by such poets as Goethe, Coleridge, and Yeats and is an accepted truth of our criticism, blurs considerably in Kafka's case.*

The Castle is indeed the new Kabbalah that Kafka saw the beginnings of in the first pages of the novel he had started to write, because hidden within it there is a secret doctrine elaborated allegorically on the basis of the literalized understanding of words and images. Literalization, which is an important element of the dream story from the very first, as it is an important element of the dream itself, is pushed in the novel to the point where commonplace words and phrases allegorically utter ultimate things, the "slightly sloping [sinking] corridor" [143] (*ein wenig sich senkenden Gang*) of the Herrenhof meaning exactly that, but also (playing on the other meaning of *Gang*) the slow running down of the world-machine. Secreted within the story's terrible dreariness and pettiness and constriction is nothing less than the world itself, grandiosely imagined on an almost Dantesque scale.

At the heart of *The Castle*'s "hidden doctrine" is K.'s striving to unite with the officials, and that bears an obvious resemblance to the Kabbalist's striving for *unio mystica*. In place however of the mystic's union with God, K. seeks union with a modern ultimate that is imperfect in its essence, so as to redeem it from its imperfection. In other words he struggles, not to unite with the divine, which does not exist, but to unite with himself and in that way cause the divine to exist, in himself and through himself in the world. (Which is not so different from the mystic's

* Perhaps it blurs in Joyce's case too. Bloom is as allegorically "ideal" (and therefore touched with a certain blankness) as he is naturalistically dense; he is as much a designed figure as a dramatized one. As realistic as *Ulysses* is, the realism is not self-sufficient, an end in itself, but is a cover for the allegory, just as the modern actuality "covers" the spiritual.

effort after all.) Kafka soars to the giddiest heights of Romanticism, wishing to create, not merely worlds like God (Joyce's ambition and the classical ambition of the great poet), but God Himself in himself (Blake's ambition). But since that is a possibility which is, "in a manner of speaking, too great to be made use of, [something that is] wrecked on nothing but [itself]," [144] he also drops to the dreariest, most disappointed depths of Realism. Kafka may say with Flaubert: "Madame Bovary, c'est moi."

The officials of the castle signify the forces working within K. himself as they emerge abstractly into consciousness; their overpowering generality of idea and his poor particularity of being make up the macrocosmic modern existence of village and castle. Conversely, the macrocosm or universe is only K.'s and everybody's microcosm spread all over the landscape. Thanks to Kafka's psychoanalytic imagination, which reached back to the old centuries and joined hands with the radical imagination of the self of Kabbalistic allegory, he is able to plant the whole huge buzzing modern macrocosm squarely inside K.'s dreaming microcosmic head.

Dostoyevsky's *Notes from the Underground* is a paradoxical composition not only because it consists of the notes of a "paradoxicalist," as the Russian writer calls his unhappy protagonist at the very end, but because it is both a story and an essay. It is a story in virtue of being an extraordinarily acute and vivid portrait of the Underground Man by the most penetrating literary psychologist of the nineteenth century or perhaps the entire modern age. It is an essay in virtue of being the Underground Man's critique of the modern scientific world view. As passionately as that critique is conducted, it remains abstract thought; what is passionate, what is concrete is the psychological man himself, fiercely uttering his ideas about himself and the world to himself. Dostoyevsky can imagine the Underground Man wrestling with the idea of the modern world, but he cannot yet imagine the idea itself of that world. The nineteenth century could think about the idea of the modern world, but it could not, within the limits of its realism, imagine that idea as a concrete reality. It could not, in other words, poetically grasp the life it lived at a level of universality comparable to that of the epic and the tragedy and the allegory of the old centuries. That is what Kafka, and the whole modern movement of the twentieth century, did.*

However the modern writers, unlike the poets of the old universal literature, stood opposed to and spiritually outside the world they lived in; they contemned its values rather than glorifying them. Heirs of Rousseau (as we all are) in weighing society in the scales of human good, rather than living in it unthinkingly as given (the lot of man before the advance of modern consciousness), they renewed the dissent of the Romantic poets with a civilization that was antipoetical, antispiritual, antivital. But unlike the great Romantic poetry, which at the beginning of the nineteenth century could still turn its back on the city and affirm the positive of Nature without being guilty of a flight from reality, the great modern literature was stuck in the world it contemned; lacking any ground to stand on, it was condemned to a negative universality. Kafka's dream-story form, when it finally embraced the entire modern world, considered as a universal idea, and forced it to submit to poetization in *The Castle,* became a kind of negative epic. It could go no further.

* This effort is what Stephen Spender calls "the struggle of the modern."

ACKNOWLEDGMENTS

The author gratefully acknowledges permission to quote from the following:

Max Brod, *Franz Kafka: A Biography,* translated by G. Humphrey Roberts and Richard Winston (New York: Schocken Books, 1960). Reprinted by permission of the publisher. Copyright © 1960 by Schocken Books Inc.

Wilhelm Emrich, *Franz Kafka* (Frankfurt: Athenäum Verlag, 1958). Reprinted by permission of the publisher. Copyright © 1957 by Athenäum Verlag GmbH Frankfurt am Main.

Ronald Gray, "Introduction" to *Kafka: A Collection of Critical Essays,* Ronald Gray, ed. (Englewood Cliffs, N.J.: Prentice-Hall, 1962). Reprinted by permission of the publisher. Copyright © 1962 by Prentice-Hall, Inc.

Franz Kafka, *Amerika,* translated by Edwin Muir (New York: New Directions, 1946). Reprinted by permission of the publisher. Copyright © 1946 by New Directions Publishing Corporation.

Franz Kafka, *Briefe, 1902–1924* (New York: Schocken Books, 1958). Reprinted by permission of the publisher. Copyright © 1958 by Schocken Books Inc.

Franz Kafka, *The Castle,* translated by Willa and Edwin Muir, with additional material translated by Eithne Wilkins and Ernst Kaiser (New York: Alfred A. Knopf, 1954). Reprinted by permission of the publisher. Copyright © 1930, 1958 by Alfred A. Knopf, Inc.

Franz Kafka, *The Diaries of Franz Kafka, 1910–1913,* translated by Joseph Kresh (New York: Schocken Books, 1949). Reprinted by permission of the publisher. Copyright © 1948 by Schocken Books Inc.

Franz Kafka, *The Diaries of Franz Kafka, 1914–1923,* translated by Martin Greenberg with the cooperation of Hannah Arendt (New York: Schocken Books, 1949). Reprinted by permission of the publisher. Copyright © 1949 by Schocken Books Inc.

Franz Kafka, *Dearest Father: Stories and Other Writings,* translated by Ernst Kaiser and Eithne Wilkins (New York: Schocken Books, 1954). Reprinted by permission of the publisher. Copyright © 1954 by Schocken Books Inc.

Franz Kafka, *Description of a Struggle,* translated by Tania and James Stern (New York: Schocken Books, 1958). Reprinted by

NOTES

Abbreviations

A   *Amerika,* translated by Edwin Muir. New York: New Directions, 1946.

B   Max Brod, *Franz Kafka: A Biography,* translated by G. Humphrey Roberts and Richard Winston, 2nd ed. New York: Schocken Books, Inc., 1960.

Br   *Briefe, 1902–1924.* New York: Schocken Books, Inc., 1958.

C   *The Castle,* translated by Willa and Edwin Muir, with additional materials translated by Eithne Wilkins and Ernst Kaiser, New York: Alfred A. Knopf, 1954.

D–I   *The Diaries of Franz Kafka, 1910–1913,* translated by Joseph Kresh. New York: Schocken Books, Inc., 1949.

D–II   *The Diaries of Franz Kafka, 1914–1923,* translated by Martin Greenberg, with the cooperation of Hannah Arendt. New York: Schocken Books, Inc., 1949.

DF   *Dearest Father: Stories and Other Writings,* translated by Ernst Kaiser and Eithne Wilkins. New York: Schocken Books, Inc., 1954.

DS   *Description of a Struggle,* translated by Tania and James Stern, New York: Schocken Books, Inc., 1958.

G   *The Great Wall of China: Stories and Reflections,* translated by Willa and Edwin Muir. New York: Schocken Books, Inc., 1946.

J   Gustav Janouch, *Conversations with Kafka,* translated by Goronwy Rees. New York: Frederick A. Praeger, 1953.

M   *Letters to Milena,* translated by Tania and James Stern. New York: Schocken Books, Inc., 1953.

P   *The Penal Colony: Stories and Short Pieces,* translated by Willa and Edwin Muir. New York: Schocken Books, Inc., 1948.

T   *The Trial,* translated by Willa and Edwin Muir. Revised, and with additional materials translated by E. M. Butler. New York: Random House (The Modern Library), 1957.

Chapter One

1. D–I, 45
2. D–I, 245
3. Matthew Arnold, in "The Literary Influence of the Academies"
4. D–II, 187
5. Klaus Wagenbach, *Franz Kafka: Eine Biographie Seiner Jugend 1883–1912* (Bern: Francke Verlag, 1958), 90
6. D–II, 145
7. D–I, 275–276
8. D–I, 278
9. D–I, 309
10. DF, 91
11. C, 80
12. *The Collected Letters of D. H. Lawrence*, ed. Harry T. Moore (New York: The Viking Press, 1962), I, 442
13. T, 286
14. J, 97
15. D–I, 288
16. D–I, 318
17. D–II, 200, 202
18. G, 302; DF, 45
19. D–II, 68
20. B, 230
21. DF, 59
22. J, 35
23. Wagenbach, 88*ff*.
24. P, 80
25. P, 143
26. Cf. Wilhelm Emrich, *Franz Kafka* (Frankfurt, West Germany: Athenäum Verlag, 1958)
27. J, 34
28. C, 241
29. Cf. Stephen Spender, *The Struggle of the Modern* (Berkeley and Los Angeles: University of California Press, 1963), 9 *et passim*
30. Cf. Heinz Politzer, *Franz Kafka, Parable and Paradox* (Ithaca, New York: Cornell University Press, 1962), 84*ff*.
31. Wagenbach, 199
32. Selma Fraiberg, "Kafka and the Dream," *Modern Literary Criticism*, ed. Irving Howe (Boston: Beacon Press, 1958), 197
33. Wagenbach, 102
34. D–I, 192
35. Br, 116
36. G, 289
37. M, 217
38. G, 289–290; DF, 39
39. M, 217–218
40. C, 3
41. M, 136
42. M, 100
43. Br, 320
44. J, 85
45. *What Is Literature?* (New York: Harper Colophon Books, 1965), 31

46. B, 109
47. Wagenbach, 175
48. D–I, 57
49. DF, 78
50. G, 293
51. J, 47
52. D–II, 213–214
53. Quoted in Martin Turnell, *The Novel in France* (New York: Vintage Books, 1958), 262–263
54. M, 59
55. M, 68–69
56. Br, 322
57. D–I, 162
58. G, 260
59. Wagenbach, 125
60. *Ibid.*, 97
61. M, 219
62. D–II, 11
63. D–II, 126
64. Wagenbach, 94
65. *Ibid.*
66. Cf. Freud, *The Interpretation of Dreams* (New York: Science Editions, Inc., 1961), 339–340
67. Published in English in *The Penal Colony*

Chapter Two

1. D–I, 250
2. Wagenbach, 237
3. DS, 15
4. *Beschreibung eines Kampfes* (New York: Schocken Books, Inc., 1946), 312
5. Wagenbach, 123
6. DS, 62
7. P, 14
8. Br, 29
9. DS, 62
10. G, 268
11. DS, 75
12. DF, 2
13. Wagenbach, 238
14. DF, 3
15. DF, 6–7
16. G, 267
17. Wagenbach, 54, 60
18. Emrich, 31–32
19. Quoted in Turnell, *op. cit.*, 298
20. *Ibid.*, 313
21. Spender, 17
22. Emrich, 67–69
23. DS, 195
24. DF, 106
25. Emrich, 99
26. G, 267–268
27. *Der Veruntreute Himmel* (Frankfurt, West Germany: Fischer Bücherei, 1952), 243; Wagenbach, 96
28. G, 263–264
29. Wagenbach, 78
30. C, 74
31. C, 73

Chapter Three

1. Erich Heller, *Thomas Mann: the Ironic German* (New York: Meridian Books, 1961), 112–113

2. T, 264
3. P, 60
4. *A Portrait of the Artist as a Young Man* (New York: The Viking Press, 1956), 308
5. "Kafka the Artist," in *Kafka: a Collection of Critical Essays,* ed. Ronald Gray (Englewood Cliffs, New Jersey: Prentice-Hall Inc., 1962), 25
6. P, 39
7. Walter Benjamin, "Franz Kafka," *Schriften,* II (Frankfurt a.M., 1955), 200
8. B, 129
9. "The Judgment," *Franz Kafka Today,* eds. Angel Flores and Homer Swander (Madison, Wisconsin: University of Wisconsin Press, 1958), 5–24
10. *Collected Papers,* IV, 180
11. D–I, 214
12. D–II, 79
13. D–II, 115
14. D–I, 279
15. DF, 177
16. DF, 177
17. DF, 191
18. D–I, 278–279
19. Benjamin, 198
20. D–II, 213
21. G, 297
22. G, 298
23. G, 46–47
24. *Mimesis: the Representation of Reality in Western Literature* (Princeton, New Jersey: Princeton University Press, 1953), 13*ff.*
25. See p. 5

Chapter Four

1. D–II, 323, note 59
2. *Image and Idea* (Norfolk, Connecticut: New Directions, 1957), 121–139
3. P, 80
4. DF, 195
5. P, 108
6. See p. 71, note
7. Emrich, 124
8. D–II, 202
9. Politzer, 76
10. G, 283; DF, 36
11. D–II, 102
12. *Classics and Commercials* (New York: Farrar, Straus, 1950), 391
13. Fraiberg, *op. cit.,* 218
14. D–II, 187
15. M, 100
16. "The Fate of Pleasure," *Beyond Culture: Essays on Literature and Learning* (New York: The Viking Press, 1965), 73, 74
17. B, 234

Chapter Five

1. D–I, 276
2. D–II, 188
3. A, 251
4. A, 30
5. D–II, 77
6. Politzer, 122
7. A, 38–39
8. Emrich, 236
9. Cf. Martin Walser, *Beschreibung einer Form* (Munich: Carl Hanser Verlag, 1961), 44–72
10. *Letters I*, 282
11. A, 227
12. J, 85
13. A, 15
14. Emrich, 247
15. A, 174
16. G, 265
17. *The Kafka Problem*, ed. Angel Flores (New York: Octagon Books, 1963), 142
18. P, 198
19. Emrich, 221
20. *Ibid.*, 223
21. G, 209–211
22. Emrich, 223–224
23. *Ibid.*, 226
24. See p. 45
25. T, 276

Chapter Six

1. T, 23
2. T, 319
3. T, 26
4. G, 287; DF, 40
5. G, 298–299; DF, 43–44
6. Emrich, 181–182, 262. My discussion of *The Trial* (and of *The Castle*) is especially indebted to Professor Emrich's study
7. T, 3
8. T, 17
9. T, 264
10. G, 270
11. T, 205
12. T, 26
13. T, 10
14. T, 26–27
15. T, 27
16. T, 7
17. T, 264
18. T, 9
19. T, 10
20. T, 19
21. T, 44–45
22. See the passages beginning "As someone said . . ." (T, 318–319) and "They went along several paths . . ." (T, 325)
23. Cf. Herman Uyttersprott, "*The Trial*: Its Structure," *Franz Kafka Today*, 127–144
24. T, 12
25. T, 282–283
26. T, 10
27. P, 204
28. T, 13–14
29. T, 77

30. T, 17–18
31. T, 145
32. T, 235
33. T, 156
34. Emrich, 282
35. T, 223
36. T, 144
37. T, 187
38. T, 9
39. T, 17
40. T, 266–267
41. T, 283
42. T, 7
43. T, 282
44. T, 33–34
45. Emrich, 275–276
46. T, 286
47. T, 37
48. T, 38
49. T, 266
50. T, 198
51. T, 278
52. Emrich, 276
53. T, 7
54. T, 8
55. T, 11
56. P, 60
57. T, 280
58. T, 285
59. DF, 101
60. T, 48–50
61. T, 61
62. T, 65
63. T, 89
64. T, 134–135
65. T, 182–184
66. T, 197
67. T, 195
68. T, 189
69. T, 269–276
70. T, 138

71. T, 277
72. T, 233
73. T, 244
74. T, 221
75. T, 242–243
76. DF, 97
77. T, 245
78. T, 286
79. T, 197
80. T, 193
81. T, 8
82. T. S. Eliot, "Religion and Literature," *Selected Essays* (New York: Harcourt, Brace and Co., 1951)
83. "Kafka's Distorted Mask," *Kafka: A Collection of Critical Essays*, 145
84. "Introduction," *ibid.*, 4–5
85. Br, 27
86. See Walser, 111–127, for a discussion of what he calls Kafka's epic form and progression by addition in the epic
87. DS, 35
88. J, 34
89. " 'Ulysses,' Order, and Myth," *Criticism: The Foundations of Modern Literary Judgment*, eds. Mark Schorer *et al.* (New York and Burlingame: Harcourt, Brace and World, 1958)
90. Quoted in Richard Ellman, *James Joyce* (New York: Oxford University Press, 1959), 169
91. "On Simple and Sentimental Poetry"

Chapter Seven

1. C, 33
2. C, 75–76
3. C, 419
4. C, 95
5. D–II, 202
6. J, 35
7. C, 3
8. G, 97
9. C, 266
10. C, 74
11. C, 433
12. D–II, 202
13. Emrich, 85–87
14. C, 12
15. C, 12
16. C, 8 (The Muirs translated "*Frau und Kind*" as "home")
17. D–II, 202
18. C, 420
19. Alfred North Whitehead, *Religion in the Making* (New York: Meridian Books, 1960), 47–48
20. C, 4–5
21. C, 9
22. C, 5
23. C, 6
24. C, 6–7
25. C, 7
26. D–II, 202
27. C, 116
28. D–II, 202
29. C, 452–453
30. C, 423–424
31. C, 21
32. Erich Heller, "The World of Franz Kafka," *Kafka: A Collection of Critical Essays,* 111
33. C, 14
34. C, 80
35. C, 465
36. C, 14
37. C, 51
38. C, 72
39. G, 296; DF, 42
40. C, 31–32
41. C, 32–33
42. C, 144–145
43. P, 161
44. C, 77
45. C, 30
46. C, 37
47. C, 92
48. C, 133
49. C, 139
50. C, 142
51. C, 95–96
52. C, 14
53. C, 15–19
54. D–II, 209
55. C, 465
56. C, vi
57. C, 96
58. C, 335–336
59. C, 422
60. C, 337–338
61. C, 59
62. C, 54–55
63. C, 56
64. C, 475
65. C, 446
66. C, 115
67. C, 116
68. C, 121
69. C, 123
70. C, 169
71. C, 258
72. C, 199–200

73. C, 111–112
74. C, 62
75. C, 65
76. C, 112
77. C, 71–72
78. C, 72–73
79. C, 151
80. C, 67
81. C, 54
82. C, 435–436
83. Emrich, 317–320
84. C, 135
85. C, 141
86. C, 182
87. C, 184
88. C, 182
89. C, 183
90. C, 178–179
91. C, 207
92. C, 62
93. C, 404–405
94. T, 282
95. G, 278; DF, 34
96. C, 258
97. C, 401
98. C, 93
99. C, 241
100. C, 239–240
101. C, 231–232
102. C, 231
103. C, 110
104. C, 231
105. C, 277–279
106. C, 279–280
107. C, 281–282
108. C, 229

109. C, 220–221
110. C, 266
111. C, 272
112. C, 267
113. Emrich, 356–373
114. C, 244–245
115. C, 256
116. C, 248
117. C, 250
118. C, 244
119. C, 273
120. C, 285–286
121. C, 300
122. C, 334
123. G, 307; DF, 48
124. C, 346
125. C, 244
126. C, 339–340
127. C, 346–350
128. C, 351
129. C, 356
130. C, 368
131. C, 369–370
132. C, 369
133. C, 373
134. C, 357
135. See pp. 190–191
136. C, 345
137. C, 412
138. P, 62
139. D–II, 197
140. D–II, 202–203
141. See p. 152, note
142. See p. 148
143. C, 359
144. C, 351

INDEX

atheism, 17, 36, 45, 111
Auerbach, Eric, 67
Austro-Hungarian Empire, 11, 24–25
authority: absolute, 112; court, 120–121, 124–129, 132–146; disrespect for, 45, 164; God-like, 17, 49; inhuman, 16, 65; supreme, justice based on, 109; ultimate, 144
autobiographical notes, Kafka's, 44–45
automatism: bureaucratic, 13; world, 94, 158, 163–164, 168, 171, 173
ax of truth, 155

"Bachelor's Ill Luck," 43–44
Beast in the Jungle, The, 149
"Before the Law," 13–14, 140, 201
Beissner, Friedrich, 52
Benjamin, Walter, 65
Beschreibung einer Form, 151
Beyond Good and Evil, 137
Beyond the Pleasure Principle, 89 n.
Biblical narrative, 66, 67
Blake, William, 173, 219
bohemianism, 25
Broch, Hermann, 30
Brod, Max, 10, 17 n., 18, 20, 23, 24, 28–30, 32, 34, 36, 70 n., 90 n., 101 n., 103 n., 177
bureaucracy, 7, 16, 50, 97, 103, 171, 179; paternalistic, 103
bureaucratic automatism, 13
bureaucratic consciousness, 15, 207

calculating consciousness, 6
Canaan, 22
Captain's Doll, The, 189

"Cares of a Family Man, The," 172 n.
Castle, The, 8, 12–14, 16, 17, 31, 40, 46 n., 48, 52 n., 65, 84, 94, 96–98, 122, 148, 151, 154–200
"Children on a Country Road," 42
Christ, 144 n.
civilization: creativity and, 7; European, conscience and consciousness of, 15
classical style, 4, 11, 13, 30, 48–50, 98
Coleridge, Samuel Taylor, 47, 52 n., 81 n., 87 n., 92, 164, 218
Colet, Louise, 22 n.
collapsing conceptions, 31–32
comedy, 94, 132–136, 138–140, 143, 145, 148, 164, 182, 205
comparison, 194–195
conceiving consciousness, 10–11
conceptions, 37–38; collapsing, 31–32; and obscure intention, 97; rival historical, 112
concrete ideas, 102
concrete images, 12, 13, 102, 103
concrete reality, 219–220
concrete universality, 164, 167, 188, 220
concreteness, 32, 96, 102, 167, 171, 173, 174
Conrad, Joseph, 37
conscience, 7; alienated, 121, 130, 132–133, 145–146; of European civilization, 15; law and, 121, 132–133
consciousness, 7–8; abstract, 167 n., 172, 219; acute, 88, 164; bureaucratic, 15, 207; calculating, 6; conceiving, 10–11; deliberating, 7; ethical, 115; of European civilization, 15;

and existence, split between, 49–50; habitual, 114; innocence and, 8, 168; modern, advance of, 220; of necessity, 200–201; official, 207–208; rational, 111; rationalizing, 7; spiritual, 169; surface, 150; true, 200–201; universal religious, 162

construction(s), 6; artificial, 6, 30, 31; intellectual, 99

contradictions, 62, 63, 159, 168, 172, 177–178, 184–185

conventional reality, 33

"Conversation with the Supplicant," 31

"Country Doctor, A," 4, 14, 157 n.

court authority, 120–121, 124–129, 132–146

creativity, 6, 7, 151

Czech literature, 14

Czech nationalism, 25 n.

Daedalus, 152

Dagon, 109

Darwin, Charles, 36

David Copperfield, 93

daydream, 35

death: Kafka's understanding of, 84–86; redemption and, 71, 83, 84, 106–107, 110, 178

Death in Venice, 48–49, 67–68

Death of Ivan Ilyich, The, 70, 134 n., 149

Dedalus, Stephen, 37–38, 50

deliberating consciousness, 7

delusions, 72, 201

dénouement, 69, 70, 84, 86, 124

Der Verschollene, 101 n.

Description of a Struggle, 29–36, 39, 45

deterministic law, 90

diary entries, 3–6, 9, 14, 15, 25, 28, 44, 59–60, 63, 68, 84–85, 93, 94, 215–217

Dickens, Charles, 93, 94

didactic-visionary talks, 194

discipline, justice and, 94, 100

disillusionment, 189, 201–203

dissociated knowledge, 128

Dostoyevsky, Fëdor, 87–90, 115–116 n., 164, 219

dramatic-psychological mode of realism, 194

dream-metaphysical narrative, 122, 162

dream narrative(s), 8–9; allegorical modification of, 217–218; concentrated poetic force of, 104; Freudian influence on, 24; images and, 13, 27, 47, 48, 53, 149, 150, 156, 157, 178; literalization and, 218; metaphysical-religious, 162; psychological symbols of, 178, 217; reason and, 155; religious history and, 108–109; rhetorical-realistic nature of, 195; simple-subtle form of, 51; and thought story, union of, 14, 157–159, 162; *see also* narrative form

dreams: Freudian conception of, 14–15; illusion and, 14; imagination and, 195; Kafka's conception of, 14, 15, 24, 26, 155; literalism and, 13, 15; and reality, 10–11, 14–15, 45, 71, 155, 195; truth revealed in, 10–11, 14–15, 26, 155, 156

drive, 89; sex, 181, 188

Duineser Elegien, 38 n.

effeminate sentimentality, 110

ego-personality, 98

Einstein, Albert, 46
Eliot, T. S., 11, 146, 152, 214, 217
empirical narrative form, 94, 95, 152
empirical reality, 51
emptiness, 18, 25, 96, 98, 99, 155, 180–181
Emrich, Wilhelm, 36, 97, 102, 107, 110–111 n., 158, 202
English prose, 4
enlightenment, 105, 124
episodic narrative, 87 n., 93, 100, 104, 122, 149, 151
estrangement, 29, 40, 41
eternal innocence, 115
eternal life, 8
ethical consciousness, 115
ethical-ontological law, 143
European civilization, conscience and consciousness of, 15
evil, see good and evil
excogitated images, 13–14, 157
expressionism, 36

failure, life-, 9, 32, 89, 114, 169
Fall of Man, 114, 117
fallen state, 116–117, 207
fallen world, 212
fear, 9, 18–19, 46, 114, 117, 138
Finnegans Wake, 38 n.
Flaubert, Gustave, 15, 22 n., 37, 219
form, see dream narrative; narrative form
Forster, E. M., 142 n., 159
fragments, 29, 33, 34, 38, 104, 147, 151, 159, 214; see also unity
freedom, 12, 41, 65, 80–81, 90, 96–97, 99, 101, 103–104; moral, 216; sexual, 130–132, 151, 181, 188; spiritual, 17
French prose, 4

Freud, Sigmund, 6, 14–16, 24, 26, 46, 47, 56, 59 n., 113

German Gymnasium, 4, 36
German nationalism, 25
German prose, 4, 40
God: belief in, 17, 18; disobedience of, 117; hidden, 67; mystic's union with, 218; as supreme bureaucrat, 65–66
Godlike authority, 17, 49
Goethe, Johann Wolfgang von, 15, 51, 99, 102, 158, 218
Golden Bowl, The, 38 n.
good and evil: knowledge of, 114–117, 121, 136, 145; truth and, 6–7
graphic pensées, 30
Gray, Ronald, 147, 148
Great Wall of China, The, 13, 147, 157
guilt: denial of, 116, 117, 121, 123, 132, 133; doubt and, 105; metaphysical, 118; sin and, 66, 84; universal, 103, 116

habitual consciousness, 114
Haeckel, Ernst Heinrich, 36
Hamlet, 87, 153, 164
Hebrew Scriptures, 109 n.
Heine, Heinrich, 46
historical allegory, 108–109
Holz, Arno, 36
Homeric narrative, 67
Howards End, 142 n.
"Hunger Artist, A," 122
"Hunter Gracchus, The," 13, 107 n., 157

ideas: absolute, 95, 112; abstract, 103, 203; allegory and, 105; concrete, 102; images and, 12, 99, 102–105; relative, 112 idiom, 4

ignorance, 7, 121, 144, 168, 185–186

illness, 16; medicine and, 19; neurotic, 17–18; and sin, 19 *n.*

illusion, 10, 74; dreams and, 14; neurotic, 18; spiritual concern and, 201

image(s): concrete, 12, 13, 102, 103; dream-narrative, 13, 27, 47, 48, 53, 149, 150, 156, 157, 178; excogitated, 13–14, 157; ideas and, 12, 99, 102–105; literal, 14, 27, 34, 47; medical, 12; Ulyssean, 152; unity of, 104, 149–153

image cumulation, 152, 178

imagination, 5, 7–9, 37 *n.*, 87 *n.*, 151, 153; dreams and, 195; psychoanalytic, 26, 47, 200, 216, 217, 219

imaginative reasonings, 13

"Imperial Message, An," 13–14, 201

In the Penal Colony, 8, 52 *n.*, 104–112, 124, 157–158 *n.*, 160

indestructible something, trust in, 17–18, 38, 83, 112, 207

indestructible truth, 145

individual truth, 143

infinite knowledge, 115

inhuman authority, 16, 65

inhumanity, 107, 110, 111, 208

injustice, 7, 99, 107, 110–112, 116, 117, 132, 134

innocence, 93, 101, 103; consciousness and, 8, 168; eternal, 115; knowledge and, 207, 209; natural, 57; of Paradise, 167; pleas of, 116, 117, 121, 123, 124, 133; universal, 116

insomnia, 19 *n.*

inspiration, 3, 6, 8, 39

instinctual truth, 7

intellectual construction, 99

intellectual equivocation, 111

intellectual provenance, 36

intellectual subtlety, 51

intention(s): obscure, 97; symbolical, 94–97

introspection, 8–9, 10 *n.*, 14, 155 n., 158, 159, 161, 209, 215–216

intuition, 6; Romantic, 173

Investigations of a Dog, 13, 42, 66, 157

irrationality, 7, 15, 49, 142, 148, 149; religious, 21

Italian novella, 51

James, Henry, 37, 38 *n.*, 149

Janouch, Gustav, 8, 10, 12, 19 *n.*, 22, 99, 155

Jesenka, Milena, 9–10, 17–18, 22–23, 25, 86, 90 *n.*

Jewish messianic tradition, 22

"Josephine the Singer," 157

Joyce, James, 11, 36, 37, 48–50, 152, 194, 214, 218 *n.*

Judaism, 25

Judgment, The, 5–6, 8, 12, 13, 16, 27, 30, 31, 38, 45, 48–67, 76, 93, 98, 133–134, 217

justice, 101, 106; absolute, 109, 110; discipline and, 94, 100; revenge and, 108; supreme authority and, 109; true 145; ultimate, 112, 146

Kafka, Hermann, 22, 24 *n.*, 62–64, 138 *n.*, 169 *n.*

Kleist, Heinrich von, 7–8, 15, 32, 36, 51, 81 *n.*, 168, 207, 212 *n.*

knowledge, 7; abstract universal, 164, 167; apple of, 117, 167; dissociated, 128; of good and

knowledge (*cont'd*)
evil, 114–117, 121, 136, 145; of indestructible truth, 145; infinite, 115; innocence and, 207, 209; of reality, 10–11; of responsibility, 114–115, 123–124; scientific, 115
Knowledge, Tree of, 6, 8, 66, 84, 123 *n.*, 167, 168

law(s): conformity to, 8; and conscience, 121, 132–133; deterministic, 90; ethical-ontological, 143; ignorance of, 121, 144; inhumanity of, 107, 110, 111; of life, 159, 167, 173, 181; of nature, 89, 142–143, 205; of necessity, 136–137, 142–143; new, 109–112; old, 109–112; of truth of things, 143; universal, 204, 207
lawless sentimentality, 108
Lawrence, D. H., 7 *n.*, 11, 37, 98, 189 *n.*
Le Poittevin, Alfred, 22 *n.*
life, laws of, 159, 167, 173, 181
Life, Tree of, 6, 66, 84, 95
life-confusion, 160, 161, 168–170
life-failure, 9, 32, 89, 114, 169
literal images, 14, 27, 34, 47
literal truth, 13, 120
literalism, 13, 15, 27, 34, 124, 215
literalization, 194, 218
literary standards, 146
"Little Fable," 24
logic, 148
loneliness, 95, 161, 172, 176
love, spiritual and worldly, 195

magic, 10, 33; sentimental, 103

Mann, Thomas, 22 *n.*, 36, 37, 48–50, 68, 214
Marx, Karl, 46
Marxism, 25
mechanical reversal, 102–103
medical image, 12
medicine, 18
Meditation, 27, 30, 39, 42, 53 *n.*
melancholy, 40, 42, 103
"Memoirs of the Kalda Railroad," 59–60
mentally constructed reality, 6
messianic hope, 21–22
Metamorphosis, The, 5, 8, 10, 16, 31, 35, 69–91, 98, 122, 124, 155, 163, 217
metaphor, 11–13, 39, 48, 51, 63, 71, 73, 86, 99, 104, 120, 150, 175–176, 179, 216, 217
metaphorical reality, 51
metaphysical guilt, 118
metaphysical narrative, 117, 160
metaphysical reflections, 118
metaphysical-religious dream narrative, 162
metaphysicality, 118
"Missing Person, The," 101 *n.*
modern consciousness, advance of, 220
modern reality, 32, 219–220
moral equivocation, 111
moral-existential symbols, 178
moral freedom, 216
moral judgment, 109–110
morality, spirituality and, 110
Muir, Edwin, 97 *n.*, 189 *n.*, 214
Muir, Willa, 189 *n.*
Musil, Robert, 30
mythopoeia, 15

narrative form, 8, 12, 33, 34, 93, 94; analytical, 34, 51; Aristotelian, 69, 86, 122, 152; Biblical, 66, 67; dream, *see* dream narrative; dream-metaphysical, 122, 162; empirical, 94, 95, 152; episodic, 87 *n.*, 93, 100, 104, 122, 149, 151; Homeric, 67; metaphysical, 117, 160; philosophical, 134, 146, 162; psychoanalytic, 34, 47, 49, 98, 120, 133, 134; psychological, 9, 47, 59 *n.*, 98, 134, 146, 178, 216; symbolical intention and, 94–97; traditional, 104; visionary, 8–9, 12, 68, 87, 132

natural history, 36, 56
natural innocence, 57
natural science, 36
natural truth, 211
naturalism, 36, 109
nature, laws of, 89, 142–143, 205
nature-cure remedies, 20
necessity: abstract, 175; consciousness of, 200–201; laws of, 136–137, 142–143; world of, 164, 168, 173, 175, 211
negative universality, 220
Neider, Charles, 147
neurosis, 16–17, 49
neurotic illness, 17–18
neurotic illusion, 18
New Eden of righteousness, 95
Nietzsche, Friedrich Wilhelm, 15, 137 *n.*
nihilistic phantasmagoria, 52
nineteenth-century realism, 219–220
Notes from the Underground, 87–90, 167 *n.*, 219
nothingness, 25, 31, 37, 41, 44–45
nudism, 20

objective reality, 65, 205
obscure intention, 97

official consciousness, 207–208
Old Testament, 109
Oliver Twist, 93
"On Poesy or Art," 81 *n.*
"On the Puppet Theater," 7–8
ontological overtones, 9
orgasmic unconsciousness, 188
Orientalizing *fin de siècle,* 30
original sin, 117
Orthodox Judaism, 25
"Outing in the Mountains," 41

parable(s), 13–14, 50, 112, 141–143, 178, 179, 194
paradigms, 178, 194
Paradise: back door to, 207, 212 n., concrete idea of, 102; door of, 212; expulsion from, 21, 191 *n.;* innocence of, 167; reentry into, 207, 212
Paradise Lost, 95
parochialism, 30, 45
paternalistic bureaucracy, 103
pathos, 73, 74, 104, 148
perception, act of, 150
phantasmagoria, 29–30; nihilistic, 52
philosophical fantasy, 94–95
philosophical narrative, 134, 146, 162
philosophical-religious solitariness, 161
philosophical unity, 151
philosophy, 134, 146
picaresque novels, 93, 94
pleasure principle, 89, 90
"Poet's Mind," 87 *n.*
poetic fantasticality, 8
poetic reality, 51
Portrait of the Artist as a Young Man, A, 152
Pound, Ezra, 152
Prager Deutsch, 26

Prague German, 11, 24, 26
prosaic realism, 8, 33
Proust, Marcel, 11
psychoanalysis, 14 n., 17–19, 89 n.
psychoanalytic imagination, 26, 47, 200, 216, 217, 219
psychoanalytic narrative, 34, 47, 49, 98, 120, 133, 134
psychological narrative, 9, 47, 59 n., 98, 134, 146, 178, 216
psychological strickenness, 162
psychological symbols, 178, 217
psychological truth, 64
psychology, 17, 137 n., 146, 216–217

rational consciousness, 111
rationalization, 115, 156
rationalizing consciousness, 7
realism, 36, 39, 95, 97, 98, 117; dramatic-psychological mode of, 194; nineteenth-century, 219–220; prosaic, 8, 33
realism-naturalism, 36
reality: concrete, 219–220; conventional, 33; dreams and, 10–11, 14–15, 45, 71, 155, 195; empirical, 51; flight from, 90, 220; ignorance of, 168; ignoring of, 193; knowledge of, 10–11; mentally constructed, 6; metaphorical, 51; modern, 32, 219–220; mystery of, 10; objective, 65, 205; poetic, 51; spiritual, 64, 155, 169, 185, 201, 203; struggle against, 178; subjective, 30, 39, 64, 71, 94, 133; unconscious, 34
reason, 7; and dream narrative, 155; essence of, 206
redemption: death and, 71, 83, 84, 106–107, 110, 178; of

fallen state, 207; psychoanalysis and, 19 n.; of world, 212
reflection(s), 30, 40, 150, 157–159, 215; metaphysical, 118
"Reflections on Sin, Pain, Hope and the True Way," 17
"Relation of the Poet to Day-dreaming," 59 n.
relative ideas, 112
relativism, 109
religious consciousness, universal, 162
religious faith, 17–18
religious history, dream narrative and, 108–109
religious irrationality, 21
"Resolutions," 41
responsibility: acceptance of, 129–131; knowledge of, 114–115, 123–124
revelation, 68
revenge, justice and, 108
rhetorical style, 7, 11, 194–195
righteousness, 102; New Eden of, 95
Rilke, Rainer Maria, 11
Romantic intuition, 173
Romantic poets, 151, 220
Romantic transcendence, 50
Romantic universality, 98
Romanticism, 219
Rousseau, Jean Jacques, 15, 22, 220
Russell, Bertrand, 7 n.

"St. Cecelia, or the Power of Music," 81 n.
salvation, message of, 141
sardonic wit, 201
Sartre, Jean Paul, 19, 69
Schiller, Johann Christoph Friedrich von, 153